SITUATING CHILD CONSUMPTION

Situating Child Consumption

Rethinking values and notions of
children, childhood and consumption

Edited by
Anna Sparrman, Bengt Sandin
&
Johanna Sjöberg

NORDIC ACADEMIC PRESS

Nordic Academic Press
P.O. Box 1206
SE-221 05 Lund
Sweden
www.nordicacademicpress.com

© Nordic Academic Press and the Authors 2012
Typesetting: Frederic Täckström, www.sbmolle.com
Jacket design: Maria Jörgel Andersson
Printed by ScandBook AB, Falun 2012
ISBN: 978-91-85509-70-6

Contents

Acknowledgements

In 2010 the Department of Thematic Studies – Child Studies, Linköping University, Sweden, hosted the 4th International Conference on Child and Teen Consumption (CTC). The conference is a biannual venture connecting people from all over the world. Different theoretical and methodological approaches to consumption, as well as children and the young, are explored during these meetings. This volume is a result of the ambitions to theoretically approach some important concepts in the field of child consumption by looking both at child and consumption research. The essays are a small selection of some of the excellent studies discussed at the conference, and frame a critical approach to child consumption with an ambition to develop methodologies and theories. The essays are written by scholars with a track record as well as newcomers in child studies and the field of consumption. Accordingly, the mix of authors represent both the generation that opened up these research fields as well as up-and-coming researchers from different national backgrounds. Together, the essays represent a wealth of insights in the complexities and rewards in researching child consumption. It has been both a joy and a learning experience to work with the authors of the essays in this volume.

The friendship and the support of colleagues have been important in accomplishing this book, and we would also like to give praise to Daniel Thomas Cook, Pål Aarsand, and Tobias Samuelsson for their valuable and firmly critical support. Annika Olsson at Nordic Academic Press has made us revise and argue for our case, while Charlotte Merton has critically evaluated our use of the academic 'lingua franca' – English. Many others have supported this book by participating in the conference, reviewing papers, and joining in the scientific discussions. We would like to express our gratitude and give credit to all of you. The book has become better thanks to you. We take full responsibility for the remaining shortcomings.

The publishing of this book has been made possible by generous support from the Department of Thematic Studies – Child Studies.

Anna Sparrman, Bengt Sandin and Johanna Sjöberg

Linköping, Sweden 2012

Situated child consumption

An introduction

Anna Sparrman & Bengt Sandin

The aim with this volume is to initiate a discussion about child consumption as *situated practices*. We have collected a stimulating set of essays on children and consumption that demonstrate the challenges and possibilities of such an analytical position. The concept of situatedness comes from Donna Haraway's (1991) concept of situating knowledge, arguing that in general neither science nor knowledge is value-neutral, but instead is made up of complex relationships that shape knowledge.

Politically and culturally, children and consumption are often associated with normative positions and moral judgments (Cook 2004a, 2005, 2009; Buckingham 2007, 2011). Different camps, be they parents, teachers, psychologists, or research traditions, negotiate what is good or bad as well as what is morally right or wrong for children. This means that child consumption, as well as childhood as such, is associated with value conflicts. Daniel Thomas Cook (2004a, 2005) argues that children in consumer culture are intertwined with moral, or what he calls even 'hypermoral', values. Hypermoral values are founded in a value system that imposes and dominates interpretations according to which consumption is intrusive in children's lives. One general idea is that marketplaces invade children's lives with vanity, obesity, and unfulfilled desires from which they need to be protected (Cook 2005). This stance informs not only children's actual consumption, but also understandings of what takes place in consumer practices.

When it comes to children and consumption, values are so ingrained in the social relations intrinsic to everyday life, policy texts, and materiality that they are difficult to identify, even for the practised eye of the researcher. What is hard to capture is the full complexity of consumption values – values that supposedly threaten to engulf children and their childhoods. As a consequence, the question of children and consumption in public debates – and in everyday performances – is exposed to a narrow, single-minded approach, leaving little space for the discovery of other values of child consumption, or of the lives of children. It is by combining the study of child consumption, child studies, and situatedness that it becomes possible to elaborate on such approaches.

The current theoretical position in childhood sociology and the history of childhood emerged during the 1980s–1990s with the idea that children are social members and actors *in* society (Cunningham 1995; Halldén 2007; Hendrick 1990; Heywood 1988; James & Prout 1990; James, Jenks & Prout 1998; James & James 2004; Jenks 1996; Sandin 1986; Thorne 1987). The development of child studies was largely a response to the criticism that children as a research topic were being neglected in disciplines such as anthropology, sociology, feminism, history, and a simultaneous questioning of the emphasis on the use of psychological theories in understanding children (James & Prout 1990). Similarly critical voices have been heard in relation to consumer theories in the last decade: these have essentially ignored the child as a theoretical figure, modelling themselves instead on the white, Western, adult, independent male (Cook 2008b), while child studies, on the other hand, have been equally remiss about considering consumption (Buckingham 2011; Cook 2008b; Martens et al. 2004). Studying children's positions in markets, as well as their relations to consumption, give rise to discussions and understandings of the notions of children and consumption, but more importantly to discussions on how the two are related. The idea that children and consumption make or *enact* one another relationally is fundamental to this book (Law & Urry 2003; Mol 2002). The point of departure taken in this volume is children as social actors in consumer practices.

Combining theories of children as actors together with consumer theories still remains a challenge. Compounding this challenge are the ever-present and powerful, if sometimes invisible, universalistic claims of developmental psychology, which, until recently, has dominated the study of childhood, child consumption, and the related field of (social) consumer behaviourism (for example, Marshall 2010; Roedder John 1999), which often runs counter to the very issues and problems that child studies set out to historicize. Briefly, much of the consumption research to date has focused on whether – and if so, at what age – children understand consumption, and how children are born as non-consumers, only to be socialized as full consumers by the time they reach adulthood. The problem, as Cook (2008b) notes, is that studies of child consumption have informed neither consumption studies nor questions concerning society in general. This volume sets out to show how child consumption is always situated in different practices, be they everyday life, politics, markets, or specific historical periods – what we have chosen to call *situated consumption*. Such an approach will transform our understanding not only of the moral indignation child consumption gives rise to, but of child consumption as such. This of course raises the question of what is being situated and what is meant by situatedness when it comes to child consumption, and it is this we will consider in this introduction. We will say a few words about children as social actors, and about our use of the concepts of markets, value(s) and practices to situate consumption. We then position each of the chapters in relation to the larger aims of the volume, suggesting ways of interlinked readings of the individual chapters.

Children as social actors and the hybrid child

As pointed out by Cook (2004b, 2009) and Buckingham (2000, 2011), marketers and academics alike have stressed that children are highly agentive and competent social actors.[1] Cook (2004a, 2008b, 2010) has, however, argued that it is time to move on from the dichotomized image of the child consumer as either competent or naive in order to create a new understanding of the child in consumer society. Approaching the same issue from a media consumption angle, David Buckingham (2000, 2011) has likewise questioned the distinction. Abandoning it, however, is easier said than done.

When the sociology of childhood established itself in the early 1990s, the idea was to distinguish children from adults and family so as to make children visible (Prout 2005). Differentiating children, however, also has a drawback in that it has a tendency to 'other' children from adults and adult worlds. Similar problems arise when equating children as social actors with children as competent actors: the competent child is often presented as being synonymous with independence and individuality, thus negating children's vulnerability (Sandin 2012; Wall 2010). As noted, the approaches common in market research configure consuming children as competent and able. Cook (2000, 2004b) and Jacobson (2004, 2008) have shown, for example, that children were looked on by the marketers as social actors as early as the turn of the twentieth century in the US. Special child departments in department stores sought to view the world through children's eyes – *pediocularity* (Cook 2004b) – and advertisers began to use children to market baby products as well as toys (Cross 2004; Brembeck ed. 2001). In this sense, the adults involved with children in consumer marketplaces began to conceptualize children as social actors sometimes decades ahead of similar constructions in scholarly theories, research, or even before the discussion of children's rights inspired by the United Nations Convention on the Rights of the Child (UNCRC) of 1989. The figure of the competent child is indeed a powerful one – witness the fact that some welfare systems are based on closer adherence to and recognition of children's rights (Sandin 2012) – but while the recognition of rights does underwrite children's agency as an expression of competence, it must be stressed that it also points to children's potential vulnerability (Sandin 2012; Wall 2010), which is a point that market research tend to neglect.

To be a social actor, we argue, is not the same as being competent. It rather means acting in society through complex systems of social relations, experiences, materialities, competencies, and, indeed, incompetencies. Such a complex understanding of social actors brings to the fore the research problems associated with approaching children as social and cultural actors. The notion of the social actor is today a well-established theme in child studies that rely on children as participants; a fact that generates both ethical and political problems that are not always reflected on in research.

Pia Christensen and Alan Prout (2002: 478) argue that one consequence of taking children to be social actors is that 'new' ethical considerations are needed. They therefore introduce the concept of 'ethical symmetry' as a way of setting the standard for the relationship between children and researchers. The concept covers both a set of values for the child studies community as a whole and an applicable approach to be used in individual research projects. Christensen and Prout (2002) divide research with children into four different categories: (*i*) the child as object – a person acted upon by others, for example adults; (*ii*) children as subjects – a person with subjectivity, but judged on the basis of cognitive abilities and social competencies; (*iii*) children as social actors, with their own experiences and understandings – no distinctions between children and adults are taken for granted; and finally (*iv*) children constituted as active participants in the research process, just as they are active participants in social life. This last approach derives from the idea that children are fellow human beings and active citizens, and serves as the basis for the concept of ethical symmetry; for by giving children a voice in research, new complexities and uncertainties arise that must be dealt with. Ethical symmetry; for Christensen and Prout, is very much about setting up a value system in which adults researching (with) children and childhood do not put themselves in a superior position to children.

This formulation of ethical symmetry mainly concerns research conducted *with* children, and not research *about* children and childhood. We argue that it is equally important to have certain standards or to establish strategic ethical values also when researching historical change or policy and politics, or when researching childhood as the object of interest for civil society organizations. The difficulty is that in these cases the focus is on notions and discourses of children and childhoods, which usually means that children's own viewpoints have to be incorporated into the analyses of historical sources when their voices are lost to us. However, the inability to see, speak to and interact with 'real, live' children – as is the case with historical research, for example – does not relieve the researcher of the necessity, the duty even, of presuming their agency in the analysis (Sanchez-Eppler 2005). Consequently, it is just as important for these researchers to think in terms of ethical symmetry if the children in their work are to be visible. In our view, the discussion about ethical symmetry also indicates that it is one element in a system of governance in which research about and with children serves a political function (Sandin 2012), further underscoring the need for self-reflexivity and a situated knowledge production when researching child consumption (see also Tisdall, forthcoming; Wall 2010).

Yet the conviction that children are ethically symmetrical to adults in no way means that children and adults are symmetrical or equal in practice. Simply intellectualizing children as having the 'same rights' to physical, mental, and emotional integrity as adults does not mean we should undermine the specificity of children's rights and everyday existence – for example their need for help and protection – as separate from the rights of adults (Sandin 2012). Neither should we neglect the fact that children, politically and socially, do not understand their position as being symmetrical. Rather, ethical symmetry points to the fact that inequalities and power relations need to be explored, not taken for granted, when considering the relationship between children and adults (Christensen & Prout 2002; Sparrman, forthcoming). Approaching children as equals when exploring child consumption means that taken-for-granted assumptions about both children and consumption can be dissected in greater detail (cf. Sparrman & Aarsand 2009), and that their practices can help us to question established consumer theories as well as notions of children and childhood.

As already stated, recent research in child consumption, like market research, has come to use the figure of the child as a social actor in a variety of ways in order to understand consumption. Combined with an unpacking of the concept of social actors, this research makes it possible for us to begin expanding alternative ways of approaching child consumption. Deleuzian complexity theory and the idea that children, like adults, are always both *being* and *becoming*, means that neither children's nor adults' life trajectories are stable: children and adults alike are always dependent, incomplete, and competent (Lee 2001). Children as actors are thus always stable *and* transitory. The notion of being–becoming expresses multiplicity in itself, and enacts a *hybrid child* who acts from multiple positions in a complex world where practical, political, theoretical and empirical issues relate and connect in a diverse set of ways (Lee & Motzkau 2011; Prout 2005). This opens up for broader analyses of values and concepts such as the market when it comes to child consumption. The relations between children, childhood, consumption, markets, and values must be situated in practices.

Situated consumption

As Manuel De Landa (2006) argues, concepts such as the market (or the state) portray abstract entities that are often simplified and reified moral generalities: 'Markets should be viewed, first of all, as concrete organizations', meaning, for example, actual marketplaces such as bazaars or supermarkets (ibid. 17). Existing physical locations such as a city, a specific region, or national, international, and global markets constitute assemblages where 'people and the material and expressive goods people exchange' co-exist (De Landa 2006: 17). Markets, local or global, are entangled with one another, and made up of people. This means it is not possible to talk about 'the market' in general terms, whether thinking of children or any other category of people. The connection between children and markets is relational in the way that they produce one another rather than defining an assumed hierarchical order. This is also true of the values that markets produce and transform.

To understand value(s), one needs to abandon the idea of applying theories of value to people, and instead turn to practices to see how value is being made. To ask what value is, Daniel Miller (2008) argues, is to ask the question wrongly; the question is rather what value does. The word value also has a rather unusual semantic range in the English language:

> On the one hand it can mean the work involved in giving monetary worth to an object ... and thereby becomes almost synonymous with price. On the other hand, it can mean that which has significance to us precisely because the one thing it can never be reduced to, is monetary evaluation, for example the value we hold dear in relation to family, religion and other inalienable possessions. I will use the term value and values for the two extremes. (Miller 2008: 1123)

Miller is struck by the fact that most people use the same concept, value, for these two very different meanings. In this he draws on Viviana Zelizer's (1985) argument about the changing value of children in the US in the period from 1870 to the 1930s. Children's value was transformed when the labour market was rationalized, and children were no longer needed as labour and thus could no longer contribute financially to their families. In the process, children, instead of being economically valuable, became emotionally valuable – priceless, in other words – which in turn led to the establishing of a new market value of the emotional child. This shows how both price and pricelessness comprise a whole cosmology of different values, including morals, emotions, and norms. By situating the analysis of consumer values in practices, it is possible to deconstruct the interrelationship between the different meanings to reveal how the values make up social, political, and material relationships.

Scholars in contemporary consumer studies call for contextualizing or, as we would put it, to situate consumption. There is, however, no single theoretical or methodological solution that will achieve this. Lydia Martens, Dale Southerton, and Sue Scott (2004), for example, argue that child consumption has generally been studied as an isolated phenomenon separate from social relations, even though most child consumption takes place within family life, with the help or company of parents or other social groups (see also Ekström 2010). Consequently, they wish to resituate child consumption in the family. Another approach to contextualizing child consumption is to conduct ethnographic studies with children in order to gain access to their own actions and doings (Buckingham & Tingstad eds. 2010; Chin 2001; Pugh 2009, 2011; Sparrman 2002, 2009; Sparrman & Aronsson 2003; Tufte & Ekström eds. 2007), in the pursuit of what is sometimes called the 'lived experiences' of consumption (Cook 2008a; for situated lived experiences, see Widerberg 2005). While some studies spring from the theories (for example Martens et al. 2004; Warde 2005), ethnographic approaches generally question theory by conducting ethnographic research (Chin 2001; Cook 2008a; Pugh 2009, 2011; Sparrman 2002, 2009; Thompson 2011; Willet 2009).

Ethnographic approaches permit us to see how meaning and identity inform markets at the same time as they question the explanatory power of general theoretical concepts. Moreover, given that culture, meaning, sentiment, and everyday life come to life by focusing on lived experiences, this implies that to research consumption is also a way to study social life (Cook 2008a). Thus, consumption is not only about the calculative dimensions of exchange, but also about the ways in which larger societal processes of consumption can create inequalities, bonds, belongings, friendships, and families (Chin 2001; Cook 2008a; Pugh 2009, 2011; Sparrman 2002, 2009) and how these aspects sometimes intertwine with and negotiate economic values (Zelizer 1985, 2002, 2005). Zelizer's studies connect the need to study child consumption as an aspect of political change with the regulation of markets, welfare, family life, child labour, and education, since such analyses reconnect to how politics and regulations are handled and reproduced in everyday life. Cultural studies has also emphasized everyday issues in relation to consumption research, accentuating the active consumer in the same way as we stress children as social actors (Mackay 1997; Paterson 2006). In a special issue on consumer practices in *Journal of Consumer Culture*, Craig Thompson (2011) also argues that by focusing on consumer practices, new theoretical light can be thrown on institutionalized (Simon 2011) or contested narratives (Brogård Kristensen, Boye & Askegaard 2011) of a political and moralistic nature. However, cultural studies, and Thompson and his colleagues, do not address and theorize the specificity of children and childhood. Nevertheless, different concepts such as everyday life, lived experience, contextualization, and practice that have been used by scholars from various disciplines point in the same direction, that can be embraced by the term *situated consumption*.

The concept of situated knowledge was developed by Donna Haraway (1991) in the field of feminist studies. Haraway argued that the knowledge produced through research is always part of the context it produces. From a feminist standpoint, situating knowledge made it possible to question the white, male vision that dominated science and research (Engelstad & Gerrard 2005a). This argument is similar to our discussion of how by situating child consumption, we can call into question consumer theories based on the independent, white, Western adult male (Cook 2008b), in an echo of Barrie

Thorne's (1987) discussion of the relationships between women's studies and child studies.

We hold that the idea of situatedness is based on multiplicity (Engelstad & Gerrard 2005a), and that if we situate consumption it is possible to bridge the gaps between the study of everyday life and the politics and policy of consumption and of childhood. If consumption is situated, then child consumption (or for that matter any consumption) can *never* be reduced to being a question simply of age, materiality, value(s), children, or any other lone entity, but must always be a mixture of different aspects; aspects, moreover, that are never predefined, but are being done or enacted in specific practices that bring actors together (Law & Urry 2003; Mol 2002).

Practice is therefore a central concept when understanding situated consumption – when thinking about what is being situated and how situatedness is being done. We draw on Annemarie Mol's notion (2002) of the plurality and multiplicity of practice, and the ways in which different practices create different 'realities'. To follow Mol, this is different from saying that, for instance, child consumption can be studied through an 'endless series of perspectives'. The point is that consumption is not a homogeneous field, but is 'being done' through an endless combination of relations:

> there is no longer a single passive object in the middle, waiting to be seen from the point of view of seemingly endless series of perspectives. Instead, objects come into being – and disappear – with the practices in which they are manipulated. And since the object of manipulation tends to differ from one practice to another, reality multiplies. (Mol 2002: 5)

Hence, there are multiple ways of signifying the ontology of child consumption, since children and consumption enact (Mol 2002) one another in different ways in different practices, generating different outcomes (see also Woolgar in this volume).

So, what is different about approaching child consumption as situated rather than approaching it as, for example, contextualized? First of all, the non-hierarchical relationality between theories, emotions, social relations, culture, and materiality is fundamental to situatedness. The same goes for the relations between historical and political processes and lived experiences. Laws, regulations, and political strategies intended to regulate consumption need to be situated in the practices in which they were developed, as well as in the practices – markets, governments, consumer organizations, family life, or peer cultures – in which they are applied.

Following on from Haraway's (1991) definition of situatedness, it is equally important to reflect on scholarly knowledge production; for example, by being aware of the notions and values of children or childhood one harbours as researchers when researching child consumption. To challenge dichotomous thinking and normative hierarchies, we must dare to stay with complexity and deal with the 'mess' that usually ensues; in other words, to see where it takes us (Law 2004). John Law (2004) argues that research needs to face complexity head-on and not try to reduce it to tidy sets of arguments or dichotomies.

The aim of this introduction is to suggest new understandings about child consumption. Consumption is understood as a cultural dimension (Arnould & Thompson 2005) constituting a material from which, for example, identities are created, in combination with the sociology and history of child studies and the idea of children as social, or even hybrid, actors and consumers. Moreover, consumption is being done (enacted) in practices, regardless of whether the practice is everyday life or historical or political processes, or whether it comprises humans or objects. This means that ambivalent consumption values such as destructive or creative are understood through practices, not as theoretical stances, when discussing child consumption (see Bocock 1993; Clarke et al. 2003; Mackay 1997; Paterson 2006). Consumption in this way involves among many other things goods, marketing, money, gift-giving, values, generations, social (intimate) relationships, imagination, and desires.

Outline of the chapters
– values of children, childhood and consumption

All the chapters in this volume share an emphasis on children as social actors in the process of making child consumption, most essays suggest that consumption is a site of active negotiation, and all elaborate more or less explicitly on the situatedness of child consumption. The authors refrain from figuring consumption as something that can be identified as a detachable item to be studied outside the practice in which it is situated. The first four chapters all challenge previous research on child consumption by disentangling concepts and reflecting on the field from within. Each chapter situates consumption in multiple ways. They point to new ways of thinking about child consumption while reflecting on the new kinds of research that might be possible and needed for future knowledge production, and how this can be accomplished. Many of the questions raised by these first four chapters are elaborated on in the subsequent ones. Steve Woolgar, with his background in science technology studies (STS), emphasizes the importance of reflecting on the ontological status when combining the concepts child, consumption, and materiality. He shows what happens when these three aspects intersect, but also how different outcomes are enacted depending on which concept of materiality is chosen. His chapter shows different ways of approaching materiality in the field of child consumption.

While Woolgar's text presents new thinking by negotiating child consumption through new theories, the following three chapters look into the future by reflecting on history. In 1985, the economic sociologist Viviana Zelizer published her now classic book, *Pricing the Priceless Child*. The book investigated the changing value of children, from being economically useful by their labour to being economically and emotionally priceless when child labour was prohibited. In this way it generated novel ideas for understanding the changing value of children and childhood over time, as much as for economic research, where Zelizer (1994, 2005) has emphasized the social and emotional aspects of the meanings of money. Two scholars of childhood, Daniel Thomas Cook and Bengt Sandin, reflect on what *Pricing the Priceless Child* has meant to them as researchers in terms of child consumption as well as child studies. Their accounts are followed by Zelizer's own discussion of how her study came about, commenting on Cook's and Sandin's reflections, and concluding by pointing to a series of new research questions.

In discussing Zelizer's book, Cook takes his point of departure in the commercial society of the US, while Sandin discusses the Swedish welfare state and consumption. Focusing on *Pricing the Priceless Child*, Cook emphasizes that Zelizer uses the history of children as a casestudy to investigate the central theoretical controversies concerning the relationship between economic and socio-cultural values. At the same time he argues that a reading of Zelizer's work can help to question and loosen up dichotomous thinking; for example, along the lines of the sacralized–commercialized child, and in approaching stability as relative.

Sandin, on the other hand, connects the emotional value of the child to the development of welfare state polices in Fifties' Sweden: the influence of economic subsidies on consumer activities, the costs associated with children, and compulsory schooling. He discusses how emotional and economic values have developed side by side through the action of the welfare system. The negotiations of monetary values in relation to children affect welfare policy as a whole, but are negotiated and transformed within families. His argument moves consumption away from an individual-centred understanding of child consumption to a collective, political understanding.

Considering Cook's and Sandin's arguments, Zelizer concludes by raising questions about what the relationship between sacralized and commercial values will look like in the twenty-first century, but also what children's consumer autonomy looks like, what children are allowed to consume, what types of money are involved in child consumption, and how the intertwinement of social and economic values is expressed. She invokes an earlier appeal for more research on money and child consumption (Zelizer 2002).

Some of Zelizer's questions are discussed in Tobias Samuelsson's essay on children's work in Sweden, Shosh Davidson's essay on Israeli children growing up in economic scarcity, and by Cardell and Sparrman in their essay on how different kinds of money or values are used in an amusement park. Samuelsson shows how the legislation on children's earnings and possessions functions, but he also situates his understanding of children's work in the children's own arguments, maintaining that the logic behind their work creates an intricate web of favours, educational aims, intimacy, time, autonomy, and money. Children's work is, however, not predominantly about creating purchasing power. Children and work are thus a contested topic that brings together many different sets of values. Children's access to or lack of money always involves adults, and is an important device in making children dependent or independent social actors.

In low-income families, children get used to negotiating for money for shopping or payment for chores they have completed. In her chapter, Davidson shows how teenage children in low-income families set out to persuade, please or flatter, or create a power game. They also differentiate between their 'own money' and their 'parents' money'. Samuelsson and Davidson show, in two different national contexts, that earning and spending money closely link children and parents. This may even be accentuated when there is a shortage of money. Moral values such as 'considerate behaviour' become a currency with which to support the family economy, as does mutual reciprocity between children and adults.

But how do children spend money when they do have access to it? Like Davidson, Cardell and Sparrman draw on Zelizer's later theoretical work (1994, 2005) on the social meaning of money and how (family) intimacy is purchased through the organization of domestic money. Cardell and Sparrman apply a twofold approach to studying the intersection between an amusement park's organization of money and monetary values, and child visitors' use of money during a visit to the park. They show how money that is situated in a special practice generates different currencies, similar to those discussed by Davidson. However, while Davidson's values concern, to use Zelizer's (1985) or Miller's (2008) term, priceless values, Cardell and Sparrman's monetary values largely intersect material and immaterial aspects such as time. Like Samuelsson and Davidson, they show that, where children have access to money, there is no simple connection between access and spending for the sake of spending. Neither the amusement park nor the children offer or create coherent systems of consumption to which either party or actor (park or child) can conform, which is why they need to create an attitude of reciprocity to each other by conforming to the other's needs. Cardell and Sparrman call this process 'sprawliness of consumption'. The three essays show how the situatedness of money in practice creates complicated monetary values, different currency systems, and differences in how money is marked (Zelizer 1994).

In her essay, Johanna Sjöberg focuses on how conservative values of parenthood are reproduced in direct advertising sent to parents of newborns. Her focus is the manner in which visual images present, or rather fail to present, fatherhood. Visual advertising is used to promote a diverse set of commodities as being essential for the newborn, even though the child cannot yet express any consumer needs or access consumer rights. Like Lydia Martens's research (2010, Martens et al. 2004), Sjöberg points to the importance of conducting research on the relatedness of child consumption to parenthood and family life, and on the rationale that consumption for babies, and indeed unborn babies (baby showers), rests on. Sjöberg's chapter shows how direct advertising visually frames parenthood as both female and heterosexual, and underlines the importance of letting consumption studies inform societal issues.

Sjöberg's essay situates the newborn child in consumer practices: between them the contributions to this volume cover children at all stages of life, from newborn to late teenage. Age is a highly relevant theoretical concept when it comes to child consumption, primarily because consumer socialization perspectives have approached the consuming child from a cognitivist, age-stage view (Roedder John 1999), but also because markets use developmental, age-based criteria to categorize their commodities – both of which aspects are discussed by Olivia Freeman in her essay on focus group discussions with preschool children. Age is used to segment the market and create as many lucrative consumer groups as possible, as is shown by Ingvild Kvale Sørensen in her essay exploring how the Disney Company in the Nordic countries deals with the quite recently established concept of the tween.

Both Freeman and Kvale Sørensen show how age is 'being done' in relation to consumer commodities such as toys and media productions when situated in interviews with children. Instead of talking about age as a chronological progression from birth to adulthood, or as biological processes connected to inner cognitive processes, they show that children use other cultural values to talk about age, such as being a 'big boy', something being 'babyish', or about themselves being 'big kids' or 'childish'. In this way, Kvale Sørensen's 12-year-old informants talk about age as an action depending on specific situations; they express that they are not 'in between' ages (child–teen), but rather continuously move back and forth between different age positions.

Freeman and Kvale Sørensen both challenge earlier research on children, age, and consumption, especially the theorization. They also dispute the idea of *age compression*, with children (aged 9–12) and adults all venturing to be teenagers, thus compressing age from two directions (Lassond 2012). Together, these two essays indicate that age is always under negotiation and transition, so that it is possible to talk about age in terms of *social age*, created in relations (Solberg 1990) with others, or/and as *cultural age*, culturally and morally connected to material objects situated in practices (Sparrman 2009). What is meant by age in the research on child consumption differs according to the practices concerned and by whom age is 'being done'.

Sue Jackson and Tiina Vares, and Sara Bragg, David Buckingham, Rachel Russell and Rebekah Willet, discuss the intersection between childhood – and more specifically girlhood – innocence, consumption, and sexuality. Both essays deal with the relation between consumer agency and childhood innocence, and discuss such concepts as 'savvy girls', 'girly girls', 'growing up too fast too soon', 'let girls be girls', and 'let children be children'. They set out to challenge the moral discourses of girls as victims of a sexualized market. Jackson and Vares use theories of post-feminism and discourse approaches, while Bragg et al. adopt a self-reflexive approach. Discussing clothes shopping, Jackson and Vares show how girls simultaneously balance and negotiate potentially amoral values of sexiness and values of childishness. The girls in focus in their essay use the same strategies as the children in Freeman's and Kvale Sørensen's chapters, positioning themselves outside prefixed categories. By situating girls' consumer habits and choices in a post-feminist framework, Jackson and Vares also position consumer studies within so-called girlhood studies (for example, Driscoll 2002).

Bragg et al. question assumptions regarding moral panics about sexualized consumer goods and childhood. Unlike the moralizing debates on child consumption, they have worked from the premise of children and parents as 'sensible' actors. Reflecting on this, Bragg et al. show that as an approach this does not generate any simple solutions, answers, or moral values, as both children and parents present complex, elaborate discussions about how childhood and sexuality come together. Both post-feminism and research reflexivity are important in understanding how girls' consumption is being done and why their consumption is perceived to be sexualized and different from that of boys.

The moralization of sexualized consumer goods is similar to the moral panic surrounding war toys and children – another hyper-sensitive combination of values. The argument presented is that by situating moral panics in practices, the logics upholding them can be investigated. In his essay, Braden Hutchinson analyses the logic of the debate on the war toy – *G. I. Joe* and the like – in Eighties Canada. He shows how the moral panic over war toys in practice concerned neither toys nor children, but rather was used as a proxy for the larger societal aims of Canadian peace activists and feminists who wished to confront American Cold War imperialism. In her essay, Helle Strandgaard Jensen takes a somewhat similar critical stance, but to the Fifties' debate on children's comics in the Nordic countries. She maintains that the teachers' and child psychologists' arguments against comics at the time did not constitute a panic, but actually followed a rationale of genuine professional concern, arguing for what they saw as the 'best interest of the child' (Sandin & Halldén 2003; Lindgren 2006). Strandgaard Jensen pinpoints the importance of situating people's actions in the specific historical contexts in which they occurred.

While Hutchinson shows that the anti-war toy panic was not about toys or boys, but about political struggle, Strandgaard Jensen underscores the fact that the professional action taken against comics was founded on an understanding of children's wellbeing. One reason is that there was a different perception of children, childhood, and the media in the 1950s. By situating consumption in practices and venturing look to the larger processes and the historical context, it becomes clear that what are called moral panics can be better understood as struggles and negotiations over whose values and norms should prevail.

All the essays in this volume present different theoretical, methodological, and empirical strategies for discussing children as social actors. However, research on child consumption cannot end with the pronouncement that children are social actors or competent consumers, or have agency, or that childhood and child agency can be perceived as hybrid. Research needs to push the argument further, by for example investigating the options children comprehend in their consumer lives or the meanings and value(s) enacting such choices. Yes, children do negotiate their choices through the production and reproduction of values and morals – but the question remains of what choices are open to children. Think only of girls' pink, sexualized choices versus boys' khaki-coloured war choices. Similarly, other values that are perhaps less visible are actualized and important to discuss in the future. What does it mean that children's toys are produced under poor working conditions by children in Asia so that markets can keep their prices down and at the same time make huge profits (Langer 2004)? Such questions are deeply political and involve not only the ethical issues about researching with children, but also the basic ethics and normative bases of consumption as such. Child consumption also constitutes the bulk of government spending on care, and parental consumption, uniting markets with governments, and large-scale historical changes with the mundane action of children and parents. It is at these intersections and intertwinements it becomes possible to see how consumer and consumption values are negotiated; in other words, observe how values are being enacted when situated in practices. By situating child consumption, and thereby exposing the complexity, multiplicity, and relationality of the social, cultural, material, and political realities in which consumption is created, pressing questions such as these will come to the fore: by situating child consumption at difficult intersections between, say, government policy decisions and everyday life (see Oware 2005), it will be possible to focus on value(s) rather than moralistic posturing.

Note

1 For research on children as social actors in consumer practices, see, for example, Buckingham 2007; Buckingham & Tingstad 2010 and all Cook's production (for example, 2000, 2004a, 2004b, 2005, 2008a, 2008b, 2009, 2010). See also Ekström & Tufte 2007; Johansson 2005; Pugh 2009, 2011; Willet 2009.

References

Arnould, Eric, J. & Thompson, Craig T. (2005), 'Consumer culture theory (CCT): Twenty years of research', *Journal of Consumer Research*, 31/4: 868–82.

Bocock, Robert (1993), *Consumption* (London: Routledge).

Brembeck, Helene (ed.) (2001), *Det konsumerande barnet. Representationer av barn och konsumtion i svensk dags- och veckopress under 1900-talet med utgångspunkt i reklamannonser* (Etnologiska föreningen i Västsverige, 34; Gothenburg: Göteborg Universitet).

Brogård Kristensen, Dorthe, Boye, Heidi & Askegaard, Søren (2011), 'Leaving the milky way! The formation of a consumer counter mythology', *Journal of Consumer Culture*, 11/2: 195–221.

Buckingham, David (2000), *After the death of childhood: Growing up in the age of electronic media* (Cambridge: Polity Press).

– (2007), 'Selling childhood? Children and consumer culture', *Journal of Children and Media*, 1/1: 15–24.

– (2011), *The material child: Growing up in consumer culture* (Cambridge: Polity Press).

– & Tingstad, Vebjørg (2010) (eds.), *Childhood and consumer culture* (Basingstoke: Palgrave Macmillan).

Chin, Elizabeth (2001), *Purchasing power: Black kids and American consumer culture* (Minneapolis: University of Minnesota Press).

Christensen, Pia & Prout, Alan (2002), 'Working with ethical symmetry in social research with children', *Childhood*, 9/4: 477–97.

Clarke, David B., Doel, Marcus A. & Housiaux, Kate M. L. (2003), 'General introduction', in eid. (eds.), *The consumption reader* (London: Routledge), 1–23.

Cook, Daniel Thomas (2000), 'The other "child study": Figuring children as consumers in market research, 1910s–1990s', *Sociological Quarterly*, 41/3: 487–507.

– (2004a), 'Beyond either/or', *Journal of Consumer Culture*, 4/2: 147–53.

– (2004b), *The commodification of childhood: The children's clothing industry and the rise of the child consumer* (Durham, NC: Duke University Press).

– (2005), 'The dichotomous child in and off commercial culture', *Childhood*, 12/2: 155–59.

– (2008a), 'Introduction: Dramaturgies of value in market places', in id. (ed.), *Lived experiences of public consumption: Encounters with value in marketplaces on five continents* (New York: Palgrave Macmillan), 1–10.

– (2008b), 'The missing child in consumption theory', *Journal of Consumer Culture*, 8/2: 219–43.

– (2009), 'Knowing the child consumer: historical conceptual insights on qualitative children's consumer research', *Young Consumers*, 10/4: 269–282.

– (2010), 'Commercial enculturation: Moving beyond consumer socialization', in Buckingham & Tingstad (2010), 63–79.

Cross, Gary (2004), *The cute and the cool: Wondrous innocence and modern American children's culture* (Oxford: OUP).

Cunningham, Hugh (1995), *Children and childhood in western society since 1500* (London: Longman)

De Landa, Manuel (2006), *A new philosophy of society: Assemblage theory and social complexity* (London: Continuum).

Driscoll, Catherine (2002), *Girls: feminine adolescence in popular culture and cultural theory* (New York: Columbia University Press).

Ekström, Karin (2010), 'Consumer socialization in families', in Marshall (2010), 41–60.

– & Tufte, Birgitte (eds.) (2007) *Children, media and consumption: on the front edge* (Gothenburg: International Clearinghouse on Children, Youth and Media, Nordicom, Göteborg Universitet).

Engelstad, Ericka & Gerrard, Siri (2005a), 'Challenging situatedness', in Engelstad & Gerrard (2005b), 1–26.

– (2005b) (eds.) *Challenging situatedness: Gender, culture and the production of knowledge* (Delft: Eburon Academic Publishers).

Halldén, Gunilla (2007), *Den moderna barndomen och barns vardagsliv* (Stockholm: Carlsson).

Haraway, Donna (1991), 'Situated knowledges: The science question in feminism and the privilege of partial perspective', in ead., *Simans, Cyborgs, and Women: The reinvention of nature* (New York: Routledge), 183–201.

Hendrick, Harry (1990), *Images of youth: age, class, and the male youth problem, 1880–1920* (Oxford: Clarendon).

Heywood, Colin (1988), *Childhood in nineteenth-century France: work, health and education among the 'classes populaires'* (Cambridge: CUP).

Jacobson Lisa (2004), *Raising consumers: Children and the American mass market in the early twentieth century* (New York: Columbia University Press).

– (2008), *Children and consumer culture in American society: A historical hand-*

book and guide (Children and Youth – History and Culture; Westport, CT: Praeger Publishers).

James, Allison & Prout, Alan (1990) (eds.), *Constructing and reconstructing childhood: Contemporary issues in the sociological study of childhood* (London: Falmer Press).

– & Jenks, Chris & Prout, Alan (1998), *Theorizing childhood* (Cambridge: Polity Press).

– & James, Adrian L. (2004), 'Constructing children, childhood and the child', in eid. (eds.), *Constructing childhood: Theory, policy and social practice* (New York: Palgrave Macmillan), 10–28.

Jenks, Chris (1996), *Childhood* (London: Routledge).

Johansson, Barbro (2005), *Barn i konsumtionssamhället* (Stockholm: Norstedts).

– (2010), 'Subjectivities of the child consumer: beings and becomings', in Buckingham & Tingstad (2010), 80–93.

Langer, Beryl (2004), 'The business of branded enchantment: ambivalence and disjuncture in the global children's culture industry', *Journal of Consumer Culture*, 4/2: 251–77.

Lassond, Stephen (2012), 'Teen is the New Fourteen: Age Compression and "Real" Childhood', in Paula Fass & Michael Grossberg (eds.), *Reinventing childhood after World War I* (Philadelphia: University of Penn Press), 51–67.

Law, John & Urry, John (2003), *Enacting the social*, Department of Sociology and the Centre for Science Studies, Lancaster University, available at <http://www.comp.lancs.ac.uk/sociology/papers/Law-Urry-encating-the-Social.pdf> accessed 1 November 2010.

Law, John (2004), *After method: Mess in social science research* (London: Routledge).

Lee, Nick (2001), *Childhood and society: growing up in an age of uncertainty* (Maidenhead: Open University).

– & Motzkau, Johanna (2011), 'Navigating the bio-politics of childhood', *Childhood*, 18/1: 7–19.

Lindgren, Cecilia (2006), *En riktig familj: Adoption, föräldraskap och barnets bästa 1917–1975* (Diss.; Stockholm: Carlssons).

Mackay, Hugh (1997), 'Introduction', in Hugh Mackay (ed.), *Consumption and everyday life* (London: SAGE), 1–12.

Marshall, David (2010) (ed.), *Understanding children as consumers* (London: SAGE).

Martens, Lydia, Southerton, Dale & Scott, Sue (2004), 'Bringing children (and parents) into the sociology of consumption. Towards a theoretical and empirical agenda', *Journal of Consumer Culture*, 4/2: 155–82.

– (2010), 'The cute, the spectacle and the practical: Narratives of new parents and babies at the baby show', in Buckingham & Tingstad (2010), 146–60.

Miller, Daniel (2008), 'The uses of value', *Geoforum*, 39: 1122–32.

Mol, Annemarie. (2002), *The body multiple: Ontology in medical practice* (Durham, NC: Duke University Press).

Oware, Percy (2005), 'Situated Development: A policy planning option for Ghana?', in Engelstad & Gerrard (2005), 101–123.

Paterson, Mark (2006), *Consumption and everyday life* (London: Routledge).

Pugh, Allison (2009), *Longing and belonging: Parents, children, and consumer culture* (Berkeley & Los Angeles: University of California Press).

– (2011), 'Distinction, boundaries or bridges? Children, inequality and the uses of consumer culture', *Poetics*, 39/1: 1–18.

Prout, Alan (2005), *The Future of Childhood: Towards the Interdisciplinary Study of Childhood* (London: Routledge Farmer).

Roedder John, D. (1999), 'Consumer socialization of children: A retrospective look at twenty-five years of research', *Journal of Consumer Research*, 26/3, 183–213.

Sánchez-Eppler, Karen (2005), *Dependent states: the child's part in nineteenth-century American culture* (Chicago: University of Chicago Press).

Sandin, Bengt (1986), *Hemmet, gatan, fabriken eller skolan: folkundervisning och barnuppfostran i svenska städer 1600–1850* (Diss.; Lund: Arkiv).

– (2012), 'Children and the Swedish welfare state: from different to similar', in Paula Fass & Michael Grossberg (eds.), *Reinventing childhood after World War I* (Philadelphia: University of Penn Press), 110–38.

– & Halldén, Gunilla (2003), 'Välfärdsstatens omvandling och en ny barndom', in eid. (eds.), *Barnets bästa: En antologi om barndomens innebörder och välfärdens organisering* (Stockholm/Stehag: Brutus Östlings Bokförlag Symposion), 7–23.

Simon, Bryant (2011), 'Not going to Starbucks: Boycotts and the out-sourcing of politics in the branded world', *Journal of Consumer Culture*, 11/2: 145–67.

Solberg, A. (1990), 'Negotiating childhood: Changing constructions of age for Norweigan children', in James & Prout (1990: 118–37).

Sparrman, Anna (2002), *Visuell kultur i barns vardagsliv – bilder, medier och praktiker* (Diss.; Linköping: Linköping University).

– (2009), 'Ambiguities and paradoxes in children's talk about marketing breakfast cereals with toys', *Young Consumers*, 10/4: 297–313.

– & Aarsand, Pål (2009), 'Towards a critical approach on children and media', *Journal of Children and Media*, 3/3: 303–307.

– (forthcoming), 'Access and gatekeeping in researching children's sexuality: Mess in ethics and methods', *Qualitative Inquiry*.

– & Aronsson, Karin (2003), 'Pog game practices, learning and ideology: local markets and identity work', in Walford (ed.) *Investigating educational policy through etnography* (Studies in educational etnography series, Vol. 8) (Oxford: Oxford): 169–192.

Thompson, Craig J. (2011), 'Understanding consumption as political and moral practice: Introduction to the special issue', *Journal of Consumer Culture*, 11/2: 139–44.

Thorne, Barrie (1987), 'Re-visioning women and social change: Where are the children?', *Gender & Society*, 1/1: 85–109.

Tisdall, Kay & Punch, Samantha (2002), 'Not so "new"? Looking critically at childhood studies', *Children's Geographies*, special issue 'Exploring children's relationships across majority and minority worlds', 10(3): 249–264.

Wall, John (2010), 'Introduction', in Wall, *Ethics in the light of childhood*, (Washington: Georgetown University Press), 1–10.

Warde, Alan (2005), 'Consumption and theories of practice', *Journal of Consumer Culture*, 5/2: 131–53.

Widerberg, Karin (2005), 'Situating knowledge – liberating or oppressive?' in Engelstad & Gerrard (2005b), 259–67.

Willet, Rebecka (2009), '"As soon as you get on Bebo you just go mad": Young consumers and the discursive construction of teenagers online', *Young Consumers*, 10/4: 283–96.

Zelizer, Viviana (1985), *Pricing the priceless child: The changing social value of children* (Princeton: PUP).

– (1994), *The social meaning of money: Pin money, paychecks, poor relief and other currencies* (New York: Basic Books).

– (2002), 'Kids and commerce', *Childhood*, 9/4: 375–96.

– (2005), *The purchase of intimacy* (Princeton: PUP).

CHAPTER I

Ontological child consumption

Steve Woolgar

As a newcomer to the field of child studies and child consumption, I am struck first by the intensity of the debates and feelings about questions of consumption associated with children, and, second, by the strength of the assumptions about the nature and identity of the key actors at the heart of these debates, and especially, of course, the child. Notions of what is right for children fuel debates in policy, academia, the media, and popular culture; debates that seem to gain much of their momentum from entrenched assumptions about what is good for children, what children need, what is in children's best interests – in short what, after all, a child *is*.

This way of capturing the situation bears an interesting resonance with key features of a seemingly far-removed academic field: science and technology studies (STS). For, in its more enlivening manifestations, STS is precisely about challenging deeply entrenched assumptions. It has, (in)famously, courted much controversy in overturning long-held epistemological assumptions about facticity and scientific knowledge. In particular, it has stressed the importance of objects and materiality in the genesis and use of science and technology. Most recently, STS has challenged us to rethink our assumptions at the level of ontology. What are our fundamental predispositions about the status of entities in the world, and how do these organize our thinking and practice? To what extent is the entrenchment of basic assumptions about objects and entities responsible for moral positioning? Authors such as Daniel Thomas Cook (2004, 2008) have shown that some of the main difficulties in the study of child consumption stem from adopting particular assumptions about what a child is. This essay widens the discussion by considering the child as part of a nexus of objects and entities about which we make consequential assumptions. It sets out to explore whether – and if so, to what extent – some of the ontological challenges recently explored by STS in relation to objects, agency, and materiality might usefully be applied to the figure of the child in consumption.

I begin by outlining some recent developments in STS, emphasizing the STS sensibilities that are useful for challenging deeply entrenched assumptions. The second section of the essay draws on these to propose a simple typology of contrasting theoretical approaches to consumption. In relation to the particular problem of child consumption, this section emphasizes the difference between studies which treat such notions as child and object 'in context', and those which explore 'the enactment' of these entities. The third section works through some specific examples of consumption in order to illustrate the difference between the in-context and enactment approaches, and considers their relative benefits.[1]

What is STS?

STS is a vast multidiscipline comprising contributions from, and to, at least: anthropology, sociology, psychology, history, philosophy, legal studies, communications, and media studies. STS draws upon and contributes to a wide range of intellectual currents including relativism, scepticism, (social) constructivism, actor network theory, anti- and post-essentialism, and feminist and post-feminist studies. In the course of its roughly thirty-year history, STS has enjoyed widespread influence and has been taken up in many, often unexpected, places (Woolgar et al. 2009). In particular, it turns out that STS has major implications for many key aspects of social theory and social philosophy, well beyond its original substantive focus on science and technology. In many of its manifestations STS is controversial and contentious, yet an important characteristic of the field as a whole is that there is no consensus about which are its central methods and procedures. It is a field in which there are fairly frequent disagreements and disputes: a multidiscipline that is productively at war with itself. Indeed, over the course of thirty years, many of its practitioners have modified or changed their positions.

It is thus problematic simply to describe *the* distinguishing features of work in STS, let alone nominate the single best examples of its practice. Nonetheless, it is possible to point to three key STS sensibilities, which, while often playing out in quite different ways, capture some of the main points of the general perspective.

The *first* and main sensibility is a commitment to deflating grandiose theoretical concepts, abstractions, and claims – and even some ordinary ones. This is especially the case in relation to concepts and abstractions associated with science and technology. Thus, notions such as knowledge, objectivity, natural order, mathematics, experiment, and measurement are all targets for demystification. As Michael Lynch (2006) sees it, the best work in STS has successfully transformed 'knowledge' into a set of pluralized and situated practices; it has dissolved objectivity into historical usage; and it has respecified the notion of mathematics as a form of number work. However, the scope of deflation spreads well beyond the focus on honorific 'philosophical' topics. STS also challenges some of the central concepts beloved of social sciences, such as social, natural, modern, market, globalization, and governance. Thus, for example, globalization is shown to depend on ordinary devices and unremarkable objects and technologies (Thrift et al. forthcoming), governance is shown to depend on the articulation and enactment of mundane objects and practices (Woolgar & Neyland forthcoming), and so on.

The general thrust of these STS deflationary moves is to point out the considerable and significant work that goes into generating and sustaining these abstractions. This then undermines claims about their obvious, taken-for-granted, accepted nature. Thus, for example, Bruno Latour (1994) declares that we have never been 'modern', meaning that the very idea of modernity should be understood as an abstract myth bearing little relation to practical action. In this same vein, neither have we ever been 'social', 'natural', part of a 'market', nor engaged in 'consumption'. The full range of potential deflation and demystification is extensive, even unlimited, or perhaps only limited by the researcher's skill and imagination. In other words, the working principle of STS is that for any apparently self-evident, obvious, entrenched, taken-for-granted situation or state of affairs, it could be otherwise.

How does STS demonstrate that it could be otherwise? A *second* sensibility is the commitment to do so by working through difficult theoretical and conceptual issues in relation to specific empirical cases. In general, STS practitioners accept that a persuasive means of illustrating and examining the work that goes into sustaining otherwise abstract claims and theories is by showing their instantiation using real-life examples.

A *third* sensibility is to pursue the 'it could be otherwise' clause by drawing on a range of theoretical and practical resources in order to convert revered and standardized ideas and concepts into objects of analysis. One can emphasize the historical contingency of a concept by reverting to a time when it was not established nor taken for granted, showing that in the past it was once otherwise. Alternatively, one can emphasize the concept's cultural specificity by identifying a cultural context in which the concept has a different meaning, showing that it is otherwise in situations other than those with which we are familiar. This approach is underscored by 'ethnographizing' the target concept – that is, by adding '-ography' to the target concept. This helps to recover the strangeness and to interrogate the cultural specificity of such concepts as scale by undertaking study in the mode of 'scalography', while the cultural relativity of the idea of ontology can be articulated by committing to an investigation which can be termed 'ontography', and so on.[2] Or, again, it is possible to emphasize the complex processes and practices involved in the becoming and sustaining of a target concept by 'gerundizing' it, where the active practices constitutive of the target concept can be emphasized by adding the suffix '-ing'. Thus, for example, instead of governance one can speak of 'governancing'; rather than ethics one can examine the practices of ethicizing; and so on. In short, the third sensibility works to demonstrate how the target concept 'could be otherwise' by drawing on resources from history, anthropology, and even literary imagination.

So, if STS offers the resources to challenge entrenched essentialisms, what are the appropriate targets in the field of child consumption? Taking the key identities that populate child consumption studies, to the extent that the literature on child consumption treats notions like 'child', 'consumption', and 'object' as reified conceptual entities, it is the strength of their entrenchment that generates the moral fervour in all quarters. So how better to theorize these entities? Is it possible to think of 'child', 'consumption', and 'object' as analogous to notions such as 'social', 'natural,' or 'modern'? As STS emphasizes, these are not givens. Instead, considerable work goes into making and sustaining these abstractions. By analogy, how to understand the considerable work that goes into making and sustaining abstractions such as 'child', 'consumption', and 'object'?

Hence a key question prompted by a consideration of STS sensibilities is how to resist the key essentialisms wrapped up in the notion of child consumption? Is it possible to generate coherent accounts and persuasive stories about 'children' and their interaction with 'objects'? How to deconstruct our too-willing acceptance of these and cognate terms such as 'decision', 'rational', 'assessment', and 'healthy food'?

Theorizing consumption

The diverse field of child and teen consumption comprises many disciplinary backgrounds and intellectual traditions, and an equally wide variety of issues. These are to do with such questions as how children become consumers, children's responses to television programmes construed as a form of consumption, the role of the media in children's identity formation, the effects of advertising, the cultural meaning of shopping, playing with toys, children online, children and food, and so on. In all this, we can ask some simple questions about the key identities and practices involved. What is a consumer? What is a child? What is being consumed and by whom? How do we know when consumption is happening, and what does it entail? In other words, how do our assumptions about these identities and practices shape our understanding of child consumption?

As a way of tackling these questions, I propose a threefold typology of perspectives on consumption. The axis of variation between perspectives is the treatment of the key identities involved. In a *first* perspective, which can be termed *naive consumption*, consumption is held to comprise certain forms of straightforward relationship between objects (or services) and actors. Schematically, the relationship here is that A consumes B, where the point is that both A and B are presumed to be stable, fixed and given entities. For example, the child plays with a toy soldier, where the nature of the child and the toy are taken as given. Questions duly ensue about whether or not the act of consumption is rational or appropriate. Should a young child be playing with a toy that embodies war and violence? Given the nature of the child and the nature of the toy, is this an appropriate engagement between them?

A *second* perspective, which can be called *consumption in context*, similarly construes consumption as a relation between objects and actors, but also goes on to consider the 'context' in which this occurs. Consumption here is not just about the relation between A and B, but also takes into account some of a wide variety of prevailing circumstances – human, social, organizational, cultural, and so on. The invocation of these circumstances draws attention to the contingency of the relation between A and B. For example, a child may no longer be seen as simply playing with a toy soldier, but might be seen to do so in the charge of parents who show little concern for the child's well-being and education. In other words, the focus on the appropriateness of the relationship in the first perspective gives way to an emphasis on the effects of the prevailing circumstances in the second.

Notably, however, this second perspective retains a degree of stability with respect to the identities of the key players. The (consuming) child and the (consumed) object are still fairly fixed, as the characteristics and capacities of each are taken as more or less given. The focus of attention is the effects of prevailing circumstances on the relation between the two. Are parents a positive or negative influence in determining whether or not the child should play with toy soldiers?

In a *third* perspective, by contrast, consumption is viewed as *ontological enactment*; that is, the practices of consumption themselves entail the enactment, or bringing into being, of the key entities involved. Enactment is a general term for all those processes variously described as constituting, constructing, creating, or performing, so that ontological enactment brings into being the nature and exist-ence of relevant objects and entities. In this case, the entities can include the child and the toy. In some STS usages, ontological enact-ment refers to an extended process over time. For example, Charis Thompson (2005) speaks of 'ontological choreography' as a way of describing the myriad organizational and institutional procedures of agencies involved in artificial inception, the gradual process of bringing into being a new biological life. In a similar vein, the term 'ontological politics' (Mol 1998, 2000) refers to the struggles that are sometimes involved in the process of bringing entities into being. In other usages, ontological enactment refers to the achievement of entity status in the course of interaction, rather than to the process of stabilization of an entity's status over a period of time. The key point in both usages is that the identities and characteristics of the entities involved are neither given nor fixed. Thus in the example of the child playing with a toy soldier, the notion of ontological en-actment suggests that the entity playing with the toy is constituted (enacted) as childlike at the same time as the toy is constituted as a thing with violent or warlike properties. In this perspective, the existence, identity, and status of the entities involved, whether they be children or objects, emerge in the course of consumption rather than simply preceding consumption.

This third perspective can seem unsettling because it disturbs our common reliance on the accepted character of key entities at the heart of the debate, and, in so disturbing these assumptions, it seems to lessen our ability to make straightforward evaluations of the situation. Yet, as I wish to argue, the unsettling of what we take for granted about the key entities is important if we are to get to grips with the current ways of understanding child consumption. In particular, the third perspective – consumption as ontological enactment – shifts the emphasis from consumption as traditionally construed (where entities consume each other) to consumption as a relationship (where entities enact each other). For our particular purposes, this third perspective suggests that consumption involves the mutual implication of entities, among them objects, technolo-gies, and the child.

So, what is involved in enactment? What kinds of processes give

rise to and sustain it? The key STS notion here is 'ontological politics', the term used by Annemarie Mol (2000) for the practices and
processes by which entities are brought into being and sustained. In
her discussion of atherosclerosis, she describes how this entity is very
different in the outpatient clinic compared to in the pathology laboratory. The practices of the clinic and laboratory are quite different,
and these practices differentially enact the disease. She emphasizes
that diseases are never isolated from their practices: there is no such
thing as the transcendental disease. Mol's is a strong argument that
the practices enact identities.

It is important to note that this is not the same as saying that the
same physical body is being looked at from different points of view.
The argument for enactment goes beyond perspectivism; it is not
just that different contexts give rise to different interpretations of
the same thing. Instead, Mol's argument is that different practices
give rise to different bodies. Indeed, the different practices exclude
each other. Atherosclerosis is done differently, and so *is* different, in
the two places. This point underscores the distinction between 'consumption in context' and 'consumption as ontological enactment'.
The former encourages the view that consumption is characterized
by different perspectives on the same entity (the child, the toy). The
latter insists that different practices enact wholly different entities.

How, then, do we come to speak of 'atherosclerosis' in the laboratory *and* 'atherosclerosis' in the outpatient clinic? On what basis do
we use the same term for two sets of mutually exclusive practices?
Mol's answer is that from time to time the different objects are
made to coincide. This is done through 'co-ordination' work. In
other words, active work is required to turn differentially enacted
entities into the 'same' thing. Their sameness is achieved – but as
the upshot of practice, not its precondition.

Enactment in practice

In recent years, many areas of scholarship have witnessed a refocusing
on objects. 'Objects are back' is Frank Trentmann's slogan (2009)
for this recent (re)turn to objects, things, materiality, and material
culture. This move has enriched the scope and insights of many

social science analyses by insisting on the inclusion of materiality alongside dimensions of practice traditionally construed as 'social'. In STS, this tendency has been especially evident in actor network theory, with its notable early advocacy of a 'generalized symmetry' – the proposal that analysts make no *a priori* distinction between the attributes and capacities of human and non-human agency.

So materiality is now much more central to the agenda of social science analysis. Nevertheless, the analytical treatment of materiality is uneven. In some analyses, objects and materiality are included while their ontological status is taken for granted; things are treated as givens, which are then subject to varying interpretations. This corresponds to the 'consumption in context' approach. In other analyses, the very status of objects and materiality is the focus of study. In line with the 'consumption as ontological enactment' approach, these analyses focus on the processes by which objects and entities acquire their status. The difference between the two treatments of materiality is subtle but important, and it is worthwhile looking at some sample efforts of challenges to essentialism in order to illustrate the relative merits of the two approaches.

First, consider some of the contributions by social historians and cultural anthropologists. For example, Arjun Appadurai (1986) examines the social and political mechanisms that regulate taste, trade, and desire with a focus on 'the ways in which people find value in things and things give value to social relations' (Appadurai 1986). In speaking of the ways in which 'things have social lives', the contributors to this work consider how things are used, circulated, bought, and sold in a variety of social and cultural settings.

Of central importance to this argument is the ironic[3] analytical stance taken with respect to the object. The pertinence of the 'it could be otherwise' principle is asserted by assuming that it is the same object that undergoes different interpretations and moves through different settings. For example, Patrick Geary (1986) discusses how the circulation of saintly relics – clothes and objects associated with them, as well as body parts – gave value to the social and cultural structures in which they circulated. Taste in specific relics changed appreciably over the centuries, as did the relative importance of relics compared to other sorts of human and supernatural powers (Geary

1986: 179). As part of a complex mechanism of circulation, the value of a relic could vary according to whether it was the subject of gift, theft, commerce, or value reconstruction.

This central feature of the argument is made explicit in the summary claim that people attribute (different) meanings to things. The implication, then, is that there is an essence of the thing, a perhaps meaningless kernel (or at least a bottom-line residual meaning) that survives all these complex historical and cultural attributions of meaning. But what could an object be without a meaning? In the context of our discussion about the move between consumption in context and consumption as ontological enactment, this is very firmly an example of the former: social and cultural variation is demonstrated, but the deeper sense of ontological enactment is overlooked. A similar point is made by Melvin Pollner (1978) in his well known critique of labelling theory. The emphasis given by some sociologists to the attachment of labels to actions and objects, especially in the sociology of deviance, overlooks the importance of how these are constituted as actions and objects in the first place.

Second, consider how objects and things feature in recent work by the social anthropologist Daniel Miller (2008). As part of his study, Miller visited thirty households in a London street and documented the lives, fears, aspirations, and frustrations of the inhabitants, especially in relation to the 'things that matter' to them. The things that matter in many cases 'turn out to be material things – their house, the dog, their music, the Christmas decorations' (Miller 2008). Miller's argument is that the meaning of material things is often a central feature of people's lives. Against the popular perception that modern life is characterized by superficial and individualistic materialistic consumption, Miller argues that material stuff provides focus and meaning to lives. Objects are 'the means by which they express who they have become, and relationships to objects turn out to be central to their relationships with other people'.

Miller's study is an exemplary ethnography of the minutiae of everyday life, in which he is keen to dispel standard social science notions of society, culture, community, and neighbourhood in favour of a focus on 'what seems to matter most to the people themselves: their ability to form relationships ... which flow constantly between persons and things' (Miller 2008: 6). For example, he shows how material culture has a central role in one householder's efforts to deal with loss and bereavement. Elia initially stored the clothes of her late mother in a box at the bottom of her wardrobe. Gradually and selectively, she gave some items away to others. Finally, after fifteen years, she began to wear the clothes herself; at first privately around the house, subsequently on special occasions, and then without feeling that she had to mark the origins of the clothing (Miller 2008: 42).

This example raises questions not dissimilar to those asked about saintly relics. In what sense are these the same clothes that are subject to varying interpretations over time? Do we want to say that the meaning of those (same) clothes changed according to the gradual attenuation of Elia's feelings of loss? Or is it more useful to say that the entities 'mother's clothing' and 'Elia' were differentially enacted in relation to each other? The third approach – stressing ontological enactment – would favour this way of to making sense of the situation, which has the virtue of sitting well with the insistence in Miller's general approach on the entanglement of objects (clothing) and persons (Elia).

Third, and more relevant to the substantive concerns of this essay, is Joan Sofaer Derevenski's analysis (2000) of the relation between children and material culture. She discusses in particular a photograph (Image 1) that appeared in the British press shortly after the end of apartheid in South Africa depicting 'a young girl dressed in an oversized camouflage shirt and shorts and holding a handgun' (Derevenski 2000: 3), captioned 'A week in the life of the "new" South Africa':

> Next to the picture, an accompanying article described how some Afrikaner children were being given military training. It also expressed shock and concern. The photograph and article provoked further comment in editorials and the letters page (Deverenski 2000: 3).

Derevenski poses the question of why the image and idea of a child with a gun have such a powerful effect on the observer.

Now, from the position of ontological enactment, one would expect an answer in terms of the ways in which the entities in the photograph are enacted. In particular, one might want to ask *how*

Image 1. 'A week in the life of the "new" South Africa.' ©Ian Berry (Magnum Photos). Originally published in Derevenski (2000) (ed.), *Children and Material Culture*, page 3.

the image at the centre of the photograph is indeed a child, how it is that the item being held by the 'child' is indeed a gun, in what way the camouflage shirt is 'oversized', and so on. Instead, Derevenski finesses these lines of inquiry by immediately asserting some 'objective' features of the photograph. She states that 'the photograph is a record of a real contemporary event, rather than the fiction of the book or a film. The child is not playing: the gun is a lethal weapon, the girl is being trained to kill' (Derevenski 2003: 3). This assertion of the photograph's allegedly objective properties is then used to explain the 'powerful effect on the observer': Derevenski claims that the photograph creates a disjunction between the encultured expectations of the modern Western reader and material reality. She states that the:

> connections which we hold with concepts of 'child' (innocent, passive, protected, happy and young) and 'weapon' (worldly, aggressive, violent, suffering and adult) are mutually exclusive oppositions (Derevenski 2000: 3).

Derevenski's analysis epitomizes the difficulty in moving from *consumption in context* to *consumption as ontological enactment*. She portrays the interpretation of the photograph as problematic. In doing so, she invokes context dependence as the key to interpretation. Yet in the same move she invokes a whole series of non-interpreted (or pre-interpreted) assertions about the facts of the matter. These include the realities of the event, of the lethal weapon, even of the character of the shirt and the training taking place. These assertions also include 'the connections we hold with concepts'. These connections then become the context in which we are encouraged to understand the asserted reality.

Thus we see that, although her analysis gestures towards the flexibility of interpretation (in line with the second approach to consumption), Derevenski's invocation of (an actual) context ('the connections we hold') is organized in relation to the asserted actual facts of the matter (that it is a real event, that the gun is a lethal weapon). In other words, the attempt to establish and explain variations in interpretation falls back on invoking the allegedly non-interpreted (perhaps non-interpretable) facts of the matter. Crucially missing from this account is any consideration of how concepts of, say, child or weapon are enacted in practice.

These three examples of attempts to challenge essentialism illustrate the differences between consumption in context and consumption as ontological enactment. Whether it be the contention that things (such as saintly relics) have social lives, that meanings are 'attached' to everyday objects, or that our 'encultured expectations' of things such as children and guns give their juxtaposition shock value, these analyses of objects fall short of articulating the enactment of the key entities in question.

To what extent can enactment help us understand significant shifts in key entities of consumption? Is it possible to demonstrate changes in the enactment of consumers and objects by looking historically at changes in the presentation of the relation between the consumer and the object of consumption? Images 2, 3, and 4 show three covers of *Which?* magazine, the primary publication of the UK Consumers' Association, from 1957, 1982, and 2007.

Here we can follow the successive differential juxtapositions of

Image 2. Front cover of *Which?* magazine, Autumn
1957. © *Which?* magazine.

consumers and objects of consumption. In 1957, the consumers
are women, dressed in what with hindsight seems somewhat drab
clothing (an effect exacerbated by the black-and-white photography), standing outside a shop window, looking in. Their gaze is fixed
on the kitchen utensils – kettles – on display. The consumption
relation is that of women purchasing useful items for the kitchen.
Twenty-five years on, in 1982, the female consumer is depicted
pushing a shopping trolley with a variety of purchases for the home
and family – cornflakes, washing-up liquid, biscuits, milk, butter,
and cheese. The consumer now appears more confident; she looks
straight at the camera. Her choice of goods seems wider, less basic;
the whole business of shopping is perhaps less austere than in postwar Britain. And some of the issues for the consumers of the day are
listed on the cover: legal advice, hair-dryers, tumble-dryers, and car

Image 3. Front cover of *Which?* magazine, October
1982. © *Which?* magazine.

safety belts. In 2007, the female consumer is a yet more confident
presence. She looks directly out of the cover, straight to camera, full
face. The issue is no longer just the purchase of goods and services
(although many of these also feature on the cover); it is now also
about the care of the consumer and her body, and about the ade-
quacy of services provided to the consumer, in this case eye care.

One advantage of understanding this transition in terms of enactment is that it emphasizes the magnitude of the shifts in the interre-
lations between humans and things. It is not just the same women
responding differently to a range of different objects over time. It
is instead a marked change in the enactment of what counts as a
female consumer. The ontological status of the consumer changes,
and does so in relation to what are variously presented as appropriate
objects of consumption.

Image 4. Front cover of *Which?* magazine, September 2007. © *Which?* magazine.

Concluding discussion

This essay has explored the possible parallels between the work of theorizing STS and of theorizing child consumption. In both fields, there has been a growing recognition of the need to include both objects and materials in analyses. But how to study objects and materialities in relation to children?

Different approaches to child consumption are characterized by markedly divergent assumptions about the relation between consumption practices and the entities at the heart of child consumption. In a *first* approach – naive consumption – the properties of all the entities involved, be they objects or children, are largely taken for granted. This approach involves a form of induction and generalization whereby the essential character of the object is deemed to give rise to certain consumption practices in a fairly straightforward way. For example, toy soldiers encourage aggressive tendencies in children. A *second* approach echoes certain STS arguments that objects and materials can no longer be considered as mere givens, highlighting the possibility of a range of alternative interpretations and reactions to the object – the same basic object can give rise to different consumption practices. Frequently, this variation is explained by reference to 'context', intervening variables, the social and political context, the prevailing circumstances, and so on. In the uncomplicated example provided here, this second perspective allows for the possibility that toy soldiers might cause deviant behaviour or psychological damage, and these alternatives might differentially arise according to the influence of teachers, family environment, peer pressure, and so on. Central to this second approach is the idea that variations in consumption practices occur in relation to the unchanging subject or object of consumption: variation is accounted for by considerations of changing context. A *third* approach inverts the direction of the relation between object and consumption by proposing that consumption practices give rise to the object, or, more exactly, that consumption practices enact the object. In our example, this means that it is the practices of consumption – the arguments, discussions, representations, and embodied practices of playing with toy soldiers – that enact the entities involved. In other words, the identity and nature both of the toys and of the child are brought into being. The radical claim is that the objects of play and their putatively violent character, just as the child and its putative innocence, do not pre-exist practices in any meaningful sense. They are instead enacted as such in the course of those practices. As noted earlier, this does not mean that different sets of consumption practices enact sets of wholly unrelated objects and entities. Instead, the environments of practice include co-ordination work: practices whereby the apparently same object is enacted in different practices.

An important implication of this argument is that it offers a better way of understanding the nature and currency of concerns about the morality of child consumption. The vehemence of those concerns and the fact that views are so entrenched may largely stem

49

from unquestioned assumptions about the ontologies involved. In other words, an unquestioning reliance on notions of what a child actually is, or of what kinds of effect consumed objects can actually have, is likely to fuel these concerns. The moral issues appear to derive 'naturally', and to draw strength, from the way things 'just are'. It is a reasonable conjecture that moral panics depend on a naive and unquestioning reliance on the way the world is. The perspectivism of the second approach does little to alleviate the situation. The argument that the meanings of consumption vary according to context will do little to perturb the absolutist view, because it leaves intact a commitment to the existence of objects and entities that lie behind the interpretation. An alternative third approach, which focuses on the situated processes and politics of ontological enactment, offers a way of more thoroughly interrogating the way in which entities – in this case children and the objects with which they engage – come to seem just what they are.

Notes

1 My thanks to Sara Bragg, Dan Neyland, Tanja Schneider, and Anna Sparrman for their helpful comments and suggestions on an earlier draft.
2 By way of reinforcing the general applicability of the 'it could be otherwise' clause, it turns out that the term 'ontography' is itself a term squabbled over by human geographers, and enjoyed usage in something like its present sense in the nineteenth century.
3 'Ironic' in the technical sense that the analytic stance claims that the object is other than it appears to be.

References

Appadurai, Arjun (1986) (ed.), *The Social Life of Things* (Cambridge: CUP).
Cook, Daniel Thomas (2004), 'Beyond either/or', *Journal of Consumer Culture*, 4/2: 147–53.
– (2008), 'The missing child in consumption theory', *Journal of Consumer Culture*, 8/2: 219–43.
Derevenski, Joan Sofaer (2000) (ed.), *Children and Material Culture* (London: Routledge).
Geary, Patrick (1986), 'Sacred commodities: the circulation of medieval relics', in Arjun Appadurai (ed.), *The Social Life of Things* (Cambridge: CUP), 169–91.

Latour, Bruno (1994), *We have never been modern* (Cambridge, Mass.: Harvard University Press).

Miller, Daniel (2005) (ed.), *Materiality* (London: Duke University Press).

– (2009), *The Comfort of Things* (Cambridge, Polity Press).

Mol, Annemarie (1998), 'Ontological politics: a word and some questions', *Sociological Review*, 46: 74–89.

– (2000), *The Body Multiple* (London: Duke University Press).

Pollner, Melvin (1978), 'Constitutive and mundane versions of labeling theory', *Human Studies*, 1: 269–88.

Schneider, Tanja & Woolgar, Steve (forthcoming, 2012) 'Technologies of ironic revelation: Enacting consumers in neuromarkets', in Susie Geiger, Hans Kjellberg & Robert Spencer (eds.), *Shaping Exchanges, Building Markets. Special Issue of Consumption, Markets & Culture*.

Thompson, Charis (2005), *Making Parents: the ontological choreography of reproductive technologies* (Cambridge, Mass.: MIT Press).

Trentmann, Frank (2009), 'Materiality in the future of history: things, practices and politics', *Journal of British Studies*, 48: 283–307.

Vikkelso, Signe (2010), 'Appropriate scales of anxiety – on the frail operation of a therapeutic technique', paper presented at InSIS, University of Oxford, 20 May.

Woolgar, Steve, Schneider, Tanja & Bartlett, Lucy (2010), 'NeuroSTS', keynote presentation to the 1st International Conference on Market Studies, Sigtuna, Sweden, 1–3 June.

CHAPTER 2

Pricing the Priceless Child
– a wonderful problematic

Daniel Thomas Cook

Viviana Zelizer's *Pricing the Priceless Child* stands as a latter-day sociological classic. It is a standard text and a must-read for anyone interested in grasping the emergence of 'modern childhood', particularly with regard to Global North or minority world childhoods. As is the case with many popularly cited texts, the original context, audience and argument can fade and become invisible among the new agendas, fields and modes of inquiry that new readers bring to bear on the material and argument. In addition, the argumentation and presentation of evidence of important works like this one, when alluded to, are often reduced to becoming a flat restatement of the thesis.

In *Pricing the Priceless Child* (hereafter *Pricing*), Zelizer maintains that US society underwent a 'profound transformation' in the social value of children in the 1870–1930 period, whereby the 'twentieth-century economically useless but emotionally priceless child displaced the nineteenth-century useful child' (Zelizer 1985: 209). It is this thesis for which the book is most often cited and identified as a contribution to knowledge. Popularity, however, can have its pitfalls. It is not an exaggeration to say that many who cite Zelizer have not read Zelizer, or have not read Zelizer as thoroughly as her work deserves. Hence, many do not recognize, acknowledge, or account for the ways in which her childhood history serves as a casestudy; an example of larger theoretical contentions about the relationship between economic and social-cultural value and explanation.

Initially pitched to economic sociologists, Zelizer's central argument sought to demonstrate that 'cultural' aspects of social life exerted influence on processes many consider to be 'purely' economic in nature. In so doing, she helped initiate a line of inquiry that has come to reject dichotomous, either/or approaches to the question of the relationship between culture and economy (see, for example, Pugh 2009). For those reading *Pricing* through the lens of the emergent field of childhood studies in recent decades, Zelizer's theoretical challenge to myopic, economistic thinking often gets lost or becomes secondary in importance to the historical thesis about the changing social value of children. It is a useful work for those who desire to locate an identifiable period and dimension of historical change regarding the conceptualization of children. Indeed, the book provides a strong case for just such a pinpoint historical pivot; one so strong that, at times, the citation of the work in research texts or theoretical tracts appears ritualistic, even perfunctory. The timing and nature of this change, in other words, has become part of the 'common sense' knowledge for various kinds of childhood studies, historical and sociological, and in the process perhaps has become dulled of some of its ability to offer insight.

Here I will offer something of a re-articulation of the import of *Pricing* in light of the overarching theoretical issues Zelizer originally addressed, with an eye to how this work may inform thinking about child consumption and children's consumer culture. The substantive issue guiding this foray into *Pricing* may be put thus: how is it that a text written over a quarter of a century ago and that focuses on issues of child labour, child insurance, and black market babies in the US context of the Progressive Era, can be relevant to the study of child consumption and inform research and thinking beyond the American experience in the twenty-first century? After all, Zelizer barely touches upon consumption in her text, except in as far as it is implied in the changing relationship between children and money in her discussion of child allowances (Zelizer 1985: 103–110). Yet it is my contention that consumption stands as one of the key sites where children's value and valuation play out, both structurally and in everyday life.

A problematic beyond the 'problem'

Pricing retains its conceptual vigour because it engages with a problematic, rather than only trying to solve a singular problem. That is, it poses issues and questions in such a way that the problems which emerge do not presuppose their own solutions or answers, but make these available for investigation in contexts and realms beyond the original topic or field of inquiry. As Zelizer (1985: 212) puts it:

> The pricing of the twentieth-century economically worthless child is thus a test case of the 'sacralization effect' of values as a counterpart to the 'commercialization effect' of money. It shows the reduction of the most precious and intangible values to their money equivalent, but also demonstrates how economic rationality and the quantification process are themselves modified.

It is the tension between profane, pecuniary value and sacralized, sentimental value that produces the generative core of Zelizer's efforts (for further elaboration, see Zelizer 1994, 2005). It is the relationship between these, not the favouring of one over the other, which enables further inquiry (for a parallel problematic from an anthropological perspective, see also Kopytoff 1986).

Seen as a dynamic interplay of seemingly incompatible 'effects' or forces, the problem of child consumption unfolds as the articulation of various values that are in conversation with one another rather than, as is often the case, as a culmination of singular economic acts, or as simply a profanation process instigated by corporate forces or by the process of capitalism itself. The framing of the issue in this way provides a theoretical underpinning for calls to move beyond an either/or approach to child consumption – beyond the child as either empowered or exploited by and in consumer culture (Cook 2004a; Buckingham 2011) – in favour of interrogating what child consumption means to various actors and from various perspectives. As a question to be engaged with rather than a problem to be 'solved', the focus on the relationship between sacralization and commercialization invites inquiry into the particular, situated articulations and understandings of the place and role of these values in social life.

I can best exemplify how the problematic marked out by Zelizer affords insights unanticipated by the original argument by discussing the key ways in which *Pricing* informed my research into the history of the US children's wear industry (Cook 2004b). While examining trade and industry documents of the 1910s to the 1930s, it became apparent that entire, thriving industries for children's goods and media were set up in this period. In addition to children's clothing, these industries included children's furniture, toys, books, decorative items, games, radio shows, commercial characters such as Mickey Mouse, and films made with child audiences or users in mind (see Jacobson 2004; Cross 1997; Sammond 2005). It also became clear that market actors, be they retailers, merchandisers, designers, advertisers, or marketers, increasingly and somewhat complacently conceptualized children as consumers unto themselves – as knowing, desiring beings – and, furthermore, designed goods, packaging, advertising, and retail space itself to speak to and appeal to this 'consumer', so constructed.

At first, I found this rise of the child consumer to be incompatible with Zelizer's view that children had become 'extra-commercium' (Zelizer 1985: 11), or outside market relations; for they were clearly implicated in consumer markets and practice, and hence in the money economy, at the precise moment she claimed they were expelled from the same. I was thus confronted with the following problem: how is it that children could remain sacralized and thought incompatible with monetary value and market relations, yet be centrally implicated in a consumer culture that would expand over the decades to include globalized, multi-billion dollar industries? In other words, how could the sacred and profane coexist in such a way?

I came to realize that the tension identified by Zelizer was not fixed in specific terms – that not all money or market action carried the same meaning as every other instance – but instead was malleable in ways that preserved the basic relations, the basic opposition. The change was not in the sacralization–commercialization relationship, but in the ways that children's goods and the 'child' itself were conceptualized in the materials I was consulting. These became framed in ways that made child consumption compatible with notions of sacred or innocent childhood. In short, I found the 'commercialization effect' of consumption was mitigated, on the one hand, when goods for children could be described as educational, developmental, or appropriately 'fun' for children. On the other hand, the levelling effect of money dissipated if children could be framed more or less as persons who have the social right and wherewithal to desire and possess goods – that is to say, if children were figured more or less as autonomous or semi-autonomous consumers. In the first case the 'goods' were no longer commercial goods per se, but rather devices to be used in support of sentimentalized constructions of childhood; in the second, children themselves emerge as actors who are less subject to commercial value as they are subjects in a consumer culture.

The extent to which these formulations may or may not hold for different studies or contexts is not at issue here – though obviously an important area to investigate. The key point to be taken from this discussion refers back to appreciating how the ways of seeing afforded by Zelizer's work can push thought and research in directions unanticipated in the initial formulation of the problem. Her general approach to the question allowed me to avoid getting trapped in dichotomous thinking, in taking sides on commercialization–sacralization, and thereby opened the way for analysis and interpretation that accounted for change that supports apparent relative stability.

An exemplary case?

Pricing, as I have contended, offers the inestimable advantage of enabling investigation and inquiry into children's consumer life in ways not specifically identified in the work itself. However, there remains a lingering question as to whether children serve only as a 'test case' of the larger problem regarding the relationship between culture and economy, as Zelizer suggests. Here, I take issue with her placement of children (and childhood) as mere exemplars of the larger conceptual point.

I think it is worth considering the ways in which children and childhood – particularly in the context of wealthy, consumer, media-saturated societies – have come to represent sacred, non-economic, sentimental value par excellence even as a commercial culture increasingly oriented to their worlds and perspectives continues apace on a global scale. Instead of standing as one example (of potentially many others) of the push and pull of commercial and sentimental worth, I contend that children and childhood have come to embody and inhabit this tension in significant ways.

The vicissitudes of capitalism, commercialism, and globalization come into starkest relief in public discourse when they are viewed from the perspective of how they impact children. From the panics about the premature sexualization of young girls in the media, via concerns about obesity and materialism and the increasing awareness of human, mainly child, trafficking, to the seemingly ever-present street children, the injurious aspects of markets and a market economy regularly play themselves out through the rhetorics of 'the child'. Put another way, the worth of children – and, by extension, of families, of relations of care and of sentiment – now serves as something of a metric for the particular kind of economic value under consideration. The rise of concern about and attention paid to children over the last century – in academic, political, and service contexts – has occurred in the very societies where capitalism and a market economy have either taken strong hold or have threatened to do so; hence, the focus on children serves as something of a moral counterweight, a 'bulwark' as Zelizer (1985: 211) puts it, to the commercialization process. This is one way to grapple with the parallel rise of childhood and consumer capitalism.

Consumption – child consumption – matters in social life to such a significant extent precisely because it confronts one as an everyday, nearly ubiquitous, aspect of living and hence involves the child wholly as a person. In the process, the child comes to stand for a moral worth that is supposed to go beyond the economic system and values that have given rise to contemporary childhoods. Parents – new parents in particular – seem fond of describing how the miracle of the birth of their child helped them rearrange their priorities away from material concerns and towards care and relationships, even as they scramble to kit out the nursery and gather the 'proper' goods to build a proper childhood. The child serves as an important modifier to economic value while enabling its varied expressions.

In this way, it is worth considering that 'the child' does not simply represent one case among many equally significant others in exemplifying a key tension in social life. Rather, 'the child' owns and exudes this tension to such an extent that it cannot be fruitfully engaged without recourse to the understandings about and experiences of children. Here is perhaps another application that most likely was not among those Zelizer intended at the time of writing. Yet these extensions and suggestions give further evidence of the wonderful, generative problematic that *Pricing the Priceless Child* presents us with as we move on towards new understandings.

References

Buckingham, David (2011), *The material child: Growing up in consumer culture* (London: Polity Press).

Cook, Daniel Thomas (2004a), 'Beyond Either/Or', *Journal of Consumer Culture*, 4/2: 147–53.

– (2004b), *The commodification of childhood: Personhood, the children's wear industry and the rise of the child consumer* (Durham, NC: Duke University Press).

Cross, Gary (1997), *Kids' stuff: Toys and the changing world of American childhood* (Cambridge, Mass.: Harvard University Press).

Jacobson, Lisa (2004), *Raising consumers* (New York: Columbia University Press).

Kopytoff, Igor (1986), 'The cultural biography of things: Commoditization as process', in Arjun Appadurai (ed.), *The Social Life of Things* (Cambridge: CUP), 63–91.

Pugh, Allison (2009), *Longing and belonging* (Berkeley and Los Angeles: University of California Press).

Sammond, Nicholas (2005), *Babes in tomorrowland: Walt Disney and the making of the American child* (Durham, NC: Duke University Press)

Zelizer, Viviana (1985), *Pricing the priceless child: The changing social value of children* (New York: Basic Books).

– (1994), *The social meaning of money* (New York: Basic Books).

– (2002), 'Kids and commerce', *Childhood*, 9/2: 375–96.

– (2005), *The purchase of intimacy* (Princeton: PUP).

CHAPTER 3

More children of better quality

Pricing the child in the welfare state

Bengt Sandin

The meaning of childhood and the relationship between children, parents, society, and state has in the West been imprinted by the construction of the welfare state and the changes to it over the twentieth century (Sandin & Halldén 2003; Fass & Grossberg 2012; Therborn 1993; Brembeck 2004). In this essay I will analyse the nature of a welfare-state childhood and focus on the transformation of the notions of childhood discussed in Viviana Zelizer's path-breaking book, *Pricing the Priceless Child* (Zelizer 1994). I will point to the relevance of Zelizer's interpretative frame for the history of childhood in Sweden in a cultural and political context defined by the welfare state. Can the framework used in her book also give meaning to some of the transformation that took place during the construction of the welfare system in Sweden? Does the state set a price on children, and how does that affect the social value of such pricing if situated in the family?

Sweden is in many ways a counterpoint to the US in terms of attitudes towards children and the provision made for them (Fass & Grossberg 2012). Sweden has a long history of left-wing governments, but also a very strong base of individual property ownership and a strong capitalist economy. Studies of value systems across the world show that Sweden holds an extreme position as an individualistic and modernistic society that sets it apart from societies in which traditional values – religion, family – play a larger role, as they do, for example, in the US. Sweden stands out for the relationship between the individual and the state; the phrase much used in this context is 'state individualism' (Berggren & Trägårdh 2009). This relationship is set in the framework of a market economy, which serves to create a complex and unique interaction between market, state governance, and families.

The importance of the state

The social and political changes that set their stamp on Sweden in the first two decades of the twentieth century resulted in the so-called child laws, for example on fostering, adoption, and delinquency. This legislation parallels developments in most other Western nations during the era of the child-saving movements, and reflects an evaluation of children as emotionally valuable. The child laws laid down the framework for the protection of those deemed valuable, but also the punishment of those who deviated from such norms. Protection of children involved the protection of society, and thus also established the fine line between protection and punishment. Normality was defined relative to what the educational system required of both parents and children from at least the early years of the twentieth century. The emotionally valuable child was entrenched in the norms of the educational system and protective legislation, such as banning the auction of children in need of care to the lowest bidder (Sundkvist 1994; Weiner 1995; Sjöberg 1998; Lindenmeyer & Sandin 2008; Lundberg 2000). The so-called romantic child made possible, and visible, the undercurrent of perceived moral danger to children in the consumption of culture – films, books, music, and theatre (Boëthius 1989). The protection of children and of childhood in Sweden evolved into a state venture. At the turn of the twentieth century, childhood took on its shape as a special period in a person's life, and children were described as having distinctive features and possessing special rights. Childhood was also defined as a period of limited capacities and growth – a period to get through as soon as possible. An important aspect of the sacralization of children was their vulnerability and need for protection, and, as a consequence of the social and cultural perils, made childhood a place in which one should not rest too long, for to be a child was to be half and incomplete. If nothing else, it could be a dangerous period if in the care of incompetent adults (Sandin 2003; Lindenmeyer & Sandin 2008).

This also brought a need to define the social commitments of the emerging welfare state at a central and local level, including the role of professionals in childcare, particularly in relation to the children of the working classes where the emotional value of children seemed most endangered. The state also created the basis for a general welfare scheme in which support was given to all, irrespective of class, gender, or income. This served to underwrite the understanding of the equal value of all Swedish children, counting them as a cost for the state and, implicitly, taxpayers (Ohlander 1980).

The relationship between the emotional and economic value of children also found literary expression, as is illustrated by the children's author Astrid Lindgren's film and novel *Rasmus and the Tramp* from the mid-1950s. The narrative demonstrates and conceptualizes the romantic value of a child who has no economic value (Lindgren 1961; Zelizer 1986). The film and its subsequent book editions are about the despair of a little orphanage boy because no one wants to adopt him. The adults who come looking for children only want girls with curly blonde hair – the ideal child, Lindgren implies. Boys like Rasmus with straight hair are of no interest to them. If the novel had been about the state of affairs a few decades earlier, Rasmus, with the makings of a good farmhand, would probably have been the first to be adopted (as in L. M. Montgomery's *Anne of Green Gables* from 1908, in which the old couple really want a boy to help on the farm). Rasmus's predicament was not just a literary invention. In the 1920s, an official at a child welfare office in Solna complained that they had a great many boys, but not enough interested fosterfamilies. The few girls they had were not enough to satisfy the demand for adoptees (Weiner 1995; Lindgren 2007).

Rasmus decides to seek a family himself, and runs away from the orphanage. He meets a tramp, who during their adventures on the road displays a moral compass well suited for a father role model. Determined to provide for Rasmus, he tries to place him in the care of a well-to-do family with a large farm. The family is very likeable, and they would like to adopt him: he has value as an heir. But will he sacrifice the relationship he has built with the good-hearted tramp?

After some hesitation, he goes on the road again and rejoins the 'father' tramp, who turns out to be a married man and a tenant with a small cottage. With this family Rasmus will not be valued as an heir, and definitely not as a farmhand; he has no economic value in such terms. Rasmus stays with a family that have nothing but love to offer him. However, emotional worth comes with the obligation to go to school and that involves a cost for the keep of a child like Rasmus. This very issue, the cost of schooling for families, was a political issue in Sweden in the years preceding the publication of *Rasmus*.

State individualism and the cost of children

The consequence of a prolonged education for the value of children posed specific problems for the politics of welfare as defined in Sweden. The understanding of childhood, and not only its pricing, was now at stake. When the education system was reformed after the Second World War, the Swedish government decided in 1947 that families needed compensation for the loss of income and increasing costs associated with children spending longer at school. However, this was compounded by the decision to finance free school meals for all children, to be introduced over the space of a decade – also to ease the burden on the children's families (Gullberg 2004). All families were given a family allowance to help support their children, without an individual evaluation of need. It was named the 'child allowance'. The parliamentary commission of inquiry that looked into the matter made careful calculations of the cost of children and the added burden of an additional school year. They also factored in the economic crisis and the need for an increase in consumption – much inspired by Keynesian economic doctrines – that had been the very foundation of Social Democratic economic policy during the 1930s. The inquiry set out to put a price on children, and it duly concluded that a child's upkeep was SEK 800 a year, and proposed that the state should support each family to the tune of 25 per cent of the annual cost (Betänkande 1946; see also Marshall 1997).

The merging of public spending with family support was entirely for the benefit of a sustained childhood protected by the state, and it was the state that set the price for the emotionally valuable child.

The Keynesian ideology was used to legitimate state influence on the economic relationships and consumption patterns of Swedish families. The state's intervention was to support the family. Nevertheless, the state did not brand the money as special by issuing coupons or vouchers to be spent on certain types of consumer goods. True, snow-suits and winter boots were initially discussed as the targeted items, but in the end it was left to the family to make its own decisions about appropriate consumption. The hand of the state was to be invisible in the market, but it clearly supported consumption to meet children's needs – much like other aspects of government spending to support increased consumption during the recession of the 1930s. However, child consumption became visible in other ways. The advertising directed at families in the 1950s and 1960s demonstrated that market actors had keenly observed the new opportunities offered to advertise special child-allowance goods to the families at the time of the monthly payouts. But all mothers were not trusted to be able to handle these resources. Historian Maija Runcis demonstrates that it led to a larger proportion of the sterilisation of unsuitable parents being done to women rather than men (Runcis 1998; cf. Marshall 1997).

Over the years the child allowance benefit has grown, albeit only slowly, and today amounts to some €112 per child and month. It is no longer close to 25 per cent of the cost of a child's upkeep, but there is a bonus for a third child, and it has been extended, or rather supplemented, with an allowance for children aged 16 to 18. This latter relates to the extension of schooling, but it is interesting to note that the legal age for children to keep and dispose of their own earnings is 16, an age set in 1949, paralleling the child allowance that covered children up to the age of 16 (SFS 1949).

The symbolic meaning of child support, however, also has changed significantly over the years. At first children's wages earned outside the home were replaced, where families could afford it, by pocket money distributed by the head of the family – again a symbol of dependence within the family. But now, some forty years later, child benefit is looked upon as children's own money, a matter of negotiation within families as to when children should be given access to their funds. It has become a symbol of adulthood – albeit within the family – and of trust in the children as independent consumers, capable of planning their individual consumption of clothing, cinema visits, mobile phones, and the like. It also opens an arena for negotiation of the social meaning of different kinds of money in the family, allowances, gifts, presents and their relationships (Zelizer 1994). For what items should the allowance be used? What are the limits of the child's independence and rights? The symbolism also resides in the child allowance benefit being an expression of the direct relationship between children and the state. Swedish children, with some variations according to class and gender, typically get access to their child allowance at the age of 15, to spend responsibly on clothing, entertainment, and similar. The child is seen as an individual within the family in this interaction between family norms and the state. In the family, the funds are a special type of income, but, and equally important, in such a way as government spending constructs the children as consumers in their own right (Näsman & von Gerber 2003; Sandin 2012; Marshall 1997). These child consumers are not the ones envisaged by the 1947 reformers. It is an unintended consequence of the interaction within Swedish families, and in many ways a new notion of childhood, that has changed the meaning of child allowance and made possible the child consumer. Still another value is associated with the extended child allowance between 16 and 18 years of age. This part of the allowance is tied to an obligation to go to school, and teachers report deviance which might lead to a revoking of the allowance. Youths are, in a manner of speaking, paid for their school attendance or perhaps compensated for their inability to participate in the labour market. As the labour market for youth is basically non-existent in Sweden, youngsters who do not adhere to the economic stimuli and take advantage of the educational provisions become an economic burden to their families. The child allowance works both as a system of support and as an instrument of discipline by the educational institutions, expressing multiple social meanings to the money spent by the government (CSN, 19 July 2012).

This also has a bearing on the character of the financial independence generated by the Swedish system in order to finance higher education. From the age of 18, young people can finance university education with a state loan, independent of the income or inclination of their parents. This system was created in the mid-1960s to replace a system of bank loans based on various guarantees from institutions and parents. Since the 1960s, young people have been individually responsible for their loans without the legal backing of their parents or institutions. Repayment is spread out until retirement and is related to an income-based repayment plan. The relationship here is formed between the young person individually (as an adult) and the state; it is not mediated by the family, nor is the relationship defined by filial identity. This decision was taken by the government in order to counteract the limits of wage-earning families, creating an individual–state relation that would promote educational expansion and accessibility for broad swathes of the population. Equal access to education promoted the idea of economic independence and an individual relationship to the state. This also had fundamental cultural consequences, as Swedish parenting does not involve saving for the education of offspring since university education is financed by taxes. Neither Swedish families nor Swedish universities have a hand in creating the special funds to shape children's educational futures: that is the responsibility of the state. The ambition to form children's path to adulthood takes other forms too, but this stands in stark contrast to the role of education in relation to the family in, for example, the US (Fass & Grossberg 2012).

Ironically, as childhood became more and more organized by the Swedish welfare system and shaped by this individualizing relationship to the state after the Second World War, the most popular figures in children's literature were to be small children in revolt against the adult world. Of these, Lindgren's *Pippi Longstocking* (2007) is the one that first springs to mind. Written at the end of the 1940s, the book depicts a motherless child living in a house all by herself with a monkey, a horse, and a knapsack full of money. She is a child who speaks out against narrow-mindedness and educational constraints and values, spends money as she pleases, sleeps with her feet on her pillow, is stronger than any adult, and lives an untrammelled life without normal limits. She refuses to observe the norms of family life and child behaviour or rules and conventions of any kind, and handles money with little respect for its value in an adult world, consuming wildly and sharing generously – and buying friendships. In her interaction with the neighbouring families and their children, she comes to represent the antithesis of middle-class norms and values – a distortion image. She represents the opposite of the norms, thus ironically confirming them as norms. The institutionalization of childhood and the increased social value of children for the state – more children of better quality – far from conjuring up notions of the child as the passive object of welfare distributions, saw the rise of the child as claim-maker and moral norm-setter (Edström 2000).

Concluding discussion

This brings us back to the original question. How relevant is Zelizer's interpretative framework when analysing a welfare state such as Sweden? Clearly, the emotional value of childhood, the transformation of value, and the marking of special kinds of monies do indeed have considerable relevance for the interpretation of the development of childhood in Sweden. The consequences, however, set Swedish developments apart from those in the US, as they allowed central government to exert a far greater influence; the consequence of social planning and views on childhood formed by society's child experts, who bought into the notion of the emotionally valuable child. The larger social undertakings of school, family counselling, and parental education were expressions of this process, as were prenatal care centres and childcare centres, with their clear intention to intervene in family life. Childcare and child welfare were definitely a matter of public interest; a crucial arena just as worthy of state intervention and regulation as other sectors of society, be it the labour market, agriculture, and the like (Sandin & Lindenmeyer 2008). The romantic, emotional child, protected by the state, was the very motif of the expansion of state intervention in families and support of children's social rights. The realization of the romantic child made state spending worth its price, as it became a part of the Keynesian policy to stimulate spending and consumption. Public consumption represents an important aspect of collective child consumption, channelled through public spending on welfare reforms that were intended to reach the general population both through the building of a welfare infrastructure and through direct support to families. The Swedish model of general welfare was inimical to visualizing such support taking the form of special kinds of money: neither welfare coupons nor state-run shops, as in Eastern

Europe, were part of the Swedish model of welfare. Families were trusted, once accepted as families, to make their own decisions about where and how to spend their child allowance. The very structure of the support given to families did indeed stimulate consumption for their children, and in due course also stimulated individual consumption by children. It was within Swedish families that the state's assistance to families was renegotiated, leaving it as support for the individual child, symbolizing the link between the state and children as well as the independent, adult responsible role of children both in their families and as consumers. This process ran parallel to an emphasis on children's political rights as individuals that, for example, led to the banning of corporal punishment of children in schools as well as in the family, but also to the young as individual beneficiaries of state support. Children's and young people's rights as citizens also make them direct objects of governance; support is withdrawn if young people do not adhere to expectations to live up to the norms of citizenship.

References

Berggren, Henrik & Trägårdh, Lars (2009), *Är svensken människa?: Gemenskap och oberoende i det moderna Sverige*. (Rev edn.; Stockholm: Norstedts).
Betänkande om barnkostnadernas fördelning med förslag angående allmänna barnbidrag m.m. Bilagor (1946), 1941 års befolkningsutredning (Stockholm: Allmänna förlaget).
Boëthius, Ulf (1989), *När Nick Carter drevs på flykten: kampen mot 'smutslitteraturen' i Sverige 1908–1909* (Stockholm: Gidlund).
Brembeck, Helene, Johansson, Barbro & Kampman, Jan (2004) (eds.), *Beyond the competent child: Exploring contemporary childhoods in the Nordic welfare societies* (Frederiksberg: Roskilde University Press).
CSN <www.csn.se/press/fakta–skolk>, accessed 19 July 2012.
Edström, Vivi (2000), *Astrid Lindgren: a critical study* (Stockholm: Rabén & Sjögren).
Fass, Paula & Grossberg, Michael (2012), (eds.) *Reinventing childhood after World War II* (Philadelphia: University of Pennsylvania Press).
Gullberg, Eva (2004), *Det välnärda barnet: föreställningar och politik i skolmåltidens historia* (Linköping: Linköpings universitet).
Lindenmeyer, Kristi & Sandin, Bengt (2008), 'National citizenship and early policies shaping "The century of the child" in Sweden and the United States', *Journal for the history of children and youth* 1: 50–62.

Lindgren, Astrid (1961), *Rasmus and the tramp*. (London: Methuen).

Lindgren, Astrid (2007), *Pippi Longstocking*. (Oxford: OUP).

Lindgren, Cecilia (2006), *En riktig familj: Adoption, föräldraskap och barnets bästa 1917–1975* (Linköping: Linköpings universitet).

Lundberg, Sofia (2000), 'Child auctions in nineteenth century Sweden: An analysis of price differences', *Journal of Human Resources*, 35(2): 279-298.

Marshall, Dominique (1997), 'Reconstruction politics. The Canadian welfare state and the formation of childrens rights, 1940–1950', in Donaghy (ed.), *Uncertain horizions: Canadians and their world in 1945* (Ottowa: Canadian committee for the history of the second world war).

Näsman, Elisabet & Ponton von Gerber, Christina (2003), *Från spargris till kontokort: Barndomens ekonomiska spiraltrappa* [slutrapport från forsknings-projektet För liten för pengar] (Norrköping: Institutionen för tematisk utbildning och forskning, Linköpings universitet).

Ohlander, Ann-Sofie (Kälvemark) (1980), *More children of better quality? Aspects on Swedish population policy in the 1930's* (Stockholm: Norstedts).

Runcis, Maija (1998), *Steriliseringar i folkhemmet* (Stockholm: Stockholms universitet).

Sandin, Bengt & Halldén, Gunilla (eds.) (2003), *Barnets bästa: en antologi om barndomens innebörder och välfärdens organisering* (Eslöv: Brutus Östlings Bokförlag Symposion).

– (2012), 'Children and the Swedish welfare state: from different to similar', in Paula Fass & Michael Grossberg (eds.) (2012), 110–38.

Sjöberg, Mats (1996), *Att säkra framtidens skördar: barndom, skola och arbete i agrar miljö: Bolstad pastorat 1860–1930* (Linköping: Linköpings universitet).

SFS, *Svensk författningssamling*, 1949:381 [Föräldrabalk] (Stockholm: Justitiedepartementet).

Sundkvist, Maria (1994), *De vanartade barnen: Mötet mellan barn, föräldrar och Norrköpings barnavårdsnämnd 1903–1925* (Linköping: Linköpings universitet).

Therborn, Göran (1993), 'Politics of childhood' in Göran Therborn & Francis G. Castles (eds.), *Families of nations: Pattern of public policy in Western democracies* (Aldershot: Dartmouth).

Weiner, Gena (1995), *De räddade barnen: Om fattiga barn, mödrar och fäder och deras möte med filantropin i Hagalund 1900–1940* (Linköping: Linköpings universitet).

Zelizer, Viviana (1985), *Pricing the priceless child: The changing social value of children* (Princeton: PUP).

– (1994), *The social meaning of money* (New York: Basic Books).

CHAPTER 4

A grown-up priceless child

Viviana A. Zelizer

Children's economic worlds have long baffled and divided specialists as well as lay observers. While at the turn of the twentieth century the battles centred on the producing child, in the twenty-first century the worries are mostly about the consumer child. Are children being morally debilitated by excessive consumption? Should parents resist their children's demands for toys, sweets, and ever-multiplying electronic wonders? If children receive an allowance, should they be able to decide how to spend the money? Different versions of such questions, to be sure, perplexed parents as early as the nineteenth century, but the explosion of consumer goods has multiplied those dilemmas. Meanwhile, children keep getting more expensive: the cost of raising a child born in 2009 to a middle-class US family to the age of 17 is estimated to be over $200,000.

Close to three decades ago, in *Pricing the Priceless Child: The Changing Social Value of Children* (1985), I set out to investigate the changing economics of childhood. This essay offers, first, a few reflections on the book's past; second, it advocates a closer exchange between childhood experts, scholars of consumption, and economic sociologists; and third, it identifies four areas of research for potential collaboration in the investigation of child consumption. Finally, it briefly comments on how Daniel Cook's and Bengt Sandin's essays in this volume advance the study of children's economic value far beyond *Pricing*.[1]

First, about the birth of the 'priceless child'. It was unplanned! I wandered into children's history almost by accident. In the late 1970s I had finished a book, drawn from my dissertation, documenting American resistance to life insurance. It focused among other things on the moral and cultural problem of pricing life and death. In one of the many industry histories I read, I had noticed an obscure footnote referring to an intense turn-of-the-century controversy about insuring children's lives. Curious about how issues of monetary valuation applied to children's lives, I investigated the dispute. After a frustrated effort to find archival materials at the Prudential Life Insurance company (a fire had ruined their files), I was fortunate to find a remarkable elderly librarian – just about to retire – at the Metropolitan Life Insurance Company, who magically unearthed a large set of documents about children's life insurance.

Studying children's life insurance drew me into the broader analysis of changes in children's economic and sentimental value. I remained intrigued by the question of how we go about setting economic equivalents for people or objects defined beyond economic value. To answer the question, I focused largely on adults' changing valuation of children in the US between the 1870s and 1930s, and the emergence of what I called the economically useless, but emotionally priceless, child. In the book, partly because of the absence of historical sources, I could not reach far into how children's own experiences and interactions changed.

Pricing centres on the construction of collective standards for the valuation of children's lives. I ask what kind of public normative systems emerged at the turn of the twentieth century in the US concerning children, and how those systems interacted with changing practices. I thus reacted against then popular psychological historical accounts that assumed a uniformity of mentalities in all ranges of social life, in particular those that argued for an overall cognitive shift among parents from instrumentality and indifference to children to affect.

The creation of a new normative system, I argued, made it hard to justify in the public arena certain explicitly economic contributions by children to enterprises and households. Following that insight, the book traced how those transformed normative systems affected commercial, legal, and welfare institutions dealing with children. Rather than a history of general mentalities, this approach produced a history of culture, institutions, and economic practices.

As I was working on the book, I thus found existing statements about children's changing value, such as Philippe Ariès's or Edward Shorter's, not fully satisfactory. Why? Precisely because they tended to map the treatment of childhood into the general mentalities of their time, rather than looking at the particularities of social relations and practices in different settings. Meanwhile, economists and demographers were providing reductionist accounts of children's value, which were equally unsatisfying.

For the next fifteen years or so after *Pricing* appeared, I veered away from the study of childhood. Paradoxically, it was the book's own fault. It happened that my analysis of children's money, such as the weekly allowances provided by their parents, coupled with the book's investigation of 'death monies' – compensation for children's accidental death and children's life insurance – as well as the multiple payments involved in the adoption and sale of children, inspired a new curiosity about how money worked. That led to my next book, *The Social Meaning of Money* (1994).

That book connected me more firmly with the 'new economic sociology' that had taken off in the 1980s. When I finally returned to the study of childhood in 2000 by teaching a new seminar on the sociology and history of childhood, I found a transformed, energized field. Fifteen years earlier, I had lamented that the sociology of childhood was practically non-existent. For example, at the first session on the topic at the 1981 meeting of the American Sociological Association, speakers outnumbered the audience. Nor were the 1980s unusual in that respect. In 1939, a text on the sociology of childhood noted that:

> Sociological writers of the past have limited their studies and researches to the consideration of problems involving the adult population and have neglected for the most part the problems of childhood, with the result that we have developed an adult sociology (Brown 1939: xxi).

Today, the study of childhood is flourishing. Around the world scholars are investigating from multiple perspectives children's culture, practices, and relations. This volume's exciting contributions exemplifies these international developments.

When children re-entered my own research agenda, the new investigations took a very different direction than that of *Pricing* (Zelizer 2005, 2006, 2007). Influenced by my involvement in economic sociology, I became interested in children as active economic agents. Despite the current absorption with children as consumers, I show that children have long participated simultaneously in production, consumption, and distribution. Indeed, in graduate and undergraduate courses in economic sociology, I regularly mainstream studies of children's distinctive forms of economic participation. Instead of devoting a separate week to childhood and economic life, I integrate relevant discussions throughout, much in the same way as I manage the teaching of gender and economic transactions. The goal in this is to identify and explain children's active participation in various types of economic transactions, and show how that varies significantly from one category of social relation to the other. How do child consumption, production, and distribution differ when they involve members of their households and other kin, agents of organizations outside households such as schools, shops, or churches, or other children?

As it turned out, however, my two intellectual 'homes' – childhood studies and economic sociology – remain remarkably alien to each other. With its specialists concentrating exclusively on adult economic activities, economic sociology, one of the discipline's most successful subfields, continues to be a 'childless' speciality. Consider the following. A quick search of the 2006 edition of a collection of 24 graduate and undergraduate syllabi (mostly from the US, but with five international contributors) prepared by the American Sociological Association's economic sociology section reveals that, besides my own undergraduate and graduate syllabi, only three others included any reading on childhood. And what would that text be? My 1981 *American Journal of Sociology* article on children's insurance. Likewise, the *Handbook of Economic Sociology* (Smelser & Swedberg 2005), the field's leading text, includes only one index item for children – a reference to *Pricing*. Other than that, children are absent from the volume's almost 800 pages.

Moreover, economic sociologists have focused their efforts on studies of production mostly by firms and corporations, oddly marginalizing the analysis of consumption. Meanwhile, noting 'the missing child in consumption theory', Dan Cook (2008) has shown how specialists in theories of consumption outside the self-defined field of economic sociology have remained largely blind to children's involvement. While recognizing a booming empirical literature on child consumption, Cook argues that those studies fail to resolve into a coherent theoretical statement. He has a point. The 'add children and mix' strategy falls short of providing an overall understanding of how their consumption works.

The exclusion of children and consumption by mainstream scholars of economic activity, combined with the neglect of children by specialists in consumption theory, creates unexpected opportunities for joint investigations. Certainly, analyses of child and teen consumption practices open up multiple issues of great consequence for the broader understanding of economic processes. Economic sociologists would greatly benefit from a conversation with childhood specialists.

Consider four examples of areas for collaborative research that I find especially promising: they deal with consumption for children, by children, among children, and of children.[2] First, consumption for children. Here, one consequential puzzle lies in the differential expenditures on children by mothers and fathers. A number of recent studies demonstrate that across the world the way in which money comes into the household affects children's welfare significantly. More specifically, mothers more often spend household monies on children's needs than do fathers. For example, if mothers rather than fathers receive child benefit payments, the money tends to go on children's food and clothing. Who is in charge of the household money thus matters for children's access to basic consumer products. Catherine Kenney (2008) for instance found that in low- to moderate-income two-parent US households, children are less likely to experience food insecurity when their parents' pooled income is controlled by their mother rather than by their father. How are such gendered spending practices established and maintained?

Second, consumption by children sets out multiple areas for

75

investigation of children's practices. Let me include in that agenda children's management of money. For example, do children differentiate between monies obtained from different sources (allowances, gifts, payment for chores)? Do they spend those monies on distinct kinds of goods and transactions? How does children's monetary earmarking vary by age, class, gender, race, ethnicity, or religion? What about monetary practices among high-earning children, such as actors, models, or athletes?

Third, consumption among children. Wherever children congregate – playgrounds, classrooms, school dining rooms, at summer camps – they construct elaborate webs of exchange for such commodities as lunches, biscuits, marbles, cards, toys, clothing, and comic books, as well as money. They barter, swap, sell, and borrow consumer goods from one another as they negotiate relations of friendship, power, and care. Often drawing boundaries between cliques via consumer goods, children create what I call 'circuits of commerce': economic arrangements in which participants manage distinctive transactions with special meanings and often with particularized exchange media. How do these child-driven circuits come about? How and when do they break down? What happens when adults intervene?

Finally, consumption of children. How should we understand emerging forms of valuation of children's lives and new baby markets? *Pricing* stopped the analysis in the 1950s. Today, new debates range from surrogacy fees paid to women for 'made-to-order' babies to the multiple payments involved in the growing and contested global market for international adoptions. At the edge of baby markets appear paid exchanges for eggs and sperm that also reflect current economic and political features of transactions involving the production of children.

Beyond untangling empirical puzzles, taking child consumption seriously contributes in distinct ways to economic sociology's relational agenda, moving emphatically away from individual-centred explanations of consumption. It also departs from exclusively status-driven accounts, where consumption matters mostly as a positional effort by establishing class or other hierarchies through the display of goods and services (Zelizer 2012). A relational approach instead treats consumption as relational work: the creation, maintenance, negotiation, transformation, and termination of interpersonal relations. As Cook (2008) notes, such relational features of consumption become especially vivid when it comes to children, as their dependence on others renders their social ties if not more real, then more visible and unquestionable.

In their essays for this volume, Cook and Sandin identify additional, crucial issues for future investigation of childhood generally and child consumption more specifically. Drawing on *Pricing*'s argument concerning the paradoxical sacralization of children at a time of capitalist expansion, Cook argues that children increasingly represent the ultimate 'moral counterweight' to advanced market economies. Child-directed consumption, from this perspective, becomes a complex interplay of commercial expansion with efforts to preserve children's special, sacred status. Ably moving away from dichotomous accounts that either celebrate or bemoan child consumption, Cook's analysis raises subtler research questions. How is the tension between commercialization and sacralization maintained in the twenty-first century? How do businesses, parents, and children navigate a world of consumption where children retain their 'pricelessness'? When, why, for whom, and with what consequences does the delicate balance break down?

Don't forget the state! Sandin warns us in his essay. We cannot properly explain children's variable consumption practices, he argues, without a close examination of state intervention. Drawing on Sweden's experience, Sandin moves the research agenda towards comparative analyses of child consumption, specifically focusing on the differential impact of state policies on children's economic status and emotional value. His fascinating historical account of the Swedish welfare state's support of families' consumer expenditures on children stands in sharp contrast with the US's persistent reluctance to spend public money on child-oriented policies.

State funds earmarked for child support independent of need, Sandin argues, produced its own distinctive version of the priceless child. Among other features, the Swedish consumer child gets his or her own state subsidy, which allows for their more independent consumerism once they get access to these funds. Multiple questions emerge. How does children's greater consumer autonomy influence their negotiations over monies with their parents and siblings? What sort of expenditures decided by children are approved or contested by their parents? Is this particular kind of child money differentiated from other sources and types of monies such as gifts, and if so, how? In what ways does the autonomous economic link created between the state and children shape broader notions of childhood, as in the case of children's political rights mentioned by Sandin?

Clearly, the study of child consumption can illuminate past, present, and future cultural understandings of children and state policies, as well as the everyday economic practices of adults and children.

Notes

1 An earlier version of this paper was presented at the session on the twenty-fifth anniversary of *Pricing the Priceless Child* at the 4th International Conference on Child and Teen Consumption (CTC) in Norrköping, Sweden, June 2010. A slightly modified version will appear as 'The Priceless Child Turns 27' in the *Journal of the History of Childhood and Youth*, 2012.

2 The goal here is to identify several key research topics but not to review relevant studies in these areas.

References

Brown, Francis J. (1939), *The sociology of childhood* (New York: Prentice-Hall).

Cook, Daniel Thomas (2008), 'The missing child in consumption theory', *Journal of Consumer Culture*, 8/July: 219–43.

Kenney, Catherine T. (2008), 'Father doesn't know best? Parents' control of money and children's food insecurity', *Journal of Marriage and the Family*, 70: 654–69.

Smelser, Neil & Swedberg, Richard (2005) (eds.), *Handbook of economic sociology, second edition* (Princeton: PUP).

Zelizer, Viviana A. (1994), *The social meaning of money* (New York: Basic Books).

– (2005), 'The priceless child revisited', in Jens Qvortrup (ed.), *Studies in modern childhood: Society, agency and culture* (London: Palgrave), 184–200.

– (2006), 'Children, "Good Matches", and policies for care', Working group on Childhood & Migration, research note 30 March, available at <http:// globalchild.rutgers.edu/research_notes.htm>, accessed 6 Sept 2012.

– (2007), 'Kids and commerce', *Childhood*, 9/4: 375–96.

– (2010), *Economic lives: How culture shapes the economy* (Princeton: PUP).

– (2012), 'How I became a relational economic sociologist and what does that mean?', *Politics & Society*, 40/June : 145–174.

CHAPTER 5

Not all about the money

Children, work, and consumption

Tobias Samuelsson

Work appears to be part of everyday life for children all over the world, and the number of working children grows globally (Hungerland et al. 2007b; Leonard 2002; Nic Ghiolla Phádraig 2007). However, in industrialized countries such as Sweden, children's work is often overlooked and discussed only as a historical phenomenon, a thing of the past, or at most something that only exists in the poor countries of the south, in developing countries. Also, most international discussions of children's work still tend to end up in a blanket 'demonization' (Arnstberg 2007) of all the different types of work children do, forgetting that most working children do not work under illegal, forced, or slave-labour conditions. Children's work in all its forms is written off regardless; condemned as harmful and threatening their very existence, their inherent right to a childhood playing and learning, sheltered from the dangers of society, and their right to undisturbed development into future citizens. Ning de Coninck-Smith, Bengt Sandin, and Ellen Schrumpf argue that there is a sort of 'cultural blindness' (1997a: 10) in society, evinced in a 'reluctance to accept children as social and cultural agents' (ibid. 9) when it comes to the question of work. Máire Nic Ghiolla Phádraig (2007) even argues that whenever their participation in work is discussed, children are often reduced not only to victims of exploitation, but also to passive objects. The children's own perspectives and motives are seldom heard, their choices and actions seldom taken into consideration. Instead, experts and policymakers tend to speak 'in the name of the child' and explain how children think and feel, and this often furthers the picture of work as a 'non-place' for children.

Several studies have shown that, historically, children never stopped working in Sweden (de Coninck-Smith et al. 1997b; Samuelsson 2008, 2011; Söderlind & Engwall 2008). Today, working children in Sweden sell products for different companies to a value of roughly €11 million every year (Flores 2011; Roxvall 2006; Tonström 2009, 2010). While far from slave labour, research has shown that this kind of work too can be exploitative, and children doing it report its distressing nature, with low pay, harmful work conditions, and the risk of abuse (Besen 2006; Leonard 2002, 2004; Samuelsson 2008). To protect children from exploitation, Sweden has a wealth of legislation to restrict the hours children are allowed to work as well as determine what they are allowed to do, yet this does not in any way prohibit children from working (AFS 1996:1).

It could be argued that children should not have to work and that their parents should provide for them financially. This is certainly a valid point. However, it implies that work is nothing more than a means to an end – that the driving force behind children going out to work is the need for money to support themselves and their family, or a desire to pay for consumer goods for their personal consumption – and a number of studies do indeed indicate that a want of money is a major incentive for working children in Sweden (Johansson 2005; Justegård 2002; Näsman & von Gerber 2003; Samuelsson 2008) as elsewhere in the industrialized world (for example, Hungerland et al. 2007b; Leonard 2002; Mizen et al. 2001). On the other hand, reports from Swedbank – one of the largest banks in Sweden – show that the majority of children receive at least enough money through their allowance to manage their day-to-day consumption without ever having to get involved in any kind of work (Samuel 2001, 2003, 2006); in other words, the majority of children in Sweden are supported by their parents.[1] Apparently, children's work is not all about the money. So why do children in an industrialized welfare state such as Sweden work?

Children and childhood

Rather than serving yet another straightforward account of the way children are exploited when they end up in 'non-places' for children, this essay takes a different approach. I use a perspective in which childhood is understood as a social construction (James et al. 1998; James & James 2004); where the definition of childhood, and how children are supposed to behave, depends on the social and cultural context. I focus on children as agents, capable both of understanding the complexities of the world and of presenting their point of view and foregrounding the strategies they use in their everyday lives. Children are thus not perceived merely as malleable objects caught up in parental or societal projects. The choice of this perspective is an attempt to go beyond the preconceived notions concerning both children and childhood that are built into cultural blindness, clouding our perception of children and childhood. However, to gain an understanding of why and how children choose and act, children's voices alone are not enough. We also have to take into account the cultural, legal, and social framework that both creates possibilities and hampers action (de Coninck-Smith et al. 1997b; Halldén 2007; James & James 2004; Prout & James 1997). By investigating 'the ways in which structure and agency combine during childhood in the process of social and cultural reproduction' (James & James 2004: 8) it is possible to chart how children interact with their surroundings and take part in the formation and transformation of childhood as we know it.

Traditionally, the majority of studies on children and childhood have focused on children's play and learning, and have been based on research conducted in different institutional settings dominated by children, such as school or family settings (James et al. 1998; Prout & James 1997). According to Pamela Reynolds (1991: xix), 'studies of children continue to be relegated to sealed-off areas where specialists focus on aspects of childhood in isolation from the analysis of broader social, economic and political forces.' These choices of settings have produced an image that this, and only this, is what children do in their daily lives. This has generated and even strengthened an image wherein children appear to spend their days only playing and learning, separated not only from adults but also from any kind of work (Zelizer 2002). This has been criticized in social studies of childhood quarters, with calls for a wider research focus (see James et al. 1998). Various scholars working in the tradition of social studies of childhood have focused on children's work, pointing out that the dominant image does not correspond to the realities of children's daily lives, which as it turns out are bound up with the same economic spheres as those of adults (Leonard 2002, 2003, 2004; Morrow 1994; Solberg 1997; Zelizer 2002). This essay contributes to this critical research tradition.

Where do Swedish children work?

To scrutinize the issue of children's work, I use material from an ethnographic study conducted between 2004 and 2006 in one rural and one urban community in southern Sweden. The point of using two communities was not quantitative, large-scale comparisons but rather to recruit informants who reflect a variety of social backgrounds in relation to work. In total, 100 children participated in the study, 66 from the rural community and 34 from the urban community. The children were drawn from school Years 4–9, and thus ranged in age from 9 to 16, although the various ages were not represented equally. The ambition was to include boys and girls of different ages from the two different communities to ensure a breadth of material, and so to be able to account for some of the possible variety I imagined would be found among the children in their relation to work. However, as I have discussed elsewhere (Samuelsson 2008), the variations between these two communities were not significant. The fieldwork involved a range of methods and sources, including group interviews, written essays, drawings, questionnaires, and participant observation. In this essay, I will only use material from participant observations, group interviews, and questionnaires.

During the fieldwork, I met children working in many places. The majority of children had a weak connection to the formal labour market, partly a consequence of the Education Act (SFS 2010:800) legislating compulsory school attendance for children most days of the week, which prevents children from working then; and partly of the labour legislation, which restricts children's chances to work legally in a large variety of workplaces (AFS 1996:1). Possibly as a result, only 9 of the 100 children, drawn only from Years 7–9, mentioned working in places that would traditionally be considered part of the formal labour market where people are doing waged work. These children mentioned that they worked either at their father's workplace, in a restaurant, at a factoring company, answering the phone at a hairdresser's, cleaning a nursery school, or on a farm.

Still, this does not mean that children in general are isolated from the world of work. While the children did not present many entrepreneurial schemes they might use to find work or to exploit new markets, several were engaged in different forms of piecework. The children's work is often intertwined with both play and learning, and is often even initiated by the institutions where they spend the larger part of the day – schools and recreational organizations. This blurs two oft-cherished perceptions of the modern world: the idea of work as a clear entity, and the idea of work as something unmistakably the opposite of play and learning. It is also notable that the work the children undertake is a mix of formal and informal activities. All of this might possibly explain why children's work is difficult to detect and why it is so often overlooked. Nonetheless, this does not make children's work any less of a fact.

Heinz Ingenhorst (2001: 145), in a study from Germany, argues that 'Child labour represents a broad range of activities, intensities and forms, which is very difficult to put into clearly defined categories.' This is also the case in Sweden. Several children mentioned that they work in their own homes, assisting their parents with chores such as the laundry, the washing-up, the gardening, and cooking. They also described taking care of family pets, walking the neighbour's dog, and helping at the livery stables at weekends. At schools, I met children who worked there: sweeping and mopping floors, and picking up litter outside the school. Many children mentioned selling Christmas magazines – a nationwide business with an annual turnover of €23–28 million (Roxvall 2006; Tonström 2009, 2010) – in the evenings after school and at weekends, over the course of a couple of weeks in the autumn. Similarly, some children mentioned that they work during the summer holidays, which are twice as long as the adults' vacation.

Children were also selling Christmas cards before Christmas and tulips in the spring to raise money for school trips, and in April they sell 'May Day flowers', small artificial flowers, in support of the charity Majblommans Riksförbund (2012). Since 1907, Majblommans Riksförbund, which claims to be Sweden's largest children's help organization, has run a variety of projects to support children and young people suffering from disease, handicap, or social problems. Children selling May Day flowers, collecting money to help other children, is the basis of the organization's fundraising activities. The organization uses the money it raises to support individual children, school projects, and research concerning children, as well as summer camps for underprivileged children. When children sell Christmas cards and tulips to raise money for a school trip, the whole class receives the money; the more than 100,000 Swedish schoolchildren who sell May Day flowers every year – collecting between €5 and 6 million – get to keep 10 per cent of the money for themselves. There is also an additional motivational factor in the sale of May Day flowers: children who have raised large amounts of money can win trips and gift certificates, and can be elected as ambassadors for the organization, thus having the opportunity to travel to Stockholm and receive a diploma from the Queen of Sweden (Majblommans Riksförbund 2012).

Finally, I met boys and girls who sold lottery tickets, coffee, and snacks at a football stadium to make money for their clubs, and girls who took care of horses at a local stable and gave pony rides on market days. Most of the time, the children who did this work were not paid in cash. Instead, through their work they financed activities for their youth teams or could go riding at a reduced cost.

Economic autonomy

The most common reason for wanting to work given by the 100 children in the study was, however, money: they both wanted and needed money, money they would use for personal consumption. It would be easy to take this as proof of the way children of today are naive, manipulated, and spellbound by consumer society. Still, much like the children in the Swedbank studies (Samuel 2001, 2003, 2006), the majority of the children had access to money without having to do any work. They received money in a monthly and/or weekly allowance; money that, they reported, covered their expenses

Children selling May Day flowers. Image printed with permission from Maj-blommans Riksförbund ©Maria Rosenlöf.

and often well beyond. To understand children's desire to work and their efforts to earn money, I would suggest we have to look beyond their perceived desire for consumer goods. Instead, we have to take the power asymmetry of family life into account.

As stated in the Swedish Children and Parents Code (SFS 1949:381), those under the age of 18 are legally minors, and are as such not allowed to decide over their own possessions. The children in the study did receive an allowance from their parents. However, this money was usually part of a parental pedagogical project, the parents' way of trying to teach their children the value of saving or handling money in what parents considered an appropriate way. Similar strategies have been shown in previous research (Hungerland 2007a; Johansson 2005; Näsman & von Gerber 2003; Zelizer 1985). As a result, the children are not really allowed to handle their allowance as they please. Much like Viviana Zelizer (1994) suggests, different money has different social meaning. The allowance provided children with economic resources, but was not really spending money. Parents often earmarked it, deciding how large a proportion the children had to save, the speed at which they were allowed to spend it, and what they were allowed to buy

(Näsman & von Gerber 2003). For example, the children were not allowed to immediately spend it all on sweets. Conversely, money the children earned themselves selling Christmas magazines and May Day flowers or in other ways gave them more leeway when it came to consumption. However, the Children and Parents Code even gives parents the right to decide over the money children up to the age of 16 have earned working (SFS 1949:381). That said, the parents did not seem to enforce this right particularly strictly. Thus work appeared to generate independent money that the children could control, use, and spend as they pleased, free from parental control. A number of scholars have shown that a desire for independence is an important motivation for work among children (for example, Leonard 2004; Mizen et al. 2001). By creating opportunities to consume, not necessarily more but as they please, the paid work the children do brings them a greater level of autonomy (Hungerland 2007a; Justegård 2002; Leonard 2003; Näsman & von Gerber 2003).

Increased self-determination

Work can thus help children attain a certain level of autonomy from their parents, giving them the possibility to consume as they please to a greater degree. Benny Henriksson (1983) argues that the role of consumer is the only meaningful role left to children in today's society and their only chance to participate. While I cannot fully agree, Henriksson is correct in some respects. Children's opportunities to move, participate, and act autonomously without supervising adults are indeed limited in many societal arenas. Children in modern Sweden live what are in many ways institutionalized lives, spending most of their day in different spheres of adult authority (Johansson 2005). School takes up a great deal of their time. All children in Sweden are obliged to attend school from the age of seven and until the summer of the year they turn sixteen, so they spend around 5–7 hours a day, 178 days a year in school, where their lives are restricted by curricula, schedules, and teachers. After school, many children attend recreational institutions where they are provided with another couple of hours of adult supervision. A feature also of many of these institutions is their extensive curricularization, so that here too, even after school, children often follow detailed learning programmes to acquire new competencies and skills. These are all settings in which adults make the decisions, be it at home with their parents, at school with their teachers, or activities under the guidance of leisure-time centre staff, sports coaches, and ballet, violin and guitar instructors. On most days, children's opportunity to make their own decisions, to decide how to use their time, to choose where to go and what to do, is thus extremely limited. However, contrary to what Henriksson argues, children still manage to locate spaces which they find meaningful and where they can act autonomously outside the consumption sphere. Work, for example, is not just a means to an end, a way to generate money for consumption; it is also an arena where children create and experience autonomy.

Work is often seen by parents, teachers, legislators, and policymakers as posing a challenge to the children's school education: taking up valuable study time, and tiring children out so they do not have the energy to study (de Coninck-Smith et al. 1997b; Leonard 2003). On the contrary, the children I met argued that work undertaken in their spare time enhanced their formal school education and gave them the chance to practise, say, mathematics when counting money in a work setting. More important still, their work provided them with a less rigid space, beyond the educational system's institutional control. Leonard (2004: 51) suggests that work next to school can be 'the first step towards achieving adult status and moving away from parental control and interference'. While this is true, we still have to remember that the work children take on in their spare time might often be in equally regulated and hierarchical organizations, or settings where adults are just as much in charge as at home or at school. Yet, despite this, the children felt less controlled when working. One explanation is that children's work often involves less obvious external control. Contrary to the situation in school, when they are working – and particularly when selling things – children seldom actually meet managers or supervisors who might interfere with their work or correct their actions. Furthermore, the often irregular nature of the piecework most children undertake offers elements of flexibility and greater self-determination both concerning time and place than children encounter in the normal course of events (Besen 2006; Strandell 2009).

Ulrik, a 14-year-old boy from a rural community, is an enlightening example of this. Ulrik, his parents, and two younger sisters live on a farm, in a house side-by-side with that of Ulrik's maternal grandparents. The farm is located in the countryside about half an hour by car from the main town in the district. Ulrik's parents work full-time away from home. His grandparents raise beef cattle and have a company assembling and selling underfloor heating systems. Both businesses operate from buildings on the farm. I interviewed Ulrik, but also paid a visit to Ulrik's home and met his family. Ulrik works most days of the week on his grandparents' farm, and, given that he also has to attend school, has a packed schedule. The amount of work does not bother Ulrik much, for as he said, he gets to decide when to work and what to do. Except for school, Ulrik spends most of his time at his grandparents'. At weekends and during the holidays, he sneaks out in the early morning and works with them all day long. Ulrik loves his parents, but he argued that it is better to spend the day at his grandparents' than being at home. At home, he said, 'you are just told to do a lot of other stuff you have to do'. Ulrik's description of being 'told to do stuff' at home tells us something important about children's daily lives. The phrase 'told to' encapsulates what Allison James and Adrian L. James (2004) see as the authority parents, and adults generally, exert over children individually and as a social category. Parents and adults, as a general rule, influence children's daily lives by making a variety of decisions, by imposing these decisions, and by telling children what to do. Obviously, children do not always support or appreciate this. Ulrik is no exception. His grandparents, of course, are also adults and if they so wished could decide over Ulrik, but refrain from doing so.

New spaces for action

Some scholars studying working children argue that children are 'working to be someone' (Hungerland et al. 2007b) rather than for economic purposes, and Beatrice Hungerland (2007a: 175) suggests that work is 'a possibility for children to go beyond the social position they have been given'. Work offers a chance to experience a feeling of being more grown-up (Morrow 1994; Solberg 1997). In a work situation, children might have to take on more responsibility than they normally would. They can make contributions that might be valued by adults and might very well be needed (Morrow 1994; Samuelsson 2008; Solberg 1997). This may foster the children's growth in their own eyes and in the eyes of others, and give them a chance to experience a greater parity with adults than they can experience at home or at school (Strandell 2009). Furthermore, by taking part in work, children can gain access to settings that are usually exclusively adult. They can both meet people and see parts of society they may not necessarily encounter otherwise, and 'extend their social networks and at least momentarily feel part of an adult world' (Strandell 2009: 206).

When I met Ulrik and his family, I was told his grandparents did not pay wages to any of their grandchildren for their work. It is thus not a straightforward business relationship, with the grandparents buying the children's labour. Ulrik's mother explained that the grandparents reward the children with additional, more expensive birthday and Christmas presents. Moreover, the grandparents do not assign the chores; rather, the children are very much free to decide for themselves, and this appears to be a more important incentive for the children than a promise of gifts. In addition, for this family working together appears to be a way of spending quality time together. Work gives the children access to their grandparents. Ulrik told me that he worked all the time he was not at school. Whilst all this work is time-consuming and even at times strenuous, Ulrik enjoys it. He emphasized all the things he is able to try and all the vehicles he is allowed to drive when working with his grandparents – tractors when snow-ploughing or ploughing fields, and quad bikes. Being around large farm vehicles, or even driving them, can certainly be dangerous for young children. Every year children are injured or killed in farm accidents when working with their families (Sandström 2000).

Of course, it is illegal for Swedish children of Ulrik's age to drive any of these vehicles, and, although they might like to, most children his age or younger would probably never get the opportunity to do so. Quite possibly this increases Ulrik's self-pride when his work gives him the chance to do what most children cannot. Much of children's daily life is structured as a developmental ladder related to chronological age (Närvänen & Näsman 2007). The school system is organized according to this system to 'provide an ordered temporal passage from child to adult status' (Strandell 2007: 55). Similarly, labour regulations have been created as a linear development ladder, or perhaps rather 'a ladder of increasing "adulthood"' (Näsman 1994: 170), along which children gradually progress towards a full working life after their eighteenth birthday. All this emphasizes that the principal way for children to gain autonomy in Swedish society is to grow up, to become adults (Näsman 1994). By working, Ulrik is able to jump several steps up the ladder without actually growing older, gaining access to a rather exclusive adult world prohibited to most other children in the communities I visited. This being the case, doing farm work all day long – work that to a bystander might appear both boring and tiring – can thus be a liberating opportunity rather than a strenuous chore.

Concluding discussion

In this essay, I have outlined some new perspectives on why children in an industrialized welfare state such as Sweden might choose to work. As I have shown, by highlighting the children's perspective we can move beyond the notion of children as naive victims and passive objects when it comes to work. It becomes obvious that children make different active choices, and that there is more to their wish to have more money and their willingness to work than a simple yearning for increased spending power and a desire for consumer goods. Rather than wanting to consume more, it is a question of autonomy – to be able to decide what to buy.

Although it is important to emphasize the children's own decision-making and agency in their daily lives, it is equally important to demonstrate that they do not live free of structure by situating their experiences in a cultural, legal, and social framework (Hungerland 2007a). By combining these aspects, it is possible to make sense of a situation that might from the outside appear irrational. Financially, the children I met do not need to work, yet even so they take part in many forms of work. I suggest that we must seek the explanation to this conundrum in the way children's lives are organized. Modern Swedish children live in very controlled environments dominated by adults who are determined to protect them, make decisions, supervise, and restrict their movements. Work gives children an opportunity to create autonomous spaces. Work can provide children with money, with its promise of consumption beyond parental control; it offers an arena in which children have greater opportunity to make their own decisions; and it gives them access to a world that in today's society is largely restricted to adults.

Finally, Swedish, like many languages, has a saying along the lines of 'Let children be children', meaning that they should be given the possibility to play freely and unrestrainedly, to explore the world and seize the day. The saying refers back to an (imagined or real) past way of life. It is sometimes invoked when children's work is debated, and then as an argument against work, which supposedly ruins children's chances of being children. Ironically, given their controlled, schedulized, and curricularized daily lives, work appears to offer children in an industrialized welfare state such as Sweden some of that (lost) freedom. Thus, rather than being a threat to children, work offers them a chance to be just that.

Note

1 There are of course exceptions. Swedish Save the Children reported in 2010 that the number of children in Sweden living in poverty is rising (Rädda Barnen 2010).

References

AFS 1996:1, *Arbetarskyddsstyrelsens författningssamling, Minderåriga*, available at <http://www.av.se/regler/afs/1996_01.pdf>, accessed 24 October 2005.
Arnstberg, Karl-Olov (2007), *Svenska tabun* (Stockholm: Carlssons).
Besen, Yasemin (2006), 'Exploitation or Fun? The lived experience of teenage employment in suburban America', *Journal of Contemporary Ethnography*, 35/3: 319–40.
de Coninck-Smith, Ning, Sandin, Bengt & Schrumpf, Ellen (1997a), 'Introduction', in de Coninck-Smith, Sandin & Schrumpf (1997b), 7–16.

– (1997b) (eds.), *Industrious children: Work and childhood in the Nordic countries 1850–1990* (Odense: Odense University Press).

Flores, Juan (2011), 'Företag tjänar på barn som säljare', *Dagens Nyheter*, 19 September: 22.

Halldén, Gunilla (2007) (ed.), *Den moderna barndomen och barns vardagsliv* (Stockholm: Carlssons bokförlag).

Henriksson, Benny (1983), *Not for sale: Young people in society* (Aberdeen: AUP).

Hungerland, Beatrice (2007a), 'Work – a way to participative autonomy for children', in Hungerland, Liebel, Milne & Wihstutz (2007b), 167–75.

– Liebel, Manfred, Milne, Brian & Wihstutz, Anne (2007b) (eds.), *Working to be someone: Child focused research and practice with working children* (London: Jessica Kingsley Publishers).

Ingenhorst, Heinz (2001), 'Child labour in the federal republic of Germany,' in Mizen, Pole & Bolton (2001), 139–48.

James, Allison & Prout, Alan (1997) (eds.), *Constructing and reconstructing childhood* (London: RoutledgeFalmer).

– & Jenks, Chris & Prout, Alan (1998), *Theorizing childhood* (Cambridge: Polity Press).

– & James, Adrian L. (2004), *Constructing childhood: Theory, policy and social practice* (Basingstoke: Palgrave Macmillan).

Johansson, Barbro (2005), *Barn i konsumtionssamhället* (Stockholm: Norstedts).

Justegård, Helén (2002), 'Earning money of your own: Paid work among teenagers in Sweden', in Merryn Hutchings, Márta Fülöp & Anne-Marie Van den dries (eds.), *Young people's understanding of economic issues in Europe* (Stoke-on-Trent: Trentham Books), 193–210.

Leonard, Madeleine (2002), 'Working on your doorstep: Child newspaper deliverers in Belfast', *Childhood*, 9/2: 190–204.

– (2003), 'Children's attitudes to parents', teachers' and employers' perceptions of term-time employment', *Children & Society*, 17/5: 349–60.

– (2004), 'Children's views on children's right to work: Reflections from Belfast', *Childhood*, 11/1: 45–61.

Majblommans Riksförbund (2012), <www.majblomman.se>, accessed 28 June 2012.

Mizen, Phillip, Pole, Christopher & Bolton, Angela (2001) (eds.), *Hidden hands: International perspectives on children's work and labour* (London: RoutledgeFalmer).

Morrow, Virginia (1994), 'Responsible children? Aspects of children's work and employment outside school in contemporary UK', in Berry Mayall (ed.), *Children's childhoods: Observed and experienced* (London: Falmer Press), 128–43.

Närvänen, Anna-Liisa & Näsman, Elisabet (2007), 'Age order and children's agency', in Wintersberger, Alanen, Olk & Qvortrup (2007), 225–49.

Näsman, Elisabet (1994), 'Individualization and institutionalization of childhood in today's Europe', in Jens Qvortrup, Marjatta Bardy, Giovanni Sgritta & Helmut Wintersberger (eds.), *Childhood matters: Social theory, practice and politics* (Brookfield VT: Avebury), 165–87.

– & von Gerber, Christina (2003), *Från spargris till kontokort: Barndomens ekonomiska spiraltrappa* (Linköping: ITUF, Linköpings Universitet).

Nic Ghiolla Phádraig, Máire (2007), 'Working children and the "descholarization" of childhood', in Wintersberger, Alanen, Olk & Qvortrup (2007), 201–223.

Prout, Alan & James, Allison (1997), 'A new paradigm for the sociology of childhood. Provenance, promise and problems', in James & Prout (1997), 7–33.

Rädda Barnen (2010), *Barnfattigdomen i Sverige. Årsrapport 2010* (Stockholm: Rädda barnen).

Reynolds, Pamela (1991), *Dance civet cat: Child labour in the Zambezi valley* (London: Zed Books).

Roxvall, Anna (2006), 'Jultidningar guldgruva för små entreprenörer', *Svenska Dagbladet Näringsliv*, 23 October, 27.

Samuel, Ulla (2001), *Veckopengen IV* (n.p.: Institutet för Privatekonomi).

– (2003), *Tonåringar och deras pengar IV* (n.p.: Institutet för Privatekonomi).

– (2006), *Veckopengen V* (n.p.: Institutet för Privatekonomi).

Samuelsson, Tobias (2008), *Children's work in Sweden: A part of childhood, a path to adulthood* (Diss., Linköping Studies in Arts and Science, 442; Linköping: Linköping University).

– (2011), 'Making money, helping out, growing up: Working children in Sweden', in Robin Price, Paula McDonald, Janis Bailey & Barbara Pini (eds.), *Young people and work* (Farnham: Ashgate), 21–34.

Sandström, Anders (2000), 'Familjeidyllen en dödsfälla', *Lantbrukets affärer*, 1: 28–31.

SFS [Svensk Författningssamling] 1949:381, *Föräldrabalk* (Stockholm: Justitiedepartementet).

SFS 2010:800, *Skolag* (Stockholm: Utbildnings- och kulturdepartementet).

Söderlind, Ingrid & Engwall, Kristina (2008) (eds.), *Barndom och arbete* (Umeå: Boréa förlag).

Solberg, Anne (1997), 'Negotiating childhood: Changing constructions of age for Norwegian children', in James & Prout (1997), 126–44.

Strandell, Harriet (2007), 'New childhood space and the question of difference', in Helga Zeiher, Dympna Devine, Anne Trine Kjørholt & Harriet

Strandell (eds.), *Flexible childhood? Exploring children's welfare in time and space* (vol. ii of *COST A19: Children's welfare*) (Odense: University Press of Southern Denmark), 49–68.

Strandell, Harriet (2009), '"It's work that has to be done": Finnish school children working during their summer holiday', *Barn*, 3–4: 205–222.

Tonström, Eva (2009), 'Barn ger förlag miljoner i julklapp', *Svenska Dagbladet*, 11 November, available at <http://www.svd.se/nyheter/inrikes/barn-ger-forlag-miljoner-i-julklapp_3781583.svd>, accessed 22 December 2010.

– (2010), 'Barnens arbete drar in miljoner', *Svenska Dagbladet Näringsliv*, 27 November: 4–5.

Wintersberger, Helmut, Alanen, Leena, Olk, Thomas & Qvortrup, Jens (2007) (eds.), *Childhood, generational order and the welfare state: Exploring children's social and economic welfare* (vol. i of *COST A19: Children's welfare*) (Odense: University Press of Southern Denmark).

Zelizer, Viviana. A. (1985), *Pricing the priceless child* (New York: Basic Books).

– (1994), *The social meaning of money* (New York: Basic Books).

– (2002), 'Kids and commerce', *Childhood*, 9/4: 375–96.

CHAPTER 6

'Consider the fact that I am considerate'

Parent–teen bargaining

Shosh Davidson

And, in the end, the love you take
is equal to the love you make.

('The End' by John Lennon &
Paul McCartney. Sony/Atv Tunes Llc.)

The increasing participation of children and teens in consumer culture has led researchers to examine how this involvement alters the
status of childhood (Cook 1995; Martens et al. 2004; Zelizer 2002).
One question that arises from this line of inquiry examines the ways
in which children's independence and autonomy are extended in
consumer culture in general (Buckingham 2000; Cook 2000) and
family dynamics in particular (Boden 2006). This essay examines
the way in which parents and teens aged 12–15 from low-income
neighbourhoods in Israel negotiate over goods and services.[1] Examining negotiations between parents and teens on consumer issues
offers a peek into what Julia Brannen and Gail Wilson (1987) call
'the black box' of the household (ibid. 1) – what happens in neglected areas such as the domestic economy, and how, in the spirit of
autonomy and competence, children develop in everyday practices
of consumption (Martens et al. 2004).

The connection between consumer practices and the exercise of
autonomy has been ideologically related to the act of 'consumer
choice' (Buckingham 2000). In a post-modern world as described by

thinkers such as Anthony Giddens (1991) and others, cultural reality does not rest on a clear and binding tradition, and consequently the individual is faced with a multitude of options (Bauman 2000; Beck & Beck-Gernsheim 1996). Individuals then feel their sense of belonging is weakened, which greatly increases their levels of anxiety (Giddens 1991; Warde 1994). Consumer culture, by this account, provides different lifestyle models from which consumers can choose and decide independently (Giddens 1991). The self is seen as a detached, separate individual who relies on himself when building his identity. A different view maintains that consumer habits should be understood in the context of social relationships (Simmel 1971; Miller 1995; Chin 2001; Martens et al. 2004; Zukin & Maguire 2004).

According to this view, people do not make purchases solely as individuals prompted by free choice, but as socially embedded agents limited in their shopping behaviour by various aspects of social life (Bird-David & Darr 2009). My essay aims to characterize the nature of the autonomy that teens develop through bargaining with their parents over financial and consumer issues (Scott et al. 2000), and will focus on various bargaining strategies which teens employ, and on the reciprocity between parents and teens that these tactics illustrate. To this end, discussion groups were conducted in seventeen classes of Years 7–9 at six junior high schools located in low-income neighbourhoods on the social periphery of Israel.[2]

Each discussion lasted 45–50 minutes – one standard school period – with the first minutes of the period devoted to the teacher's explanation of the nature of the activity, and then my presentation. After a general presentation, I asked the pupils to be my 'research assistants' and to tell me about their experiences and insights. In conducting the discussion groups, I adopted the strategy of questioning known as 'the interested adult', or 'the interested idiot' (Darbyshire et al. 2005), playing the role of the adult who has forgotten or never knew what children do. In this case, it meant asking the teens to explain things about their daily life on subjects relating to shopping, such as What do you buy? Where does the money to go shopping come from? and the like. General statements made by participants such as 'You know not to go overboard', or 'Ask reasonably, know when to push' were the openings I needed to ask for examples and anecdotes on the subject.

Participants also discussed various comments from previous discussion groups about independence and responsibility. In addition, 12 in-depth interviews were conducted with 11 mothers and 1 father, whose children participated in the discussion groups.[3]

In four of the families, only one parent worked, and one family was headed by a single mother. The interviews, which were conducted at the homes of the interviewees and lasted one-and-a-half hours, were characterized by various ways of focusing on the questions, How do you cope with requests by your teenage children to buy them things? What do you think about teenagers and shopping? How does your household deal with this subject? The essay will first describe teens' discussions of their sources of income and the methods they employ to increase their income. I then present the quality of reciprocity created between parents and teens in light of and through the material exchange, and finally examine the nature of the autonomy that teens develop through discussing and bargaining over financial and consumer issues with their parents.

Parent–teen bargaining

Teens' income sources and their methods of increasing their income, as presented in the class discussion groups, extend along an axis of relative dependence to independence. The sources of income are work outside the home, presents, working for one of their parents, allowances, allowances conditional on achievements or the completion of a specific chore, and payment for various chores done around the house. Based on the class discussion, it seems that teens draw a very clear distinction between 'money from parents', which is money they have to ask their parents for and entails convincing them of the necessity of the expense, and 'my own money', which they don't have to ask their parents for and which they can spend without their their consent. These categories may coincide or overlap sometimes – for example, an allowance that changes according to needs that parents approve of, or money received from parents on special occasions – yet teens distinguish between the different sources of income, manipulate them, and use the different sources of income differently.

SITUATING CHILD CONSUMPTION

In her book *The Social Meaning of Money* (1997), Viviana Zelizer analyses the modern use of money as a social medium, which provides visibility to certain types of relationship and social meaning, with their inherent implications. The various sources of income available to teens extend across the continuum of the financial and personal independence that they grant. On one end of the continuum is 'money from my parents', which is given based on parents' judgement. The fact that parents are the breadwinners, which gives them authority in general and validation for their financial decisions in particular, is accepted and understood by many teens. However, the picture is not so simple, for as one teen put it: 'Parents are a little bit considerate of their children' (girl, 13). It seems that parental authority is justified by virtue of their hard work and caring for the family, and does not derive solely from a 'natural', legal, or normative right.

The transfer of money from parents to children changes the nature and value of the currency: 'The moment they give you the money and it's in your hands, it's yours' (girl, 15). In the discussion groups, teens describe different ways of turning 'money from my parents' into 'my own money'. One teenager said: 'There are some things we want but parents don't allow us to get. *So that's why you argue*' (boy, 14, my emphasis). The first bargaining strategy teens use is to attempt to persuade parents of the necessity and worthwhileness of the purchase. Its necessity could stem from the fact that 'everyone' has the same product, as one child explained: 'You tell them "everyone" uses it. Everyone has it – everyone has a cell phone. Everyone has it, only I don't' (girl, 14). Another rationale that strikes a sensitive chord with parents is the product's importance to the teen's development or academic success; or, as one girl commented: 'Tell them it's a thinking game, that it helps you learn' (girl, 13).

The other bargaining strategy is negotiation, marked by power games – as one of the teens suggested, 'We have power. Let's put it like this – if they don't buy us what we want, we'll make them suffer' (boy, 14), or the explicit threat of another teen: 'There's a better way, just say – buy it or I won't study!' (boy, 14). A different strategy takes the form of pleasing and flattering, as one teen described his way of getting what he wants: 'I approach Mum when she's not tense, I make her laugh so she'll be in a good mood and then I tell her [wheedling] please, Mom, buy it for me' (boy, 14). The other significant type of money in the life of the teens is 'my own money', is defined by its ownership and the ability to spend it without having to justify this to their parents. The 'purest' kind of 'my own money' is that which is earned by having a 'real' job, outside the family household. Work is seen as an educational experience that teaches, in the most tangible way, the value of things; as a teen from one of the classes stated: 'Anyone who works for their money knows what money means' (boy, 13). However, work is still uncommon among the teenagers who participated in the study.

One of the characteristics of 'my own money' is the different attitude teens have towards spending it, compared with expenditures that rely on money from their parents. Zelizer (1997) shows how people earmark different monies for different social interactions. According to her analysis, not only do people think or feel differently about different monies, they also spend them differently by limiting the use of money from a certain source to a certain goal. A girl in one class made a clear distinction between 'my own money' and 'money from my parents': 'With my money I buy all kinds of stuff, and then I go shopping with my Mom – that money [my money] has nothing to do with it' (girl, 14). It seems 'my own money' is rarer, more valuable, whereas 'money from my parents' is more 'spendable'.

Pocket money, or an allowance, is a sum of money given regularly by parents and put at the disposal of the teen. An allowance slightly increases the teen's autonomy, yet still enables parental control of the family's expense budget. Making the allowance conditional on good behaviour is one way of 'commercializing' parent–teen negotiations. According to this exchange system, desired behaviour is rewarded and bad behaviour is punished. As one of the teens said:

> I tell my parents to buy me something and if they don't want to, then I set conditions – if I do this for them, they'll do that for me … I told her – you know what? I'll tidy the house all week … if you buy it for me. (boy, 14)

A central debate in social anthropology concerns whether kinship groups should be treated as a special category of social relationships characterized by a commitment to share resources without thought of personal gain (Finch & Mason 1993). Anthropologists who oppose this view argue that kinship group relations are not characterized by a distinct 'moral property', but can be explained in the same way as other relationships and examined according to the material and financial benefits they provide individuals. Commercializing the care and aid relationships in families is often decried by both parents and teens. The fact that this is a controversial issue evoking strong emotions on the one hand, but practised in many families on the other, raises questions regarding the moral property of reciprocity between parents and teens. The accepted view expects teens to take care of the home while parents are out at work. It seems that different approaches to reciprocity, which include ample room for bargaining and negotiations about chores and rewards, are applied in many families. One girl described her own family:

> I used to get paid for babysitting my sisters, but now it's become a regular thing. My mum bribes me ... for example, if we're at the pool and I don't feel like helping my sisters shower, she tells me – if you shower your sisters, you'll get this or that amount of money. (girl, 14)

Examination of these strategic interactions points to the nature of reciprocity, and the meaning of fairness in moral and strategic bargaining between parents and teens. It seems that teens are paid to do household chores more often than they are willing to admit; not always as an explicit agreement, but as part of their 'favour-for-favour' daily interactions. As one girl said:

> I have two younger brothers and when my parents ask me to help with my brothers and stuff, I help, and when I want to go out or I want money for something, they give it to me, they don't ask questions. (girl, 14)

In other words, the daughter's helpful and desirable behaviour leads her parents to grant her requests, not necessarily in a direct exchange for her services as a babysitter, but as a form of reciprocity and to encourage the desired behaviour (Macintosh & Punch 2009). The use of payment for chores, even when it is in the form of a conditional allowance, is seen at times by the teens as a way of increasing their autonomy. This system of exchange increases the children's status as active agents who influence their own financial situation. This category of child income demonstrates the ways relationships and children's status within the family are negotiated by defining the value and significance of money transactions (Zelizer 2002). In order to understand the bargaining that takes place between parents and teens, I will now turn to the moral quality of reciprocity created between parents and teens in light of and through the material exchange.

The currency of considerate behaviour

Candour and openness are the first strategy that parents use to handle financial interactions with their teens. Sharing with the children the family's financial situation, and in some cases its financial hardships, helps parents explain the need for restraint in their children's shopping requests. A father explains the directness and non-defensive style in which he explains to his children the family's financial situation: 'We let them know in advance that we can't, even if we want ... give them what they are asking for' (Interview 5, father). An example of strengthening the feeling of belonging in the family takes place when parents emphasize to their children the family's situation in comparison with their friends' families, and use the restriction to strengthen family identity and to match the child's expectations to the situation. As one mother says: 'You explain to him – his friend's parents are not like me and Dad. You explain the situation' (Interview 3, mother). Denying the teen's request to buy something, while accompanying the refusal with an explanation of the family's financial options, increases the teen's possibility for belonging.

Children's understanding of the family's financial limitations and parents' willingness to cater to children's needs within a modest financial budget are described by parents and teens as requiring mutual consideration. Considerate behaviour is the children's way of participating in the effort to support the family. Contemporary parenthood (Seiter 1993), and motherhood in particular (Cook 2009), is embedded in consumption. Elaine Bell Kaplan (2000) suggests that including the world of consumption directly into the context of mothering highlights the play and force of children's subjectivities relative to practices of care, as the following example demonstrates. Leehi is the youngest daughter in a single-parent family. Her parents have been divorced for a number of years, and she lives with her mother and older brother, a high school student. Einat, Leehi's mother, has a graphic design studio and works long hours away from home.[4] This is how Einat described the family's financial situation:

> When I got divorced there was initially a period when we hadn't reached a financial settlement, and it was very important for me to buy this house... and I took out a second mortgage ... and both kids had to be part of that. You can't maintain the same lifestyle as before, you have to be more calculated and level-headed. We talked about it a number of times, and these days, you know, they consider everything. Even the electricity bills; if the bills are unusually high, they're involved. (Interview 9, mother)

Einat describes the demands made of the children to understand and adapt to the new financial situation as their way of participating in supporting the family: 'If you don't treat them as partners, they won't be partners. I don't, umm, send them out to make money, yeah, but ... they're involved' (Interview 9, mother).

In their book *Connecting Children*, Brannen et al. (2000) write that care as a concept is the engine of family life. Care implies the realization of control, and places the caring, responsible person in a position of power (see Walkerdine & Lucey 1989). In the context of food, for example, mothers and children fight about, negotiate, bargain, and enact relationships of super- and subordination, of caring and sharing (Cook 2009; Kaplan 2000). Analysing considerate behaviour shows that children, like adults, are active participants in care relationships. Children's caring includes a wide range of behaviours and emotions that build cooperation and solidarity (Brannan et al. 2000) and thus raises children's status in the family. Considerate behaviour, therefore, is a direct continuation of openness, and is a currency that teens can contribute to the effort to support the family. In Hebrew, the word *hitchashvut* (consideration) comes from the root *h.sh.v*, which has several meanings, and, beyond the accepted meaning of using judgement, also carries a meaning of 'calculation', educated, and calculated examination. This double meaning reflects the complexity and symbolism involved in the considerations of material exchange between parents and teens. The reciprocity that parents and teens speak of expresses belonging, which is learned and exercised in consumer interactions and is an inseparable part of those interactions. The child, guided by his family to consider the financial situation and the family's budget, is intertwined in his own consumer behaviour within the family context and the need to see and understand all the needs and limitations of the family (Miller 2001).

The issue of reciprocity is very important to teens, and they often mention their considerate behaviour as a significant contribution that parents should take into account when they consider their children's purchase requests. Thus, for example, one teen indicated the reciprocal nature of considerate behaviour: 'Stand by your parents, help your parents, like, don't be selfish and think only about yourself: "get me this and get me that". *Parents should also take into consideration the fact that I am considerate*' (boy, 14, my emphasis). If the parents' strategy of openness expresses the closeness and belonging of the teen to the family group, then considerate behaviour constitutes a significant contribution by teens to the family finances. It provides a feeling of self-worth and control that stems from caring for their parents.

Another theme that arises from the mothers' interviews regarding teens' shopping requests indicates that approving the requests involves parents reflecting on their own childhood, and children reflecting on their future adulthood. Lydia Martens et al. (2004: 175) suggest that reflexivity lies 'at the heart of what can be understood as children's consumption'; Craig Thompson (1996), that parents (especially mothers) are fully aware that through their consumption they employ memories of their own childhood. The following section will describe the way parents share with their children memories of the difficulties they experienced during their own childhood, and at the same time say they want to compensate them for those hardships as well as compensate themselves for everything they lacked in the past. All the while children listen carefully to their parents and see the future image of what their parents want for them and their central role in their parents' success.

Parents' consumer childhoods

Parents describe their childhood as a time when people were strangers to luxury, life was simple, the demands upon children were higher, and therefore education was more effective. The way parents view their childhood incorporates their values about autonomy and building character through hardship. One of the teens ridiculed the ethos expressed in the stories of poverty and austerity their parents told in response to their children's complaints and requests: 'If you want something and they don't give [it to] you, then they give this answer [self-righteously]: "I grew up with seven siblings, we all slept in one bed " – I know!' (boy, 14). The teens share an aversion to the image of a child whose every material whim is immediately indulged by his parents, and describe such an attitude as a slippery slope that ends in dependency and an inability to cope. In one of the classrooms, one teen summarized the fate of such a child: 'He won't earn more than a piece of gum a month ...' (boy, 13). However, alongside the message of resisting temptation, parent–teen relationships also contain an aspect of material reward for desired behaviour and compensation for financial hardship (Pugh 2004).

Ma'ayan's parents timed the purchase of her new mobile phone to coincide with her being awarded a certificate for outstanding achievement at school: 'I knew that she was going to receive a certificate of excellence, so when she came to sit with me, I gave it to her ... we found the right time' (Interview 6, mother). A different kind of reward that mothers tell of is given as compensation for the experience of 'doing without' and the need to share with their children information about the difficulties of making a living. Some mothers say they feel the need to compensate their children and thank them for the sacrifice and devotion they show their family, its problems, and hardships. Moran's story demonstrates the part children play in sharing the burden and the parents' desire to thank and compensate them.

Moran is thirteen years old, the eldest child in the family. Her mother is a housewife, her father an electrician who works as an independent contractor, and she has a younger brother and sister. Orly, Moran's mother, praises her unique and considerate nature compared with the squandering and extortionate behaviour of other teenagers: 'These days they suck and suck till they suck you dry … but Moran is a considerate girl'. Moran's father is the family's sole provider, and every purchase for the children is based on the mother's explanation or persuasion, since it's the mother who spends all day at home with the children. Orly tends to convince her husband to buy things for Moran as compensation and reward for her behaviour:

> I tell him, look, I really appreciate what she does. I tell him – this is the kind of a girl you won't find just anywhere, like, really, and I see children her age when I sit here with the neighbours. (Interview 4, mother)

Moran's help was most significant during her mother's illness:

> It was before Passover, it was Moran's birthday, and I had back surgery … I was post-surgical and it was very difficult for me. Moran behaved like a grown-up. I wasn't here for ten days, and Moran cleaned the house, Moran did laundry, Moran cooked, Moran took care of her siblings. (Interview 4, mother)

Moran asked for a new high-end mobile phone to replace her old, broken one. Her mother expressed her wish to compensate Moran for that difficult period and to thank her for her sacrifice and devotion:

> I don't know how to thank Moran for that whole period … I told my husband that for the time being, anything Moran wants she gets, because really I had no way of thanking her. You don't understand, she would even help me shower! (Interview 4, mother)

The use of compensation terminology indicates the mother's wish to reciprocate for her daughter's help in running the household.

However, as mentioned earlier, compensation is not just for the cur-rent hardships, and mothers describe shopping for their children as compensation for the hardships and humiliation they suffered during their own childhood and the past feeling of helplessness they are now trying to rectify by buying things for their children. Leehi's mum said:

> Recently Leehi wanted a new pair of shoes ... I have a traumatic memory from my childhood, from the day my father didn't let me buy Adidas shoes, and I had to imagine the stripes of the Adidas on my plain white sneakers ... I said to myself, at least I will com-pensate myself. (Interview 9, mother)

A unique aspect of the mothers' desire to correct their own expe-riences through their children is seen in the way they encourage them to invest in their studies so they can be successful and secure financial well-being for themselves and their future families. This subject came up in interviews as an important message that is re-lated to family discussions of financial and consumer issues, and as a reflection over their own personal history and their hopes and dreams for their children. Moran's mother explains:

> I give her myself as an example ... I didn't study ... if you be like I want you to be ... you'll make me proud, make me happy; what I couldn't do, I want you to do (Interview 4, mother).

This aspect of reflexivity – parents reflecting on themselves by observing their children, and children reflecting on themselves by observing their parents – is therefore the heart of the tangled skein where the parents' past is intertwined with the present and the children's future, and emphasizes the relationality that is expressed through bargaining over consumer matters between parents and children (Martens et al. 2004).

Concluding discussion

The nature of autonomy, as expressed in the teens' bargaining with their parents over increasing their income and their part in con-sumer culture, matches the view of selfhood that emerges from the feminist notion 'relational autonomy'. This is an umbrella term that encompasses a variety of perspectives, which stem from the shared assumption that people are socially embedded, and that their identity is shaped in the context of relationships and by complex and intersecting social elements (Mackenzie & Stoljar 2000). This model of autonomy challenges, politically and morally, the ideal of personal autonomy that stems from liberal ideology and is seen as the opposite of dependence and social ties. In contrast, according to the relational autonomy approach, people are fundamentally social creatures who develop the ability to be autonomous through interacting with others. Children's increasing participation in the consumer world and bargaining interactions over financial issues within the family can be understood from a re-examination of the term autonomy which takes into account the way the self is embedded in social relations (Cooke 1999).

Autonomy, according to this view, does not rely on free choice, but rather on dealing with limitations and familial commitments (Boden 1996) which provides a unique possibility for belonging; a feeling of value and mutual caring between parents and teens that is expressed in various methods of bargaining. The first way teens increase their autonomy in interactions with their parents over consumer issues is accomplished through 'market-oriented' bargaining. The proactive, considerate behaviour of teens towards their parents which they weigh against their parents' consideration of them, the care which teens and parents show, are all used in bargaining interactions and constitute the fulfilment of their share in supporting the household. Anna Sparrman (2009) indicates that children's pester power includes the sense of negotiation; an evaluation of the level of investment as compared to what benefit can be gained from it. Similarly, the teens who participated in this study bring the market into the relationship with their parents in a way that changes the balance of power in the family. The expectation of compensation for the children shouldering some of the family responsibilities highlights the negotiated aspect of consumption processes.

Responsibility and care place those who provide them in a position of power (Brannen et al. 2000). Feminist sociologists have recognized the fact that care combines love and labour (Finch & Groves 1983;

Graham 1991), while it also has a clear moral dimension (Mason 1996), in the sense that people frequently feel responsible for and committed to provide it, although in actual practice they are acting not only out of a sense of commitment but also negotiating the 'guidelines' for the way in which they will actualize this commitment (Finch 1989). Like adults, children are active participants in caring relationships both as receivers and as givers. Mutual consideration serves, then, as negotiable currency between parents and teens, and contributes to the children's status and sense of competency.

The second way in which teens increase their autonomy in bargaining interactions is through reflection. Critical reflection is a key for the development of autonomy because it enables the person to shape his attitudes and to guide his activities (Blöser et al. 2009). In contrast with the individualistic bent of philosophical views of autonomy, autonomy can only develop in the context of relationships, traditions, and social institutions (Meyers 2005) that expose teens to the way parents see themselves and their children. This interpretation of autonomy emphasizes the ability to participate in a dialogue which Bachtin terms 'answerability'; an ability that consists of finding the appropriate tone and content, and understanding the relationship with the others and the self (Bachtin 1986). According to Michail Bachtin, the self 'steps across to experience the other's subjectivity and then returns to its own interior position' (Burr 2009: 325). The negotiable aspect of buying permission portrays the bargaining interaction as forms of speech event, where parents and children 'interact via language in some conventional way to arrive at some outcome' (Yule 1996: 57) or some agreement.

As distinct from the unfavourable connotations of pester power, the reflexive nature of parent–teen bargaining over consumer matters in low-income families addressed in this essay carries an aspect of fitness and autonomy. Examining the sacralization of childhood in her book *Pricing the Priceless Child* (1985), Zelizer writes that from the children's point of view, 'the creation of an ostensibly useless child never segregated children from economic life ... children engaged actively in bargaining, contesting and transforming their own relations with the economy' (Zelizer 2002: 391). In bargaining with their parents, the teens argue and influence as well as listen to their parents and

understand them, and they express their autonomy by being interlocutors worthy of talking and arguing with. This combination of
the economic sphere with the sphere of social relationships is a key
component of social life, in which money and intimacy are closely
intertwined (Zelizer 2005). To paraphrase the Beatles, the love and
care teens take in discussing consumer matters with their parents is
bargained and considered along with the love and care they make.
The relational autonomy expressed in parent–teen bargaining suggests
an additional use of commercializing processes for negotiations over
the status of childhood (Zelizer 1985; Cook 2010).

Notes

1 This essay is based on part of my Ph.D. research at the University of Haifa
on consumer education, as part of which such education was examined in
different arenas of teenagers' lives. I am grateful to my supervisors, Professor
Tamar Katriel and Professor Nurit Bird-David, for their helpful comments.
2 The concept 'social periphery' combines the term 'periphery', in the sense
of a distance from the geographical centre of Israel, with socio-economic
distance from the centres of power in Israel.
3 In discussing data from the interviews, I will refer to 'mothers'.
4 The names of the participants in the study have been changed.

References

Bachtin, Michail (1986), *Speech genres and other late essays*, trans. Vern W.
McGee (Austin: University of Texas Press).
Bauman, Zigmunt (2000), *Liquid modernity* (Cambridge: Polity).
Beck, Ulrich & Beck-Gernsheim, Elizabeth (1996), 'Individualization and
precarious freedoms: Perspectives and controversies of a subject-orientated
sociology', in Scott Lash, Paul Heelas & Paul Morris (eds.) *Detraditionali-
zation* (London: Blackwell), 23–48.
Bird-David, Nurit & Darr, Assaf (2009), 'Commodity, gift, and mass-gift: On
gift-commodity hybrids in advanced mass consumption cultures', *Economy
and Society*, 38/2: 304–25.
Boden, Sharon (2006), 'Another day, another demand: How parents and
children negotiate consumption matters', *Sociological Research Online*, 11/2.
Blöser, Claudia, Schopf, Aron & Willaschek, Marcus (2009), 'Autonomy,
experience and reflection: On a neglected aspect of personal autonomy',
Ethical Theory and Moral Practice, 13: 239–53.

Brannen, Julia & Wilson, Gail (1987) (eds.), *Give and take in families: Studies in resource distribution* (London: Unwin Hyman).

– Heptinstall, Ellen & Bhopal, Kalwant (2000), *Connecting children: Care and family life in later childhood* (New York: RoutledgeFalmer).

Buckingham, David (2000), *After the death of childhood: Growing up in the age of electronic media* (Cambridge: Polity Press).

Burr, Jennifer (2009), 'Exploring reflective subjectivity through the construction of the "Ethical Other" in interview transcripts', *Sociology*, 43/2: 323–39.

Chin, Elizabeth (2001), *Purchasing power: Black kids and American consumer culture* (Minneapolis: University of Minnesota Press).

Cook, Daniel Thomas (1995), 'The mother as consumer: Insights from the children's wear industry, 1917–1929', *Sociological Quarterly*, 36/3: 505–22.

– (2000), 'The rise of "the toddler" as subject and as merchandising category in the 1930', in Mark Gottdiener (ed.), *New forms of consumption: Consumers, culture and commodification* (Lanham, MD: Rowman and Littlefield), 111–29.

– (2009), 'Semantic provisioning of children's food: Commerce, care and maternal practice', *Childhood*, 16: 317–34.

– (2010), 'Commercial enculturation: Moving beyond consumer socialization', in David Buckingham & Vebjørg Tingstad (eds.) *Childhood and consumer culture.* (Basingstoke, UK: Palgrave), 63–79.

Cooke, Maeve (1999), 'Questioning autonomy: The feminist challenge and the challenge of feminism', in R. Kearney and M. Dooley (eds.), *Questioning ethics: Contemporary debates in philosophy* (London: Routledge).

Darbyshire, Philip, Schiller, Wendy & MacDougall, Colin (2005), 'Extending new paradigm childhood research: Meeting the challenges of including younger children', *Early Child Development and Care*, 175/6: 467–72.

Finch, Janet (1989), *Family obligations and social change* (London: Polity).

– & Groves, Dulcie (1983), *Labour and love: Women, work and caring* (London: Routledge & Kegan Paul).

– & Mason, Jennifer (1993), *Negotiating family responsibilities* (London: Tavistock/Routledge).

Giddens, Anthony (1991), *Modernity and self-identity: Self and society in the late Modern Age* (Cambridge: Polity Press).

Graham, Hilary (1991), 'The concept of caring in feminist research: The case of domestic service', *Sociology*, 25/1: 61–78.

Kaplan, Elaine Bell (2000), 'Using food as a metaphor for care: Middle school kids talk about family, school and class relationships', *Journal of Contemporary Ethnography*, 29/4: 474–509.

MacIntosh, Ian & Punch, Samantha (2009), '"Barter", "deals", "bribes" and "threats"', *Childhood*, 16/1: 49–65.

Mackenzie, Catriona & Stoljar, Natalie (2000), *Relational autonomy: Feminist perspectives on autonomy, agency, and the social self* (New York: OUP).

Martens, Lydia, Southerton, Dale & Scott, Sue (2004), 'Bringing children (and parents) into the sociology of consumption: Towards a theoretical and empirical agenda', *Journal of Consumer Culture*, 4: 155–82.

Mason, H. E. (1996), *Moral dilemmas and moral theory* (New York: OUP).

Meyers, Diana (2005), 'Decentralizing autonomy: Five faces of selfhood', in John Christman & Joel Anderson (ed.), *Autonomy and the challenges to liberalism* (Cambridge: CUP), 27–55.

Miller, Daniel (1995), 'Consumption and commodities', *Annual Review of Anthropology*, 24: 141–61.

– (2001), *The dialects of shopping* (Chicago: University of Chicago Press).

Pugh, Allison (2004), 'Windfall childrearing', *Journal of Consumer Culture*, 4/2: 229–49.

Schoenberg, Sheila (2008), *Autonomy and education – Current perspectives* (Tel-Aviv: Resling Publishing) (in Hebrew).

Scott, Stevi, Jackson, Sue, Backett-Milburn, Kathryn & Harden, Jeni (2000), *The Impact of risk and parental risk anxiety on the everyday worlds of children* (Final report for UK Economic and Social Research Council).

Seiter, Ellen (1993), *Sold separately: Parents and children in consumer culture* (New Brunswick, NJ: Rutgers University Press).

Simmel, Georg (1971), *On individuality and social forms*, ed. and intro. Donald N. Levine (Chicago: University of Chicago Press).

Sparrman, Anna (2009), 'Ambiguities and paradoxes in children's talk about marketing breakfast cereals', *Young Consumers*, 10/4: 297–313.

Thompson, Craig (1996), 'Caring consumers: Gendered consumption meanings and the juggling lifestyle', *Journal of Consumer Research*, 22/4: 388–407.

Walkerdine, Valerie & Lucey, Helen (1989), *Democracy in the kitchen: Regulating mothers and socialising daughters* (London: Virago).

Warde, Alan (1994), 'Consumption, identity-formation and uncertainty', *Sociology*, 28/4: 877–98.

Yule, George (1996), *Pragmatics* (Oxford: OUP).

Zelizer, Viviana A. (1985), *Pricing the priceless child: The changing social value of children* (New York: Basic Books).

– (1994/1997), *The social meaning of money: Pin money, paychecks, poor relief and other currencies* (Princeton: PUP).

– (2002), 'Kids and commerce', *Childhood*, 9/4: 275–96.

– (2005), *The purchase of intimacy* (Princeton: PUP).

Zukin, Sharon & Maguire, Jennifer S. (2004), 'Consumers and consumption', *Annual Review of Sociology*, 30: 173–97.

Entrance to the Liseberg amusement park, Gothenburg, December 2009.
©David Cardell.

CHAPTER 7

Enacting money
at an amusement park

David Cardell & Anna Sparrman

It is getting dark outside and thousands of lights have been lit to signal the Christmas event at the Liseberg amusement park. An eye-catching, pink-floodlighted portal frames the entrance to the park, a landmark in the Gothenburg city event area in Sweden. Outside this monumental construction, people gather in different groups to prepare for their visit. Some are cheerful and attract attention from passers-by as they chat loudly and laugh. Others hurry to get inside the park, rummaging for their wallets to pay the entrance fee. The entrance, with its portal and cash desks, serves to separate the mundane, outside world from the experience of the spectacular space of Christmas carefully designed with artificial snow, real reindeers, trees, lights, and booths selling Christmas decorations and presents.

Previous research has highlighted aesthetic concepts such as spectacle and the artificial that have bearing on the description above, discussing how the design of amusement parks includes strategies to create an atmosphere of happiness in order to maximize profits (for example, Bryman 1995; Mitrašinović 2006). Although design and content are commonly seen in relation to the economic rationalities of capitalism (for example, Lainsbury 2000; Lukas 1998; Marin 1984; Sorkin 1992), few studies go beyond management and corporate concerns to empirically look at consumption as a practice that involves amusement park visitors as consumers.[1] This essay seeks to explore how different values and social meanings of money are enacted in these particular entertainment and consumption practices.[2]

Viviana Zelizer (1994) argues that money is generally an under-analysed social phenomenon in research, and that most analyses of consumer culture stop when it comes to money. This observation is equally valid for research focused on amusement parks, as consumer spending and profits are presented as bald numbers rather than as involving social dimensions and monetary considerations that affect consumer choice. Zelizer provides a theoretical framework for exploring different values of money where social relations, culture, and economics are interrelated, and should be understood as such (Zelizer 1985, 1994, 2005). Moreover, she discusses the social meaning of money, suggesting that it is labelled or earmarked, and not just simply spent. It is valued differently depending on when and where it is spent and from where or whom it comes. By taking this line, the argument becomes that 'people are constantly creating different kinds of money' (Zelizer 1994: 1). Zelizer even talks about variations in monies to explain the process of how money is constantly transformed into other objects or physically distinct markers. The earmarking of money creates a variety of social relations and what Zelizer (2005) calls intimacies – that is, that economic transactions always are part of the creation of intimate relationships, like for example families.

Similarly, Daniel Miller (2008) argues that economic theories have applied an abstract concept of value, using it in a universalistic way while ignoring everyday practices. With an ethnographical methodology, relations between the economy and (plural) values are addressed, demonstrating how value is approached in practice and how it varies according to location or group (Miller 2008). Drawing on Zelizer and Miller, we begin our analysis where researchers of amusement parks have halted. We will look at the practice of money.

John Law and John Urry (2003) have demonstrated how the concept of enactment can be used to discuss how different social realities are made in practice (see also Law 2004; Mol 2002). Enactments not only present something that is already made, but instead have 'powerful productive consequences' (Law 2004: 56). This means that the 'real' is both 'real' and at the same time made (Law & Urry 2003). Reality is a relational effect, and, instead of talking about perspectives of different realities, one should acknowledge the fact that all realities are enacted. Enactment is sometimes used as a synonym for performance; however, John Law (2004) argues that, unlike performance, its focus is not only human conduct but also non-human materiality. Another important aspect of the concept is that it underscores 'difference and multiplicity to be chronic conditions' (Law 2004: 158).

In this essay, we approach the organization and use of money as a productive process, focusing on how money as a material entity is intertwined with other entities, and how monetary values come into being through practices (cf. Mol 2002). This means that the *activities* are central in order to investigate how money through a 'combination of people, techniques, texts, architectural arrangements and natural phenomena' is enacted (Law 2004: 56). If one accepts that money is one material aspect to the production of an amusement park's ontology (Law & Urry 2003), the question then becomes what a visit to an amusement park such as Liseberg can tell us about the values of money and value practices. When, how, and by whom is money made (in)valuable? What is money intertwined with in the amusement park? Whose money is enacted, at what times, and in what ways? It is in the complex relationships between money, children, and the park that value is enacted, and our aim is to investigate the productive consequences of those relationships. By investigating children's enactment of money, it is possible to address the fruitfulness of such an approach.

Consumer actors

The consequence of the praxis-based approach adopted here is that children are held to be respected, knowledgeable social actors informed by their own experiences. A focus on children's actions is very different to a focus on children's potential cognitive abilities as they relate to, say, age (Christensen & Prout 2002): in the latter instance, children's actions are interpreted using mental charts, while approaching children as social actors focuses on their actual doings. Accordingly, children in this essay are approached as *consumer actors*, reflecting the notion of children as *social actors* common in childhood sociology (Christensen & Prout 2002). The idea is that they are to be understood as actors *in* society, not on its margins. Translated into the consumption context, this means that children act *in* consumer society and are not solely acted upon.[3] In this way, aspects of vulnerability or dichotomies such as either/or (Cook 2003, 2004), being/becoming (Lee 2001), or competence/non-competence become theoretically irrelevant, since the primary analytical grounds for studying how money and values are enacted by children are taken to be practices and actions (cf. Mol 2002).

Approaching children as consumer actors contradicts earlier research on amusement parks, in which adolescent and adult visitors are more generally approached as cultural dopes or robots (for example, Baudrillard 1983; DeAngelis 1997; Eco 1986; Gottdiener 1982; Marin 1984; Pine & Gilmore 1999; Ritzer 2008; Urry 1990; van Wert 1995). Moreover, the ethnographical approach applied in this essay challenges not only current thinking on the rational *individual* consumer of economic theory (and critiqued by Cook 2008), but also ideas about families as a static, *collective* visitor category envisaged in earlier amusement park research using a non-participating, 'top-down' perspective. There are a handful of studies of amusement parks based on actual practices and conducted 'from below' that have included children (Mathiesen Hjemdahl 2003; Raz 1999; van Wert 1995), and this present study is a contribution to a body of research that is child-oriented.

Visiting an amusement park

A three-hour pilot visit to Liseberg was carried out in December 2009 with two 12-year-old boys. Our methodological inspiration for this participatory observation came from works on visual ethnography (Pink 2007a) and on the practice of 'walking with' (Cele 2006; Lee & Ingold 2006; Pink 2007b). We asked to 'walk with' the boys through the park while documenting their activities using video and still images.

It turned out that conducting field work at an amusement park has its own particular challenges, with rapid shifts between activities and the special intensity of the place. It can be noted that the documenting process was challenged by the speed the boys moved at, having declined the offer to film each other, leaving us to pursue them as best we could, running after them instead of 'walking with' them. The technology became an obstacle instead of a means to generate knowledge. That said, the methodological challenges did however help us realize that speed and time are fundamental aspects of consumer practices. We will return to the issue of the methodologies of investigating amusement parks elsewhere, and instead move on to the key themes of money enactments in the park: the materiality of money; the value of efficiency; time is money; and the boys' use of their own money.

The materiality of money

There are many different ways of paying admission to Liseberg. One can either buy an annual gold pass, which includes unlimited rides; a yearly season ticket, that only includes entrance to the park; an all-day entrance pass; a special ride pass that allows unlimited rides during the day; or single coupons for individual rides. Admission can be purchased either at the park or online, and prices are set to reflect the amount of time spent at the park, frequency of visits, and the season. The different types of ticket take a variety of forms, each making money increasingly invisible. The special ride pass can, for example, only be bought online, which means you can enter the park without using money at the location. The all-day pass is a wristband that gives the wearer access to all the rides. Accordingly, money is exchanged for paper tickets corresponding to certain values or for wristbands or passes with infinite value for a day, in this way acting as a money equivalent in much the same way as cigarettes in prison, gambling chips, luncheon vouchers, and collectible cards; strategies which work only because people agree to them (Zelizer 1994, 2005). This means that the conversion of money into other objects such as wristbands can render the cost of the visit invisible, at the same time as the objects themselves on leaving the park become tokens and material memories. The only time the visitor pays for a ride with cash – that is, coins or notes – is when they buy coupons from one of the ticket vending machines that dot the park.

A common practice when setting admission prices for children's entertainments is to go by age and sometimes by family grouping

(Sparrman 2011); yet neither age nor family is mentioned in Liseberg's list of prices, which are instead determined by height. Children shorter than 110 cm have free entrance to the park, and their ride passes are cheaper because they are not allowed on all the rides for safety reasons – shorter adults have to pay for park entrance, however. The two other required minimum heights for rides are 130 cm and 140 cm. For those taller than 140 cm, all the rides in the park are accessible, although there is a maximum height of 195 cm for rides such as Kanonen and AtmosFear (Liseberg 2011a, 2011b). However, being too tall does not give a reduction in price; neither is being too tall signalled by a prefix similar to that for being too short, which is labelled 'children' and 'mini'. This indicates that height is something especially important when it comes to children.

Next to all the ticket offices is a height indicator to measure children's heights. While waiting for the authors to purchase ride tickets, the two boys posed next to a height indicator, which showed that they were taller than the 140 cm required to go on all the rides. This demonstration of their height soon turned into an enactment of the changing heights of childhood, with one of the boys pretending to shrink and stretch to show different stages of growth. His visual presentation literally embodied the different consumer potentials, showing what it means to be a consumer actor inside the park. Their remarks on the different heights also show that the boys were enacting knowledge about how the park system works through their bodies. However, height was not described by the boys as a static category beyond all possible challenge. They talked about how using thick-soled shoes and drawing yourself up to your full height were possible solutions if you were not tall enough. This situation seems to suggest that being a child, lack of the right height can be intertwined with consumer desires. Height also becomes an incentive to return the next year, since there possibly would be more possibilities as a consumer at that time.

However, as already noted, other parks 'age-ify' their admissions and also offer special family prices, which emphasizes a generational visit shared by adults and children (Sparrman 2011). Liseberg focuses instead on individuals, without any predefined, traditional relations to other people. Or do they? That is how it appears at first glance. In fact, Liseberg sets out to attract families, but not by age or concepts such as family, but rather by using the strategy of an *absence* of entrance fees for children under 110 cm in height. In this way the park takes into consideration that families do not want to pay for things they cannot use, and by that enacts them as a visitor category. The organization and earmarking of the price of admission thus takes into consideration the connectedness and intimacy between people, implying a family unit, and suggesting that young children not should visit the park on their own. The price structure points to a complex nexus of money, objects, and people sanctioned through the purchase and use of various different admission strategies. This in turn shows that the cost of admission is used to chisel out and configure putative visitors (Woolgar 1991).

The boys negotiated different value systems – body height, thick-soled shoes, money, and time – in order to enact a visit. By doing this, they were also enacting the park, showing that the strategies produced by the park are enacted as a complex materiality. This suggests that structurally oriented theories of amusement park management are not enough to understand (child) consumer actors.

The value of efficiency

Speed is an important factor in consumption at amusement parks. In *Fast Capitalism,* Ben Agger (1989) argues that capitalism has speeded up through the compression of time and the reduction of significant time-consuming practices, be they at work, in everyday life in a wider sense, or specifically related to leisure activities (see also Agger & Shelton 2007). Consequently it is argued that capitalism cannot afford to have people at rest, which suggests that the need for speed is enacted socially, economically, and culturally within capitalism. It can also be seen that some visitors to Liseberg literally buy into this enactment of speed by purchasing a product called 'Quick Pass'.

During the summer, when the amusement park is packed, some visitors run between attractions so as to be able to go on as many rides as possible in the time available, while others buy a Quick Pass, which makes it possible to jump the worst of the queues and go straight to the rides. This implies that money is not only exchanged for different material objects but also that time is sold as a commodity (Zelizer 1994). By investing in a Quick Pass, the time spent queuing is reduced, which in turn suggests that the efficient use of time is assumed by management to be something attractive to park visitors. The ultimate experience would thus be to spend as much time as possible on the rides, or alternatively as little time as possible off them. The irony, though, is that Quick Passes only work if very few people purchase them. The more people who buy them, the less valuable they will be, since the Quick Pass queues will then grow. This is something that Liseberg's management has thought of, as the number of times each visitor can use a Quick Pass is limited to three per visit at a cost of €6 only when buying a special ride pass in advance online. Speed can thus be bought as an additional service, which moneywise equates to plus-sized meals at McDonald's, where additional quantity is added to a product already bought. Unlike McDonald's, however, at Liseberg the total number of available Quick Passes per day are limited. This means that the park consciously sets out to ensure that the Quick Pass queues never grow so long that it is not worth spending money on non-material things like speed and time. The time spent on most of the rides does not equate to the time the majority of visitors, who do not have a Quick Pass, spend queuing. A ride only takes a few minutes, while queuing can take up to 30–40 minutes per ride. By selling and buying Quick Passes, time is enacted as a luxurious commodity only available to a limited amount of visitors. While McDonald's offers everyone the chance to add extras to their plus-size meals, Liseberg amusement park only offers extras to those who can afford it, plan ahead, and adjust to the fact that money is time.

The number of people visiting Liseberg varies according to the day and season. During the summer in particular parts of the park are crowded. The day we visited Liseberg, in December, not all the attractions were open so it was easy to move between rides, and access was quick to most attractions and shops. At this time of the year, a Quick Pass is superfluous. The park does work to accelerate visitors' consumption in other ways, however. The visit started off with a meal before moving on to the rides. Looking at the food map supplied by the park, we chose a place serving waffles. It turned out to be on a corner and was organized like a fast food restaurant, without chairs or tables (Ritzer 2008: 60). Both doors to the restaurant were wide open, creating a cold December draft. The organization of the food intake was neither relaxing nor peaceful, so we all ate very fast in order to move on quickly. Since sitting-down and relaxing is time-consuming, it might also delay other consumers. To keep up the speed of consumption, a scaled-down spatial arrangement is a very powerful tool to persuade consumers to keep on the move (Ritzer 2008).

The way the park organizes the speed of consumption enacts quantity as quality. The consequence is the more you do during a visit, the better the visit, with the effect that the more money is spent – for example, on Quick Passes and fast eating – the more fun the visitor will have. It could be argued that the capitalistic enactment of the park is hard and single-minded, as it enacts a Tayloristic-like organization of leisure time (Cardell 2010) in which speedy actions and efficiency are central. A very simple cause and effect relation between speed, money, and fun is thereby created by the park, which in turn generates a very robotlike or single-minded view of visitors (Eco 1986) – a view, however, which partly seems to work, since our meal speeded up. Though not fully aware of it at the time, we accommodated ourselves to the organizational principle of 'money is time' and quickly moved on from the restaurant to spend more money elsewhere. Money is enacted as time, and time is enacted as a commodity in the park. From this it follows that money, as argued by Zelizer (1994, 2005), enacts values beyond its economic value, so that money–time is enacted as a currency within the park.

Time is money

Money is time, then. However, it also turned out that time is money. Since the aim of the visit was that we, as researchers, wanted to know more about what children do at the amusement park, the boys were left to decide the length of the visit and what to do: they were to show us 'their' Liseberg. Both of them had visited the park on a yearly basis throughout childhood. Since this visit took place on our initiative and the boys were doing us a favour, funds for the visit – including admission, tickets for rides, and food – were provided by the research project, so money was not an issue. Despite this, and without any explicit restrictions on our part, the two boys argued for limits on the time they were to spend there and the tickets to buy, and consequently how many rides would be possible. They asked only for coupons, not the ride passes where all the attractions are included and can be experienced an unlimited number of times. This came as something of a surprise, but their argument was that single tickets would be more cost-efficient.

This points to the fact that a visit to an amusement park is an orderly, planned undertaking. The fact that the boys had free access to money, but still chose to discuss, negotiate, and plan the visit shows that such strategies are probably enduringly important to how a visit is enacted by these boys. The planning might set the standards for how they evaluate the visit afterwards: was it a good or a bad visit in relation to what was planned? Not every visit will, however, be the same, as they will vary according to when you go and with whom. For example, the two boys did not like the same kind of rides: one liked rides that spin while the other liked fast rides. Getting the best out of a visit, no matter whose money is being spent, thus boils down to what can be done *together*. Togetherness can be seen as one aspect of what Zelizer (2005) calls the purchase of intimacy. Instead of simply spending as much money as possible, the boys seemed to organize and value their purchase through orders of intimacy.

Given Zelizer's (1994) argument that people earmark money, it is worth pausing to reflect on what type the researchers' money was, and what it became. The money used during the visit came from the Swedish Research Council – it was not any one individual's money – and we made it clear to the boys that it was not money from our own pockets. Thus it was viewed as official funds that did not belong to any special person. It is difficult to tell whether this sort of money is easier or harder to spend, although what can be said is that it came with certain preconditions and responsibilities attached as we spoke of its origins. That children act responsibly when handling this type of money has also been shown by Elizabeth

Chin (2001), who in her study of children in low-income areas gave children money to go shopping. They spent the money on things they needed, such as shoes, but also on presents for their parents or siblings. For a consumer actor it might well seem a necessary and responsible thing to go on amusement park rides when knowingly participating in the social context of this research study. However, to do so does not imply excess or consumption running amok; instead, the consumption level is decided by considering different types of values in relation to one another (Miller 2008).

One last thing to consider is that time is also money for the boys. Purchasing a ride pass means spending more time in the park to use its value – and spending more time with us researchers. To buy single tickets may well mark the right amount of time for the boys to invest in us. Applying a buy-and-sell system, it could be argued that we were purchasing the boys' time and knowledge, and how much they were prepared to sell was decided by the boys themselves. The way they govern their knowledge, their time, and the worth of the visit to them enacts the value of the research money. By approaching children as consumer actors, and not as cultural dopes, robots (Eco 1986), or naive innocents (Cook 2003, 2004), while avoiding the temptation to judge them as either competent or incompetent, it becomes possible to see how money during a visit is enacted in different ways.

Values of (own) money

The boys had also brought some money of their own, just as they would if they were visiting Liseberg with their families. Own money, they argued, was however always to be spent only on sweets and perhaps a souvenir to take home. As well as all the various rides, the park offers an assortment of games of chance, such as wheels of fortune. At several locations, it is possible to gamble by betting on a specific number on the wheel, which in turn gives the chance to win prizes such as home appliances, soft toys, crisps, and sweets. Several of the wheels of fortune are branded, so it is possible to see from a distance which products are offered as prizes.

Noticing one of these gambling locations, the boys started to talk about how it worked. They told us that most prizes from the wheel of fortune are won early in the day so that they are seen throughout the amusement park being carried around by the winners. By distributing the products early, the boys argue, a special way of marketing is promoted encouraging others to try their luck later. These elaborate ideas about the way strategic marketing is presented suggest that the management of Liseberg is consciously manipulating visitors. By the boys' account, little was left to chance, since everything about the wheel of fortune was said to be predetermined.

Older political debates and social commentaries show that accusations of companies manipulating games of chance are neither new nor unique to this context (Husz 2004). What makes the boys' comments at Liseberg particularly interesting was that one of the boys, despite commenting on the strategy, still invested his own money in taking a turn on the wheel of fortune labelled with a famous Swedish chocolate brand. He selected one group of numbers and paid about €2, but when the wheel stopped it was clear that he had won nothing.

The boys' discussion about the fortune wheel draws on the idea that nothing at the amusement park is there by chance, but instead is well-thought-through to create the most profit by visitors' consumption. Still, accommodating to Liseberg's organization is not a single-minded action. As argued earlier in this essay, little is gained by discussing the boys' actions in terms of competence and incompetence, or naivety and innocence (Cook 2003, 2004; Prout 2005). The example instead shows that the boys, like most people, approached the visit as appealing and indulging, living up to combined feelings of delight and nerve-tingling excitement when they toyed with the possibility to either lose or win by gambling on the wheel of fortune.

The fact that the boys convincingly described the systematic tricks of a profit-seeking amusement park at the same time that they joined in may seem paradoxical. Peter Sloterdijk (1988: 26) argues that such tension between knowledge and practice is to be understood as *enlightened false consciousness* – people are aware of systematic deceptions, but nevertheless still act. What is interesting here is that money was at stake, not as income, but potentially as expenditure without any return. Thus, while perhaps prepared to be deceived as long as he might win, the boy who gambled stopped immediately when he failed to do so. This suggests that the boy accepted what can be called the humbug industry, which encompasses both the practice of gambling and only limited repetitions. The boy neither used more of his money nor asked for research money in order to gamble, suggesting that an enlightened false consciousness was operating at that point of the visit, but not throughout the entire visit. We would argue, contra Sloterdijk, that enlightened false consciousness, rather than being systematic and totalizing in character, is enacted in practices.

Since the money invested was his own, had the boy won when playing the wheel of fortune, the prize would have been his. Gambling with research money could have led to a discussion about the prize's rightful owner: would it be the group of four or any particular individual? Commodities and material possibilities are, so to speak, related to political and economic concerns about ownership. The way in which the collective and/or the individual are valued as risk-takers and (potential) winners directly affects consumption practices. By not asking us to pay for the wheel of fortune, the boys stuck to a well-established routine, probably established during their visits to Liseberg with their families. Using one's own money to gamble with guarantees to whom the prize belongs.

After this event, the boys wanted to purchase some sweets. One of them went over to one of the booths selling Christmas sweets to ask what things cost. When he heard the price of the exclusively packaged almonds and other nuts – roughly €11 – he froze, and his body posture turned rigid. He later told us he was playing a waiting game. After a moment of active passivity, a smaller and much cheaper cone of almonds was also presented, which he duly bought for about €3.

In this situation, two different pricing systems were enacted. All prices at Liseberg are pre-set and standardized, yet the Christmas booths offering sweets, meat, Christmas decorations, and so on do offer some opportunity to bargain. This was something the boy was aware of. His silence and body posture were a way of negotiating; waiting out the vendor to see if anything else was on offer. When they later entered a sweet shop elsewhere in the park, nothing like this took place, and the boys then took the prices at face value. Thus they were able to move between different economic practices, knowing full well how to assess the spending power of their own money while enacting the park as a pre-set system.

When spending, the boys acted with care, and did so within three different monetary frameworks: humbug (by the boys' account), fixed prices, and negotiable prices. Moving between locations, these different economic rationalities were observed and adhered to. The examples above show that investment is one part of being a consumer actor, but within the social world of an amusement park so is non-consumption – one can risk being duped or losing money, but not all the time. This flexibility between economic rationalities, consumption, and non-consumption thus points to children's amusement park practices relying on both social agency and conditions of a systematic character set up by the park management at one and the same time.

Concluding discussion

By investigating the relationships between an amusement park, money, and children, and approaching them as equal actors, this essay empirically and theoretically questions research in which money is viewed as a static, coherent system and amusement park visitors (children) as cultural dopes. In our analysis we have looked to the connectedness between realities produced by the various actors rather than pursuing dichotomies.

The analysis shows that the way money is ordered both by the park and by the child consumers creates relations between social actors, material entities, and different economic frameworks. The use of *enactment* as a concept to investigate the value of money in practice poses a challenge to static consumer theories (Cook 2008; Zelizer 1994) by highlighting ontological multiplicity (Law 2004; Mol 2002). We have also chosen to work on the assumption that children are *consumer actors*, again questioning earlier research where children are described either as completely naive or fully competent, or as if their actions are only the expression of their age-based cognitive abilities.

However, it is not enough to say that the world is complex, without then asking in what ways it is complex; or in this case, in what ways money is enacted in complex ways. The analysis shows that social and material complexity is enacted through what we would like to call a *sprawliness of consumption*. Our argument is that – even though there is a connectedness between realities and relations between social actors, materiality, and economics – neither the amusement park nor the boys' actions form a coherent system of consumption. The boys simultaneously enacted money by drawing on family routines, using consumer experiences from their earlier visits, criticizing the park's system of consumption, accommodating to the park's speeding up of consumption, and using different strategies to negotiate with the researchers and sales assistants. In doing so, they enact a variety of economic systems, monies, and values. At the same time the park management, on the one hand, configures visitors as (rational) individuals with great spending power, while on the other hand, by the absence of entrance fees considers families' consumer abilities, naturally in the hope of generating even more consumption. The argument is that the consumer activities which take place in the park enact values of money in a multitude of unpredicted and unsystematic ways, but, crucially, without coming together as a coherent, static system. One can ask how the park still functions when so many different monetary values are enacted simultaneously. The key element here is not complexity through connectedness, but complexity through distribution and sprawliness of consumption. We suggest that sprawliness of consumption, whether that of the management of Liseberg or the boys, is a resource rather than a problem when understanding what makes the park function. The sprawliness creates a situation in which both the park and the boys (visitors) need to pay careful attention to accommodating one another's strategies. Consequently, it is the sprawliness that makes the park function, giving it an exciting character.

Notes

1 Our discussions of previous research in this chapter include studies focused on both amusement parks and theme parks.
2 The authors of this article are placed in alphabetical order. The research project is funded by The Swedish Research Council – Humanity and Social Science (Dnr 2009-6137), and led by Associate Professor Anna Sparrman at Linköping University. It runs from 2010–2013.
3 A consumer actor might seem something of a tautology; however, in the present case the concept denotes that child consumption is always situated in social, cultural, and material practices.

References

Agger, Ben (1989), *Fast capitalism: A critical theory of significance* (Urbana: University of Illinois Press).
– & Shelton, Beth Anne (2007), *Fast families, virtual children: A critical sociology of families and schooling* (Boulder: Paradigm Publishers).
Baudrillard, Jean (1983), *Simulations* (New York: Semiotext(e)).
Bryman, Alan (1995), *Disney and his worlds* (London: Routledge).
Cardell, David (2010), 'The funzone and industrial play: The choreography of childhood spaces in a Swedish context', *Entertainment and Sports Law Journal*, 8/1. <http://www2.warwick.ac.uk/fac/soc/law/elj/eslj/issues/volume8/number1/cardell/cardell.pdf>, accessed 26 June 2012.
Cele, Sofia (2006), *Communicating place: methods for understanding children's experience of place* (Diss.; Stockholm: Stockholm University).
Chin, Elizabeth (2001), *Purchasing power: Black kids and American consumer culture* (Minneapolis: University of Minnesota Press).
Christensen, Pia & Prout, Alan (2002), 'Working with ethical symmetry in social research with children', *Childhood*, 9/4: 477–97.
Cook, Daniel Thomas (2003), 'The dichotomous child in and of commercial culture', *Childhood*, 12: 155–59.
– (2004), 'Beyond either/or', *Journal of Consumer Culture*, 4/2: 147–53.
– (2008), 'The missing child in consumption theory', *Journal of Consumer Culture*, 8/2: 219–43.
DeAngelis, Michael (1997), 'Orchestrated (dis)orientation: Roller coasters, theme parks, and postmodernism', *Cultural Critique*, 37 Autumn: 107–129.
Eco, Umberto (1986), *Travels in hyperreality: Essays* (San Diego: Harcourt Brace Jovanovich).
Gottdiener, Mark (1982), 'Disneyland: A utopian urban space', *Journal of Contemporary Ethnography*, 11/2: 139–62.

Husz, Orsi (2004), *Drömmars värde: Varuhus och lotteri i svensk konsumtionskultur 1897–1939* (Diss.; Stockholm: Stockholms universitet).

Lainsbury, Andrew (2000), *Once upon an American dream: The story of Euro-Disneyland* (Lawrence: University of Kansas Press).

Law, John (2004), *After method: Mess in social science research* (London: Routledge).

– & Urry, John (2003), 'Enacting the social', Department of Sociology and the Centre for Science Studies, Lancaster University <http://www.comp. lancs.ac.uk/sociology/papers/Law-Urry-encating-the-Social.pdf>, accessed 1 November 2010.

Lee, Jo & Ingold, Tim (2006), 'Fieldwork on foot: Perceiving, routing, socializing', in Simon Coleman & Peter Collins (eds.), *Locating the field: Space, place and context in anthropology* (Oxford: Berg), 67–86.

Lee, Nick (2001), *Childhood and society: Growing up in an age of uncertainty* (Maidenhead: Open University).

Liseberg (2011a), *Allt om Liseberg 2011* (Gothenburg: Liseberg AB).

– (2011b), <http://www.liseberg.com/en/home/>, accessed 23 Aug. 2012.

Lukas, Scott A. (1998), 'Signal 3: Ethnographic experiences in the American theme park industry' (Rice University Electronic Theses and Dissertations) available at <http://hdl.handle.net/1911/19282>, accessed 1 June 2012.

Marin, Louis (1984), *Utopics: Spatial play* (Atlantic Highlands, NJ: Humanities).

Mathiesen Hjemdahl, Kirsti (2003), *Tur–retur temapark: oppdragelse, opplevelse, kommers* (Kristiansand: Høyskoleforl).

Miller, Daniel (2008), 'The uses of value', *Geoforum*, 393: 1122–1132.

Mitrasinovic, Miodrag (2006), *Total landscape, theme parks, public space* (Aldershot: Ashgate).

Mol, Annemarie (2002), *The body multiple: Ontology in medical practice* (Durham, NC: Duke University Press).

Pine, B. Joseph & Gilmore, James H. (1999), *The experience economy: Work is theatre & every business a stage* (Boston: Harvard Business School).

Pink, Sarah (2007a), *Doing visual ethnography: Images, media and representation in research* (2nd edn., London: SAGE).

– (2007b), 'Walking with video', *Visual Studies*, 22/3: 240–52.

Prout, Alan (2005), *The future of childhood* (London: RoutledgeFalmer).

Raz, Aviad E. (1999), *Riding the black ship: Japan and Tokyo Disneyland* (Cambridge, Mass.: Harvard University Press).

Ritzer, George (2008), *The McDonaldization of society 5* (Thousand Oaks, Calif.: Pine Forge Press).

Sloterdijk, Peter (1988), *Kritik av det cyniska förnuftet* (Stockholm: Alba).

Sorkin, Michael (1992), 'See you in Disneyland', in id. (ed.), *Variations on a theme park: The new American city and the end of public space* (New York: Hill and Wang).

Sparrman, Anna (2011), 'Barnkulturens sociala estetik', *Locus*, 3: 25–44.

Urry, John (1990), *The tourist gaze: Leisure and travel in contemporary societies* (London: SAGE).

van Wert, William F. (1995), 'Disney World and posthistory', *Cultural Critique*, 32: 187–214.

Woolgar, Steve (1991), 'Configuring the user: The case of usability trials', in John Law (ed.), *A sociology of monsters: Essays on power, technology and domination* (London: Routledge), 57–99.

Zelizer, Viviana A. (1985), *Pricing the priceless child: The changing social value of children* (New York: Basic Books).

– (1994), *The social meaning of money* (New York: Basic Books).

– (2005), *The purchase of intimacy* (Princeton: PUP).

CHAPTER 8

Fatherhood through direct marketing

Johanna Sjöberg

As the first country in the world to do so, Sweden introduced paid parental leave for fathers in 1974. This was a unique challenge to the traditional division of duties between men and women. Since then, a great many political reforms have been carried out to strengthen the participation of fathers in children's lives (Klinth 2008) and to create a gender-equal, dual-earner/dual-carer family in which both parents can combine work and parenthood (Berggren 2005; Forsberg 2009). Becoming a parent in Sweden today, one in different ways is met by these political aims. At the same time, socialization into parenthood is also pursued, for example, by the private consumer market. Direct marketing to new parents begins at an early stage, advising them what to buy and how best to take care of their infant. Such advice can be seen as complementing or competing with the policies promoted by state officials. This essay discusses the potential clash of values between the Swedish state and visual consumption in the medium of direct marketing.

Why look at fathers?

Caring for a child is associated with expenditures realized through the market. Consuming for children, and hence initiating their participation in marketplaces, begins even before a child is born. To understand children's part in the market society it is vital to understand the role of parents, as neither children nor parents are independent actors in relation to consumption (Cook 2008). Since parents as a category are

133

relational and gendered, it is important to critically examine differences and similarities in parental child consumption.

Daniel Thomas Cook (2009) points to the close connection between motherhood and consumption, emphasizing the particular importance of considering mothers when conducting research on child consumption. As he argues, 'There has been little or no recognition of women *as mothers* – and thus of accompanying caring obligations and ties – in general approaches to consumption and consumer culture' (Cook 2008: 231). Recognizing children in the field of consumption, he claims, 'necessarily places the lives and experiences of mothers directly in the crux of the inquiry' (ibid.). This viewpoint is challenging as it backgrounds the role of fathers, and consequently there is a risk that research takes stereotypical parental roles for granted and reproduces them.

In Sweden, stereotypical roles of parenthood do not go unchallenged, for the male breadwinner system is weak and mothers have been active in the labour market for a long time (Hirdman 2001; Nyberg 2000; Sommestad 1998; Klinth 2008). Traditional divisions of labour, where mothers care for children at home and fathers are family breadwinners, are thus not applicable to Sweden. Swedish men are also increasingly apt to be engaged in the lives of their children and have appropriated the norm of an 'involved fatherhood' (Forsberg 2009: 117–19). As the involved father, or 'new man', is connected both to participation in the family and to a consumerist lifestyle (Aarseth 2009), fathers should be recognized as consuming in order to benefit the household and care for their children. The *involved* father is therefore an interesting figure in the study of child consumption. Yet the same is also true of the *breadwinner* father, performing traditional fatherhood: being the main provider, he can have a great say in negotiations about what to buy for the family and at what price.

A study from the US shows that single fathers spend less on child-specific goods than do single mothers and married parents (Ziol-Guest 2009). Whether Swedish fathers likewise make consumer decisions for their children that differ from the mothers', and whether they relate differently to the child market, has yet to be established. At least the child market relates to fathers in other ways than it does to mothers (Pugh 2005). Conducting research on how fatherhood is shaped, and how fathers are involved and positioned in everyday consumption, is therefore just as important as studying mothers. Research has to recognize men *as fathers*, and their caring obligations and ties to consumption and consumer culture, to paraphrase Cook (2008). In investigating how men as fathers are represented and addressed by the market, this essay is a contribution to the understanding of how fathers are invited and constructed through visual advertisements and consumption.

The chosen source material is direct mail from Swedish and international businesses received by a Swedish first-time father, here called Mike, during his daughter Stella's first year of life in 2008–2009. The aim is to discuss the adverts' visual approach to fatherhood in relation to gender-equal parenthood and the dual-earner/dual-carer norm promoted by the Swedish state, asking how fathers are represented and addressed as childcare consumers, and how advertisements relate to notions of involved fatherhood and Sweden's policies on parenting.

In investigating these questions, theories and methods of visual discourse analysis (Rose 2007) and visual culture (Sturken & Cartwright 2009; Mitchell 1994; 2002) have been employed. Special attention has been paid to the visual address (Sturken & Cartwright 2009) and recurring visual patterns and contradictions (Rose 2007). The material has been approached from a visual point of view, where words are seen as part of the visual communication. It is at the intersection of image and text (Mitchell 1986, 2002) that discourses about fatherhood are activated and negotiated.

In the direct mail Mike received there are 31 images in which men appear (printed in total 45 times). The procedure has been to use these images as a focal point and to study them in isolation and in context. Despite the fact that some images of men were published several times, the immediate impression from the material is that there is a lack of representations of men. Not only are they numerically outnumbered by images of children and women; of the 31 images, fully 14 show men out of focus, or only in part, or the images are extremely small, demanding a very close look to interpret them as men. The 31 images of men position them as fathers, but while there are also other positions evident, such as journalist and

Image 1. All direct mail sent to Mike during Stella's first year. ©Johanna Sjöberg.

bridegroom, there are for example no grandfathers, male nurses or physicians. Images of fathers are closer in number to the 18 images of elderly women (labelled grandmothers) than they are to those of children (604) or women (236).

Economic values of children and parenthood

In Sweden, as in other Western countries, the notion of children and childhood has been re-evaluated during the past 150 years. As children's contribution to the family has shifted from an economic contribution through labour to an emotional contribution, children's value being discussed in terms of pricelessness means that families can now spend a great amount on money on children in the name of this emotional value (Zelizer 1985; Sandin 2003).

Large amounts of commodities are purchased for children to-day, partly out of sheer necessity, but also because commodities construct, express, and provide identity positions related to gender, age, ideology, status, and the like. Commodities also play a part in transitions into parenthood (Uth Thomsen & Sørensen 2006).

While most children are co-consumers, influencing and negotiating family consumption (Ekström 1999; Johansson 2005; Cook 2008), infants have little or no influence on what is bought for them. The act of materially defining who they are is therefore left in the hands of others. Being dressed by someone else means adapting to the other's view of oneself (Lurie 1992), and the same holds true for other symbolic matters that impact on infants. Parents are therefore in powerful positions to express their thoughts and wishes about the infant's identity, who can then be thought of as an extension of the parent's self (Johansson 2005).

That children are worth spending great amounts of money on is true not only in the family context; it is also seen in how the Swedish state spends tax revenue on child benefits. Motivated by a characterization of children as bearers of the future, many costly political reforms benefiting children have been implemented (Halldén 2007). The conditions for childhood have thus been closely connected to the building of the Swedish welfare state (Sandin & Halldén 2003c; Sandin in this volume).

Today, publicly financed institutions supporting families are strongly established and well developed.[1] At baby clinics and visits to local drop-in preschools, parents meet authorities and professionals who support and govern their parenthood. The state is in this way involved in the family, blurring the borders between public and private (Sandin 2003). Not least, the Swedish state governs the lives of families through the design of the parental insurance system. Under the present system, parents have 480 days' paid leave per child, of which 60 days are earmarked for each parent. An additional 10 days are reserved for the father immediately following the birth – for those 10 days, parents are allowed to be on parental leave together. The remainder of the days can be divided between the parents as they see fit, but they cannot both be on leave at the same time. Either parent can take full care of the child a few months when the other is working, or both can work part-time, taking daily or even hourly turns caring for the child (Försäkringskassan 2012). Despite this flexibility and a slow increase in men's uptake, fathers used only 23.7 per cent of the parental leave in 2011 (Orpana 2012). The success of creating gender equality in Sweden is thus a matter of some doubt.

While a parent is on leave the family's income falls, as the parental benefit only covers up to about 80 per cent of the individual salary. However, tax reduction is given to couples who divide their parental leave equally between them (Försäkringskassan 2012), and a child allowance of about €112 a month is paid to all children up to the age of 16 (Försäkringskassan 2010). With this financial support, the state tries both to increase gender equality and to ensure a certain material standard for children (Berggren 2005). It is also an encouragement for parents to consume, and to create or maintain strong bonds to the consumer market through their child. In this way the welfare state society and the consumer market are woven together and intersect.

Addressing Mike?

In Sweden, companies can first get access to addresses of newborn babies' parents only eight weeks after the birth (SPAR 2012), but Mike received his first direct mail concerning child consumption when Stella was 11 weeks. During the first year Mike was an involved father, sharing parental leave with Stella's mother. Since she had chosen to make her personal data at Sweden's SPAR Register unavailable to companies that use direct marketing, all the direct mail that came to their home was addressed only to Mike.[2]

In total, Mike received 24 separate mailings, including postcards, brochures, coupons, and free samples. It is a complex, visual material, often three-dimensional in physical character. The mailings often contained several items printed on both sides, and every now and then several companies were promoted in the same delivery. One envelope, for example, contained eight leaflets from separate companies. A special edition of the glossy magazine *Föräldrar & barn* called *Föräldrar & barn, baby – gratis specialtidning till dig som just fått barn* ('Parents & child, baby – free special magazine for new parents') also arrived. The magazine consisted of editorial copy functioning as an advertisement in itself, encouraging the reader to buy or subscribe to the magazine. It also contained adverts for subscription, and numerous adverts for other companies. In total, the collected material used in the present study comprised 107 different pieces of marketing.

Viviana Zelizer (2005) argues that economy and consumption

Image 2. Libero Club letter with envelope. ©SCA Hygiene Products AB and Johanna Sjöberg.

permeate all relationships and are under constant negotiation. Even those relations primarily considered emotional rather than economic have economic implications, and hence also the relationship between parents and infants. The message from Mike's direct mail is clear: the relationship not only has economic implications, it is dependent on consumption. Being a good parent demands being a consumer of a range of commodities.

The commodities promoted by the adverts were mainly related to five themes: children's bodies,[3] children's play,[4] knowledge,[5] memorabilia,[6] and motherhood.[7] Fathers are visible in marketing for all these types of commodities except for those related to motherhood, which highlighted the pregnant and breast-feeding body. Since the advertisements were sent to Mike in his capacity as a new father, one might expect him to be offered products of particular interest to men, for example from a growing daddy-gadget market, but that was not the case.

The first delivery was a letter from the largely Swedish-owned

Image 3. Libero postcard. ©SCA Hygiene Products AB.

company SCA's nappy brand Libero, offering membership of the 'Libero Club'. The letter began: 'Hi Mike. Congratulations on your baby – I hope you are enjoying this first wonderful time together with your family.' This joyful and personal tone is repeated throughout the advertisements. By using Mike's given name, it seems as if Libero is making their offer to him exclusively; however, that is not the case, as the letter used the plural form of the Swedish word for 'you' – the second person pronoun can be singular or plural, which makes it easy to tell if one or more people are being addressed – and hence the offer was also directed at Stella's mother. The interpretation that Libero was speaking to her is strengthened by the fact that the club members' introductory gift pack shown not only included nappies, disposable bibs, toys, and baby socks, but also sanitary towels. Libero seems to assume that all potential 'Libero Club' member families include a woman. When sending the letter to a man, as in this case, a nuclear heterosexual family norm is being articulated; had the letter been sent to a woman, a father would only be present hidden in the word 'family'. As the gift pack is intended to reach a woman, it seems as if it is mainly mothers who are thought of as potential members of the club – and as nappy buyers.

In a postcard also sent by Libero (Image 3), the central element is an infant with a man visualized as a safe background. His cropped face hides his identity, but it is still possible to interpret him as smiling, looking down at the infant in his arms. The gaze correlates with the text saying 'Enjoy seeing how your child develops'. As the plural 'you' is used, fatherhood is represented in both image and words, but positioned as something cooperative and shared by a spouse.

In the rest of the direct marketing material, the second person plural is seldom seen. When it is, it is not used consistently in an unambiguously inclusive mode of address. The global company Procter & Gamble sent several advertisements for its brand of nappy, Pampers; for example, in two issues of the booklet *Pampers Village Magasin*. In one of the booklets, exercises to help the reader avoid getting a bad back from carrying the growing infant are discussed. The topic could be of interest to both mothers and fathers, and the text first addresses a non-gendered singular 'you'. However, the text is accompanied by five images of women doing gymnastic movements, visually turning the address to mothers. The interpretation that women are the intended audience is reinforced later in the text, where the neutral singular 'you' is changed to mean 'you the mother' by making the connection between a sore back, pregnancy, and breast-feeding.

Jane Sunderland (2006: 507, 512) uses the concept of 'slippage', showing how texts about parenthood start out in a gender-neutral way, using inclusive neutral words such as the plural 'you' and 'parents', but then slowly slip into addressing only mothers. For example, a plural or gender-neutral heading is followed by a section of text that only refers to mothers, or positions the reader as a woman, with the result that fathers are excluded or positioned as less important. As I have shown here, it is not only the texts but also the visual elements that create this slippage towards mothers. Both the images of sanitary towels and those of exercising women are examples of what I would term *image slippages*, where mothers are highlighted and fathers are quietly excluded. In the material as a whole, there is a tendency for mothers to be constructed as both important in collaborative parenthood and as an independent parent, while fatherhood is invisible, or, when included, is something shared by a woman.

Competent, masculine, and intimate

Studies of advertisements, parenting books, and parenting magazines from the US and UK show that fathers are positioned as less important to the child and less competent than mothers (Kaufman 1999; Pugh 2005; Sunderland 2000, 2006). As paternity leave is more common in Sweden than in most countries, it might be expected that representations of fathers in Swedish adverts would show a different tendency. If depicting an equally shared parenthood, they should, according to Sunderland (2006), consist of a genuine inclusiveness, with both fathers and mothers varyingly and directly addressed; they should offer representations of a variety of parents and types of family; and they should explicitly construct both men and women as social actors. If aligned with the official policy, Mike's direct mail would also portray fatherhood as competent and involved. The adverts could even resemble Swedish government-initiated paternity leave campaigns that highlight men's ability to care (Klinth 2008).

Mike's material does portray fathers in ways that could be argued to visualize competent, 'involved fatherhood'. A father is seen loading a car, reading a book to a child, looking in a bathroom cabinet and, according to the text, fetching medicine for a child with a fever. Men are also seen cuddling and supporting infants learning to walk and swim, but most often fathers are shown holding the infant in their arms or in a baby carrier.

In the advert for Spacebabies (Image 4) and the feature in *Föräldrar & barn, baby* (Image 5), men are shown carrying infants next to several women. Being outnumbered among women, fatherhood

Image 4. Spacebabies©, *Föräldrar & barn, baby – gratis specialtidning till dig som just fått barn*, 2008, Issue 1: 34. ©Spacebabies.

Image 5. *Föräldrar & barn, baby – gratis specialtidning till dig som just fått barn*, 2008, Issue 1: 38–39. ©*Föräldrar & barn* and Maria Rosenlöf.

becomes a visual exception to a female norm of parenthood. The fathers are not only different by sex, but also in their interaction with the infant and the camera. In the *Föräldrar & barn, baby* feature, the man is the only one looking down to make eye contact with the infant, focusing all his attention on the infant, and seemingly unaware of the photo shoot, while the women confidently face the camera. In the Spacebabies advert, two women look down at their infants while the man puts his face down close to kiss and smell the infant's head. In both images, the fathers are more intimate towards the infant, leading them to stand out as the visually most attentive and loving parents. At the same time, fatherhood is marginalized and subordinated to the norm of motherhood. That fathers are seen and mentioned in the adverts should accordingly not be understood as being examples of slippage towards fatherhood; rather, fathers are treated as special, positioned as the marked others (Pugh 2005; Sturken & Cartwright 2009) in relation to a powerful female norm.

Images of men with infants have been used to promote a range of commodities since the 1970s, owing their origin to the earliest paternity leave campaign (Hagström 1999) that showed the famous Swedish weightlifter, Lennart 'Hoa Hoa' Dahlgren posing with an infant (Image 6). Roger Klinth (2008) argues that the image showed that even the most masculine of men can be a competent and responsible parent. It reassured people that caring for an infant and being on paternity leave does not undermine a man's masculinity. Charlotte Hagström (1999) points out that images of men together with infants often are sexualized, and that the infants function as symbolic proof of the man's virility. This means that images of men involved in (female) tending can reinforce masculinity rather than the opposite.

The visualized relationships between fathers and infants in Mike's direct mail are close – in fact, more intimate than the image from the 1970s promoting paternity leave. Especially intimate is the image on a flyer from the Swedish Portrait Club (Image 7), which shows an undressed man holding an infant in his arms. The man's secure grip and affectionate look puts the focus on the small infant, who becomes the most important element in the image. The man is not muscular and hyper-masculine like the weightlifter in the 1970s paternity leave campaign, but everything about him signals manhood. That no clothes are seen makes the image unusual, as undressed men are rarely seen in advertisements (Schroeder & Zwick 2004), but Patricia Holland (2004) argues that intimate closeness to a baby can legitimize nakedness in an image. The man's naked-

Image 6. Barnledig pappa! Försäkringskassan (The Swedish Social Insurance Office), 1976. ©Försäkrings-kassan and Reijo Rüster.

ness gives the presumably staged image a very private character. He is stripped of all symbols of working life, which turns him into a solely private individual, an emotional father who is there for his infant. Without clothes to date the photo, its character becomes timeless. Therefore it could be argued that the nudity ties the father and infant to nature, emphasizing the father–child relationship as a natural, private and timeless bond. The sexual aspects of the man's naked body as an object for a gaze of desire exist side-by-side with the purity of the new father–child relationship. The image turns masculinity, fatherhood, and sexuality into a romantic state where fatherhood is seen as something highly desirable.

145

Image 7. Image from a leaflet sent by The Swedish Portrait Club. ©Den Svenska Porträttklubben.

Jonathan Schroeder and Janet Borgerson (1998) argue that women in advertisements are often portrayed as combining two types of social symbols: aggressiveness and attractiveness. 'Female models may seem to adopt the powerful stance similar to a stereotypical man's: however, this is tempered by signals of glamour and submission' (ibid. 172). In this material where women are visualized mostly as mothers, such aggression is not seen. However, Schroeder and Borgerson's discussion is interesting in relation to how fathers are portrayed in Mike's advertisements where the fathers seem to adopt the stereotypical mother's role, which is a powerful stance in this context. The stereotypical mother's role is, then, tempered by a distinct masculine body expressing affection and closeness to the infant. It seems that an effort has been made to show men as loving parents. Since motherhood seems to be understood to equate loving parenthood, mothers need not to be overtly portrayed as such, while fathers, on the other hand, are visualized as exceptionally good and loving parents.

Image 8. The story 'Put to bed by Dad' in 'Daddy's corner',
Pampers Village Magasin Month 11–14: 12. ©Pampers.

Caring as a joyful choice

Looking closer at the images of the loving father, his practical involvement in childcare is seen to have limits. Men are not seen doing everything women do; for example, feeding children. In *Pampers Village Magasin*, fathers are singled out as special, and a separate section, called 'Daddy's corner', is dedicated to men. As there is no 'Mummy's corner', it can be argued that the other ten sections mainly address mothers. But not even in 'Daddy's corner', where anecdotes formulated as real-life stories describe men participating in their children's lives, are fathers fully involved.

In a story entitled 'Put to bed by Dad' (Image 8), an anonymous

147

man describes putting his son to bed. The story is accompanied by an image of father and son wearing similar green shirts. Again, the man gives all his attention to the child, keeping him close by holding a firm hand on the child's tummy as if hindering him from moving away from the bed. A gold wedding ring is visible on the man's right hand, placing him and the boy in a nuclear family setting. The mother herself is not seen in the image, but is present in the text.

> When Marcus was about 9 months old his mother had an extremely hard week with toothache and it just happened that I put him to bed the whole week and then it just automatically continued. Before that we used to take turns, but usually [Marcus's mother] did it anyway most of the time. As time went by I started looking forward to our evening rituals. And so did Marcus, I think. Like many dads I wasn't on parental leave much in the beginning, so I never got to spend much time with him when he was really young. … So the bathing and putting to bed became our little moment together and I always tried to get home early – even if it meant that I was forced to go to work at five o'clock the following morning to finish something. (*Pampers Village Magasin Month 11–14*: 12)

The story starts from the position that men do not normally participate in daily childcare activities. It describes the mother as responsible for the boy and the father as out at work and not as involved in his care. Because of a severe situation, the father has to help the mother out. He is content with letting the bedtime routine continue, discovering a positive side that is worth maintaining. The moral is that to become an involved father one has to find a joyful task to engage in. That men are encouraged to engage in joyful childcare constructs caring as neither obviously rewarding in itself, nor something that must be done whether it is satisfying or not. Implying that the rest of the child's care falls to the mother, motherhood is positioned as a responsibility, while fatherhood is a fun commitment to engage in when it suits. This constructs the father as the secondary parent, similar to that seen in previous research on toy adverts and parenting magazines and books (Pugh 2005; Sunderland 2000, 2006). These constructs of parenthood are not in line with the Swedish dual-earner/dual-carer family norm. However, the story is one of few in the material studied here where parental leave is explicitly mentioned. As the father is said not to be on parental leave much, just 'like many dads', Pampers is normalizing fathers taking fewer days' parental leave.

The difficult period that follows parents' return to work from parental leave is discussed in the two *Pampers Village Magasin* folders. By textual and visual slippage, the topic of combining work and home is framed as a problematic issue – for women:

> Share housework equally
> Make sure you share the housework equally: as a working mother, you're busy during the day. It's now really important that you and your child's father share the cleaning, the laundry, and the cooking equally, or that he takes most of the responsibility for the housework *if* he is on parental leave. (*Pampers Village Magasin Month 11–14*: 17, my emphasis)

According to this, fathers seem to have a choice whether to take parental leave. Also, it assumes that housework will not have been shared to begin with, and that the father would only take on a major responsibility for the housework *if* he is on parental leave. Paternity leave is thus not requested. Elsewhere in the booklet, nursery school and grandmothers, but not paternity leave, are mentioned as alternatives when a mother is about to go back to work.

Fathers' childcare and housework are not seen as something self-evident, but men are expected to be competent enough to step in and take more responsibility, suggesting that they have an accommodating approach to participation. Fathers are thus constructed as capable, but only marginally involved in family duties. Equal responsibility is not framed as something that men might want, or as an issue of equal interest to both sexes. Instead, the historically recurring theme of positioning women as the ones to find solutions to inequality issues (Hirdman 2001) is reiterated when mothers are encouraged to make sure that the housework is shared. Fathers (lack of) involvement is framed as a problem for individual women, and the task of changing this situation is assigned to them. Mothers are positioned as gatekeepers, encouraging (or preventing) dual-earner/dual-carer parenthood.

Swedish politics visualized

To promote genuinely shared parenting, texts and images have to 'mirror current social realities and practices', Sunderland argues (2006: 506). From a feminist perspective, however, she proposes that such representations be even more progressive, challenging parental gender stereotypes. The present analysis of direct marketing addressed to Mike shows that the direct mail he received certainly does not align with a feminist viewpoint. Instead, it minimizes the importance of fathers in infants' lives, positioning fatherhood in a subordinate relation to motherhood. Heedless of the state's norms of gender equality, the adverts present Mike with messages of a traditional division of family life. There was one exception where the stereotypes were challenged, though: an advert for the now defunct Swedish company allt-i-tyg.se, published in *Föräldrar & barn, baby* (Image 9).

The text of the allt-i-tyg.se advert emphasizes their cloth nappies and carriers as an investment in an environmental friendly future. Both the products and the hopes for the future seem to spring from an alternative lifestyle, and signal an alternative future when it comes to gender roles. In the image, a strong-looking, unshaven father carries an infant while keeping a firm grip on a broom. Confidently facing the camera, as he performs both childcare and cleaning, this man seems to be in charge of his duties, not merely helping out. Visualized as independent and fully competent, he simultaneously embodies the male parent while carrying out domestic chores. The intimacy and attentive paternal gaze of earlier images are not repeated here. Facing the camera, his portrayal is closer to that of the mothers in Image 5, and his parenthood seems just as self-evident as theirs. There seems to be no need to impress this father's love and care on the viewer.

The text promises products for the 'whole family', yet the visualization of the family concept is represented by two infants and a lone man. Acknowledging the variety of real family constellations, he could be read as a single parent or a parent in a homosexual relationship. Yet, if interpreting the image from a gender-equal dual-earner/dual-carer perspective, it is quite possible to imagine

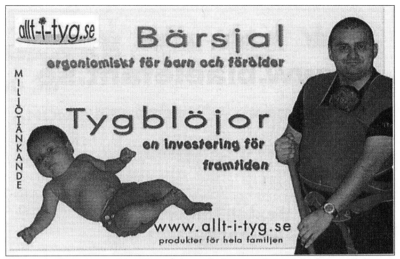

Image 9. allt-i-tyg.se, *Föräldrar & barn, baby – gratis specialtidning till dig som just fått barn*, 2008, Issue 1: 47. ©allt-i-tyg.se.

a female spouse; a mother off at work while the father performs the domestic work.

Concluding discussion

When communicating what products infants and new parents need, akin to parenting self-help books, advertisements give advice on parenthood and infant care (Pugh 2005). Gayle Kaufman (1999) suggests that adverts may act as socializing agents for parents and particularly for fathers, who may be more inclined to look to role models for comparison at a time when involved fatherhood is widely expected. From a gender-equal perspective, child consumption would be conducted by either parent. Likewise, if promoting 'involved fatherhood', companies would encourage fathers to engage in consumption. Yet that is not the case, and the role models Mike was offered to compare himself with were few, however portrayed as very affectionate. Fathers were positioned as involved, yet not as much as mothers were. The fact that the adverts mainly address women and promote items related to motherhood shows that mothers – rather than parents, or for that matter mothers *and* fathers – are the focus for the companies that approached Mike. Even though his name is on all the direct mail, Mike seems not to be the ideal consumer. It might even be that he was not thought of as the recipient in the first place, and was only sent this mail because Stella's mother had blocked direct marketing to her name. The adverts strongly signal that Mike and other fathers are not seen as being consumers and child carers equal to mothers.

Since visual representations in adverts can influence individual, as well as cultural, conceptions of identity (Schroeder & Zwick 2004), the way parents and children are visualized both produces and reproduces societal notions and expectations of childhood (Cook 1999; Higonnet 1998) and parenthood. The recurrent positioning of the father as a secondary parent could be partially explained by the fact that some of the companies which approached Mike are not originally Swedish, and thus the advertisements might be translated from other languages and other cultural contexts where involved fatherhood is not expected. However, Swedish companies also re-produce this image. It was an advert produced by a small Swedish company that adopted the most alternative stance on fatherhood, showing it not only as involving love but also household duties. By demonstrating that masculinity can embrace both childcare and housework, it takes the image of fatherhood in the marketing sphere a step further. Here, masculinity and fatherhood are forced towards the officially promoted discourse, showing the implications of the dual-earner/dual-carer ideal. It is an image that probably would not cause a stir if used in a paternity leave campaign – but it is surprising to find it in the direct mail sent to Mike, as the to-tality of the marketing he received merely strengthens stereotypes and undermines gender equality. Even though only one image, its existence shows that state-promoted norms of gender equality, and the identity and contents of an involved fatherhood, are being negotiated at the consumer levels of Swedish society.

Notes

1 There are, for example, several state-financed allowances to apply for when one has a child, and health services for children and pregnant women are free. All children are also guaranteed daycare at a low cost, and free compulsory elementary education including lunches (Halldén 2007).

2 The Swedish SPAR Register, administered by the Swedish Tax Agency, contains personal records of everyone resident in Sweden and can be used by companies trying to target a specific group of consumers; for example those who have just became parents. If someone is blocked in the register, companies are not allowed/able to use those records for marketing purposes (SPAR 2012).

3 The category covers products such as clothing, nappies, skin care, prams, baby carriers, child seats for cars, and products for feeding.

4 Products for play sometimes have educational aims, so it is not obvious whether baby gyms, for example, should be classified as entertaining toys or as products to stimulate children's knowledge and development, the third category.

5 The category covers products that focus on learning and on developing skills. It includes those educating parents about children's development and upbringing through books and magazines, but also products aimed at increasing infants' knowledge and physical, cognitive, and intellectual development, such as children's books and baby swim classes.

6 The products in the category emphasize the uniqueness of infancy, marketing products such as cameras, professional portrait photography, printed matter, and objects decorated with the child's name or hand- and footprints.

7 The category covers, for example, maternity clothes, breast-feeding equipment, and prenatal vitamins.

References

Aarseth, Helene (2009), 'From modernized masculinity to degendered lifestyle projects: Changes in men's narratives on domestic participation 1990–2005', *Men and Masculinities*, 11/4: 424–40.

Berggren, Stina (2005), *Kunskapsöversikt över förmåner riktade till barn och barnfamiljer/An overview of the Swedish family benefits – goals and development* (Working Papers in Social Insurance 2005:1; Stockholm: Enheten för forskning och utveckling, Försäkringskassan).

Cook, Daniel Thomas (1999), 'The visual commoditization of childhood: A case study of children's clothing trade journal, 1920s–1980s', *Journal of Social Sciences*, 3/1–2: 21–40.

– (2008), 'The missing child in consumption theory', *Journal of Consumer Culture*, 8/2: 219–43.

– (2009), 'Semantic provisioning of children's food: Commerce, care and maternal practice', *Childhood*, 16/3: 317–34.

Ekström, Karin (1999), 'Barns påverkan på föräldrar i ett engagemangskrävande konsumtionssamhälle', in Karin Ekström & Håkan Forsberg (eds.) *Den flerdimensionella konsumenten* (Gothenburg: Tre böcker förlag), 81–101.

Försäkringskassan (2010), *Barnbidrag och flerbarnstillägg*, available at <http://www.forsakringskassan.se>, accessed 7 Aug 2012.

Försäkringskassan (2012), *Till alla som väntar eller just fått barn*, available at <http://www.forsakringskassan.se>, accessed 7 Aug 2012.

Forsberg, Lucas (2009), *Involved parenthood: Everyday lives of Swedish middle-class families* (Diss., Linköping Studies in Arts and Science, 473; Linköping: Linköping University).

Hagström, Charlotte (1999), *Man blir pappa: Föräldraskap och maskulinitet i förändring* (Lund: Nordic Academic Press).

Halldén, Gunilla (2007), 'Inledning', in ead. (ed.) *Den moderna barndomen och barns vardagsliv* (Stockholm: Carlsson bokförlag).

Higonnet, Anne (1998), *Pictures of innocence: The history and crisis of ideal childhood* (London: Thames & Hudson).

Hirdman, Yvonne (2001), 'Kvinnorna i välfärdsstaten', in *Kvinnohistoria: Om kvinnors villkor från antiken till våra dagar* (Stockholm: Utbildnings-radion), 203–218.

Holland, Patricia (2004), *Picturing childhood – The myth of the child in popular imagery* (New York: I.B.Tauris).

Johansson, Barbro (2005), *Barn i konsumtionssamhället* (Stockholm: Norstedts akademiska förlag).

Kaufman, Gayle (1999), 'The portrayals of men's family roles in television commercials', *Sex Roles*, 41/5–6: 439–58.

Klinth, Roger (2008), 'The best of both worlds? Fatherhood and gender equality in Swedish paternity leave campaigns, 1976–2006', *Fathering*, 6/1: 20–38.

Lurie, Alison (1992), *The language of clothes* (London: Bloomsbury).

Mitchell, W. J. T. (1994), *Picture theory: Essays on verbal and visual representation* (Chicago: University of Chicago Press).

Mitchell, W. J. T. (2002), 'Showing seeing: A critique of visual culture', *Journal of Visual Culture*, 1/2: 165–81.

Nyberg, Anita (2000), 'From foster mothers to child care centers: A history of working mothers and child care in Sweden', *Feminist Economics*, 6/1: 5–20.

Orpana, Lena (2012), *TCO granskar: Pappaindex 2011#2/12* (TCO, Avdel-ningen för kommunikation och opinion).

Pugh, Allison, J. (2005), 'Selling compromise: Toys, motherhood, and the cultural deal', *Gender & Society*, 19/6: 729–49.

Rose, Gillian (2007), *Visual Methodologies* (London: SAGE).

Sandin, Bengt (2003a), 'Barndomens omvandling – från särart till likart', in Sandin & Halldén (2003c), 221–40.

– & Gunilla Halldén (2003b), 'Välfärdsstatens omvandling och en ny barndom', in Sandin & Halldén (2003c), 7–23.

– & Gunilla Halldén (2003c) (eds.) *Barnets bästa: En antologi om barndomens innebörder och välfärdens organisering* (Stockholm: Symposion).

Schroeder, E. Jonathan & Borgerson, L. Janet (1998), 'Marketing images of gender: A visual analysis', *Consumption, Markets & Culture*, 2/2: 161–201.

– & Zwick, Detlev (2004), 'Mirrors of masculinity: Representation and identity in advertising images', *Consumption, Markets & Culture*, 7/1: 21–52.

Sommestad, Lena (1998), 'Welfare state attitudes to the male breadwinning system: The United States and Sweden in comparative perspective', in Angélique Janssens (ed.), *The rise and decline of the male breadwinner family?* (Cambridge: CUP), 153–74.

SPAR [Statens personadressregister], <http://www.statenspersonadressregister. se>, accessed 7 Aug 2012.

Sturken, Marita & Lisa Cartwright (2009), *Practices of looking* (New York: OUP).

Sunderland, Jane (2000), 'Baby entertainer, bumbling assistant and line manager: Discourses of fatherhood in parentcraft texts', *Discourse & Society*, 11/2: 249–74.

– (2006), '"Parenting" or "mothering"? The case of modern childcare magazines', *Discourse & Society*, 17/4: 503–27.

Uth Thomsen, Thyra & Sørensen, Elin Brandi (2006), 'The first four-wheeled status symbol: Pram consumption as a vehicle for the construction of motherhood identity', *Journal of Marketing Management*, 22: 907–27.

Zelizer, Viviana (1985), *Pricing the priceless child: The changing social value of children* (New York: Basic Books).

– (2005) *The purchase of intimacy* (Princeton: PUP).

Ziol–Guest, M. Kathleen (2009), 'A single father's shopping bag: Purchasing decisions in single-father families', *Journal of Family Issues*, 30/5: 605–22.

CHAPTER 9

'I do like them but I don't watch them'

Preschoolers' use of age as an accounting device in product evaluations

Olivia Freeman

In many countries, by the time a child attends preschool, chronological age has become a defining component of self-concept.[1] Preschoolers have passed myriad developmental milestones, many of which have been accomplished through the utilization of age-graded material objects from consumer culture. Birthdays, 'a visible marker of age awareness' (Cook 2004: 99), have been celebrated and accompanied by festivities and gift-giving by family and friends. Chronological age is of course a key segmentation variable for marketing purposes; not least across the childhood demographic, which is neatly divided up into a number of discrete categories by marketing theorists and practitioners alike. For example, the online Lego store carves childhood into six distinctive age categories (<http://shop.lego.com/ByAge/>) and the Toys "R" Us British online store offers seven distinctive, age-based browsing categories (<http://www.toysrus.co.uk/browse/product/toys>). Traditionally, the consumer socialization perspective (Gunter & Furnham 1998; John 1999; McNeal 2007) has offered a cognitivist, age-stage-based view of the child consumer. For example, Deborah Roedder John (1999: 186) proposes that consumer socialization can be viewed as a developmental process that sees the child consumer proceed through a series of three age-based stages as they mature towards adulthood: (*i*) perceptual (ages three to seven); (*ii*) analytical (ages seven to eleven); and (*iii*) reflective (ages eleven to sixteen). In a similar vein, James McNeal (2007) argues that consumer development, motor development, and cognitive development are intertwined, and that 'consumer behaviour is thus the medium of social development and its resulting social relations' (ibid. 87). He follows a similar age-stage formula and posits five stages of consumer development: observation (birth–6 months); requesting/seeking (6–24 months); selecting/taking (24–48 months); co-purchase (48–72 months); and independent purchase (72–100 months).

Alternative perspectives focus on child consumers as 'knowing, meaning-making beings' (Cook 2009: 279). These views derive from the 'new paradigm' in childhood studies (see James & Prout 1990; Qvortrup et al. 1994), the biggest theoretical legacy of which remains the reconceptualization of children from 'social becomings' to 'social beings'. Childhood is viewed as brought into being by children's negotiation and manipulation of material, linguistic, and interactional resources with other children and adults, and thus serious engagement with children's consumer culture as produced by children themselves necessitates an examination of what and how consumer goods mean to them. This essay presents findings from a broader study that explores preschoolers' production of consumer selves and relations through talk-in-interaction about the material artefacts of consumer culture in a focus group setting. An examination of children's talk-in-interaction about consumer products reveals that the concept of age is drawn on to make sense of and evaluate products. The act of evaluating the objects of material consumer culture sees the evaluations produced used as a form of social currency between children, with which in the cases addressed here they create age-based consumer identities, and differentiate themselves from or align themselves with other focus group members.

Mary Douglas and Baron Isherwood (1996: xvi) emphasize the communicative aspects of consumer goods, arguing that 'goods are neutral, their uses are social; they can be used as fences or bridges.' While their theorizations of consumer culture do not discuss the 'child consumer' explicitly, a lack that is typical of consumption studies more broadly (for 'the missing child' in consumption studies, see Martens et al. 2004; Cook 2008), their emphasis on the social uses of consumer goods is reflected in work addressing children as consumers (Chin 2001; Goodwin 2006; Langer 2002; Langer & Farrar 2003; Pugh 2009; Seiter 1993).

Beryl Langer's (2002) theorization of the child consumer emphasizes the social aspects of doing choice. For Langer, learning to shop involves developing the ability to make choices and be discerning in those choices. Ellen Seiter (1993) argues that children's desire for involvement in consumer culture cannot be explained only through 'greed, hedonism or passivity', but rather through the 'desire for community and for a utopian freedom from adult authority, seriousness, and goal directedness' (ibid. 49). Elizabeth Chin (2001) and Randi Wærdahl (2005) support her claims, arguing that children must learn how to interpret consumer goods in terms of their 'status value'. Allison J. Pugh (2009) uses an ethnographic approach to explore children's consumer cultures in California, coining the phrase 'economy of dignity' to describe the realms within which 'children transform particular goods and experiences into a form of scrip, tokens of value suddenly fraught with meaning' (ibid. 7). Scrip is a term used to describe a source of social currency. Such scrips do not necessarily require actual ownership; Pugh's empirical analysis reveals that 'what made something count as scrip was that it allowed entry into the ongoing conversations of his or her peers', but equally what counted as scrip was 'fluid and dynamic' (ibid. 55). This results in an exchange rate that is forever in flux and that varies across several different economies of dignity; for example, at school, in the neighbourhood of home, or at an after-school club. Children made the most symbolic value out of 'claiming access to popular culture' (ibid. 56), and that access came in many shapes and forms, from actually owning and using to knowing about various heavily advertised objects of popular appeal.

The brief overview provided above posits that displaying knowledge or possession of a consumer commodity is exchanged for kudos within social environments, and thus this knowledge provides a type of social glue that facilitates relationships between group members. The expression of tastes, desires, and evaluations of material consumer culture is used as social currency between children, whereby producing the 'socially acceptable' evaluative judgements in interaction is as, if not more, important than owning the material possessions themselves.

Having provided a discussion of the theoretical background, consideration will be given to how a conversation analysis approach can be utilized to explore product evaluations, with two data extracts analysed in order to investigate how age is used and produced in talk-in-interaction about consumer commodities. The data presented in this essay is taken from a project comprising fourteen activity-based focus groups with preschoolers aged between two and five years, held in a number of settings including privately owned Montessori schools and community-based preschools in Dublin, Ireland (for a more detailed discussion of activity-based focus group methodology, see Eder & Fingerson 2003; Freeman 2009).[2] The talk-in-interaction so produced was transcribed using the conventions detailed in Appendix A.[3]

The aim of the research from which this essay derives is exploratory, taking a bottom-up approach to the broad question of how preschoolers make sense of the commodities of consumer culture as displayed through their talk-in-interaction with a focus group moderator. The transcribed data revealed that many of the sequences of talk centred on the requesting of product evaluations (predominantly moderator work) and the provision of product evaluations (predominantly participant work). These products derived from children's consumer culture and included characters from children's television, fast food and drink products, toys, and films. The aim of this essay is to address the question of how preschoolers use age as an accounting device in product evaluations.

Doing evaluation

A CA-informed discourse analytic approach[4] is used to focus on the construction of consumer selves and relations (for other discourse analysis work on children's consumer culture, see Sparrman 2009; Keller & Kalmus 2009). In line with this approach, product evaluations are understood to be fluid and shifting social constructs produced through talk-in-interaction, and not inner mental states revealed through language. Evaluations are thus understood as 'interactional expressions' and not ' "private" motivational states' (Schegloff 2007). 'Age' emerged as a central thematic thread, and hence the research presented in this essay addresses the question as to how preschool consumers use product evaluations to build 'aged' selves and relations. 'Age' is thus understood as something that is made meaningful for and by children through their talk-in-interaction about toys, media, consumables, and other commercial artefacts.

Before addressing the data, it is necessary to provide a brief outline of how the acts of evaluating or providing assessments are understood from a conversation analysis perspective. Marjorie Harness Goodwin (2006: 195) posits that the activity of assessing an object entails the expression of a positive or negative evaluation by a speaker using contrastive verbs such as 'like' and 'hate', and 'statements containing assessment adverbs and adjectives which position the participant with respect to the object'. An examination of the language utilized by speakers provides ways to understand the significance of issues, popular culture, or material objects to those speakers in a social context. Goodwin's (2006) analysis of 'assessment sequences' (Pomerantz 1984) in her work on girls' social worlds revealed that the activity of assessment provides a resource with which speakers can display to one another 'a congruent or divergent view of the events they encounter in their phenomenal world' (ibid. 183). The terms evaluation and assessment are often used interchangeably, but rather than 'ready-made cognitive objects' are understood to be worked up and performed to suit the social action being accomplished (Puchta & Potter 2004: 20). Analysis of assessment sequences brings a number of conversational features into focus, including preference structures and the accounting device.

Evaluation is an activity that prevails in focus group talk about children's consumer culture. The question of whether children 'like' something is one for which the preferred response is a positive 'yes' and the dispreferred response is a negative 'no'.[5] The theory of preference structures would suggest that where a negative assessment (dispreferred response) is provided, an account is then required or demanded by the moderator, but where the preferred response is provided, an account is not expected. The term accounting refers to talk where an individual accounts for something by providing an explanation or a justification (Goodwin 2006). In summary, evaluations assess things and accounts justify assessments.

The analysis below focuses on how 'age' is used to provide the substance of an account, and hence age is referred to as an accounting device. An examination of two lengthy assessment sequences offers a rich and textured analysis of the social activity of doing evaluation, revealing the ways in which the child participants and the moderator utilize consumer products discursively through expressions of 'evaluation' for social ends.

Doing age through objects

Age is first introduced as a *marked* social category by myself (the moderator) as I ask each child for his or her name and age during the ice-breaking phase of the focus group. Subsequently, the age category is intermittently produced and made salient by the children themselves for various social ends throughout the period of interaction. Whether age is evoked in the context of a spontaneous evaluation or whether it is utilized as an accounting device, it has a number of interactional consequences. Firstly, it sees speakers comply with regular conversational conventions by providing an account (age-based) of or a 'reason for' a stated negative response (disagreement, negative evaluation) to a prior utterance of another speaker, and thus passing the interactional floor back to the first speaker or allowing room for another speaker to enter. Secondly, it sees speakers position themselves and/or others in age-based terms in relation to the consumer object under discussion. Thirdly, it provides evidence of the ways children make sense of products in age-based terms in the social context of the focus group. Two extracts have been selected that serve to illustrate how age is evoked in the doing of product evaluations.

The first sequence (see Extract A) chosen for analysis is taken from a focus group comprising four children: Josh, Cian, Millie, and Ciara. Having completed a creativity collage-style exercise, I (the moderator) invite each child to talk the group through the various consumer-related objects they have selected to use in their

Image 1. Video still. Josh talking to Olivia and the group members through the consumer objects he selected for his collage – 'show and tell' style. (Left to right – Millie, Josh, Cian.) ©Olivia Freeman.

Image 2. Video still. The children taking turns to select images for their collages from the selection laid out in front of them. (Left to right – Harry, Ruth, Nancy, Chris, Olivia (moderator).) ©Olivia Freeman.

collage. It is important to note that the methodological perspective employed here is not concerned with seeking the truth or ascribing 'true' inner states to individuals, but rather argues that truths are constructed in the here and now of interaction, are fluid in structure, and serve differing functions across contexts. The analysis is thus not motivated by an interest in what sort of toys preschoolers 'really' like, but rather how preschoolers utilize them as resources in social interaction. The data presented here was collected in 2006, a time when *Teletubbies* and *Barney*, discussed below, were popular (characters that remain available, but have not retained the currency and popularity they had at the time).

This assessment sequence centres on *Teletubbies*, a BBC television series aimed at preschool viewers. It features four colourful main characters who live in 'Tellytubbyland'. The concept incorporates a large array of spin-off merchandise, including DVDs and character-licensed products. Linn (2004: 41) cites figures from The Itsy Bitsy Entertainment Company, the distributor for North and South America, which estimated that the programme was reaching one billion toddlers worldwide in 2001.

The sequence sees Josh produce a complex age-based account in response to a question from me about whether he 'likes *Teletubbies*'. Josh's account for why he does *not* watch *Teletubbies* is illustrative of the fact that preschool consumers categorize the artefacts of consumer culture in terms of age (in)appropriateness. In distancing himself from *Teletubbies*, he employs an 'age-based' repertoire (Potter & Wetherell 1987) that weaves through the consumer culture discourse produced by the focus group members and me, the moderator. Josh thus accomplishes an 'aged' consumer self through talk-in-interaction. While he does not give his age in years, he does contrast his persona – 'a big boy' who likes but does not watch *Teletubbies* – with that of a 'baby' persona, who not only likes, but, as implied by Josh, also watches *Teletubbies*. His initial assessment is met with very limited support from me, and silence from the other members of the focus group, with the exception of Cian, who produces spontaneous parallel and separate preferences related to other consumer artefacts, including *Care Bears* and *Scooby-Doo* (lines 696 and 704). This lack of support might explain

Extract A – ' I do like them but I don't watch them'

```
Clip Time: 62 seconds

      686   Olivia:      °Excellent° that's great thanks Cian
                         Josh >can I take a picture of ↑your one
                         ↓now<
      687   Josh:        No- I- have to tell you first
      688   Olivia:      Fir- tell me first [okay]
      689   Josh:                          [ I  ] ha::ve Scooby
                         Doo Figure (1.5) Fifi (1.0)(with)
                         Flower Tots Fifi (.) >Fifi and the
                         Flower Tots< Teletubbies Postman Pat
                         (1.5) >there you have it<
→     690   Olivia:      >Very good< (1.0) and do you ↑like
                         Telletubb↓ies
→     691   Josh:        Well em- I- I don't watch them but I I
                         do ↑like them but I dont' watch them.
→     692   Olivia:      Why do you not watch them.
→     693   Josh:        'Cos I'm a ↑big boy now.
→     694   Olivia:      Oh
→     695   Josh:        Only ba↓bies watch them. but I do like
                         them but I .hh I don't
                         [really watch them]
      696   Cian:        [I    love     care ] bears
→     697   Olivia:      Do you ↑like Teletubbies ↓Millie
→     698   Millie:      °Em::::: yeah° ((looks to Josh))
→     699   Olivia:      Do you watch them sometimes
→     700   Millie:      °Yeah°=
      701   Olivia:      =Yeah
→     702   Claire:      I watch them sometimes too
→     703   Olivia:      °Great°
      704   Cian:        I love (.) scooby doo
      705   Olivia:      Okay(.)did I take a picture
                         [>I didn't take one yet did I< ](.) =
      706   Cian:        [            (    )               ]
      707   Olivia:      = >'Cos you were tellin' me first< so
                         I'll take one now?
      708   Cian:        Noddy ( )
      709   Olivia:      °You hold it for me there that's great
                         (.) well done just turn it this way so
                         that I can see it with the camera
                         (1.5)
      710   Josh:        ((Holds collage towards the camera))
      711   Olivia:      Very good
```

Josh's subsequent downgrading from 'don't watch' to 'don't really watch' across just two turns (line 695).

Josh's very clear distinction between liking and watching potentially allows other members of the group, namely Millie and Claire, to position themselves, like him, as 'liking' but not 'watching' *Teletubbies*, without compromising their status as 'big girls' and 'not babies'. However, they do not confirm his account, instead affirming that they 'watch it sometimes'. While this might see them positioned in Josh's 'only babies watch it' category, his preceding downgraded claim to 'not really' watching it, as opposed to 'never' watching it himself, muddies the waters with regard to exactly what level of liking and watching is socially acceptable. What is also noteworthy here is the interaction taking place between Millie and Claire. Goodwin (2006: 195) argues in the context of assessment sequences that one way of 'constituting and displaying alliances is through affirming similar perspectives with respect to an event'. Claire is active in supporting Millie's claims in respect of liking *and* watching *Teletubbies*, as demonstrated in her spontaneous use of a me-too utterance (line 702).

By the end of the sequence, Josh has successfully utilized an age-based account in his evaluation of *Teletubbies*. No member of the group has explicitly challenged his account and he has, thus, firmly asserted a 'big boy' consumer self in opposition to that of a 'baby'. To this end, he has successfully utilized this material resource to make sense of his own place on the chronological ladder. Claire and Millie have used the opportunity to reinforce their own alliance. Meanings surrounding *Teletubbies*, however, and specifically the age at which it is acceptable to like and/or watch it, remain unresolved, and thus its social kudos as an age-defining product is somewhat in flux.

The second sequence (see Extract B) chosen for analysis is taken from a group comprising two boys, Chris and Harry, and two girls, Ruth and Nancy. The children are taking turns to select images from a large array of possible choices drawn from children's consumer culture with which to create a collage. *Barney and Friends* stars the eponymous large pink dinosaur who appears alongside children aged between eight and ten; an all-singing, all-dancing, larger-than-life character, he is targeted at preschool consumers aged between one and five.[6] The Barney character is licensed across a huge range of products and, like *Teletubbies* above, is therefore omnipresent in the consumer landscape of preschool children. He is an icon of children's culture and a recognizable and familiar character for the children in this group.

Here, Ruth utilizes her possession of a 'Barney toy' and her experience of watching the television programme to take the floor (line

Extract B – 'Barney's for Babies'

```
Clip Time: 42 seconds

              459   Olivia:   Okay? (.) now Chris again (.) quick
                              quick (1.5) would you ↑like this ↑one
                              ((Barney sticker))
→             460   Chris:    ((Shakes his head))
→             461   Harry:    >Bar-ney's< for ba-bies!
              462   Chris:    I wanna' get another Tigger one
→             463   Ruth:     I have Barney at home and Tigger(.) and
                              Winnie the Pooh
              464   Olivia:   And do you like↑ Barney Ru- Ruth
→             465   Ruth:     ((Slight nod)) (3.5) =
→             466   Chris:    Every ( ) [      (later)      ]
              467   Harry:               [I got (.) I got]=
→             468   Ruth:     = [No I don't ]((coughs))
→             469   Harry:    = [Two Tigger ]cards
→             470   Olivia:   Why not.
→             471   Ruth:     We watched Barney before (Barney)
              472   Olivia:   Do you like ↑it
              473   Ruth:     ((Shakes head))
→             474   Olivia:   No why not
→             475   Ruth:     °No I don't° ((folds her arms around
                              her knees and looks down))
→             476.1 Olivia:   You just don't? (.)Okay
```

463) and, as is typical in focus group talk, her stated declaration of ownership of this particular commodity leads to a request for elaboration on the topic from me. However, Ruth appears stifled in her freedom to provide elaboration. While initially affirmative in 'liking' *Barney* (line 465), she engages in a u-turn midway (line 468) and remains emphatic about 'not liking' *Barney* throughout the rest of the interaction. While the concept of age appropriateness is not alluded to by Ruth, an earlier utterance by Harry has very clearly provided the frame within which meanings around *Barney* are to be understood. His emphatic '*Barney*'s for babies' (line 461) contrasts sharply with Ruth's whispered 'No I don't' (line 475) offered at the completion of this interaction.

Ultimately, Harry's evaluation of *Barney* presents Ruth with what Billig (2001) refers to as an 'ideological dilemma'. It is impossible for her to marry her ownership, experience of, and apparent 'liking' for Barney in this forum without falling into Harry's categorization of being 'a baby'; a pejorative label for preschool-aged children. Ruth is not innovative in negotiating this dilemma, instead allowing her statements of ownership, experience, and initial liking to sit uncomfortably alongside later statements of unaccounted dislikes. However, her discomfort is apparent in her body language and whispered tones, and ultimately her refusal to comply with conversational conventions (providing an account for a dispreferred response) is accepted by me.

In terms of social ends, Harry uses his evaluation of *Barney* to exert some leadership in this interaction. His assessment of *Barney* is not challenged by Chris or Ruth, nor indeed Nancy (who does not participate at all) or myself. Harry does not actually state explicitly whether he likes *Barney* at any point in this sequence, but his emphatic and animated evaluation provided early on in the interaction serves to set the scene for the interaction that follows, constructing *Barney* as a low-value product in social exchange terms.

The CA-informed discourse analysis perspective used here allows a focus to be placed on the 'how' of doing product evaluations. A focus on 'age' reveals that consumer objects are made sense of in terms of age (in)appropriateness: popular characters from consumer culture, including *Barney* and *Teletubbies*, were variously constructed as being 'babyish'. Harry's spontaneous, age-based assessment of *Barney* appears to impact on the interaction that follows as *Barney* is constructed as a low-value product in social exchange terms. Goodwin (2007: 371) argues that 'providing a next move to an assessment entails important interactional competence, as the appropriateness of one's move is itself subject to evaluation by interlocutors to the present interaction'. Ruth's change of heart from her stated liking for *Barney* to dislike, and her subsequent discomfort when pressed for an account for her negative evaluation, demonstrates the extent to which assessments are subject to scrutiny by other group members. Josh introduced the experiential dimension of 'watching' as distinct from 'liking' in his assessment of *Teletubbies*. His logic suggests that liking something that is age inappropriate is acceptable, but watching it is not, thus illustrating the complexities involved in doing consumption evaluations. However, his construction of *Teletubbies* as 'babyish' had a limited social impact, because Millie and Claire were allied in their claims of watching this television programme 'sometimes', leaving the extent to which *Teletubbies* might be viewed as an age-defining product somewhat unresolved.

Concluding discussion

A concern with how much, or conversely how little, the '*developing*' child consumer knows and understands about how the marketplace operates, and how they fit within it as a 'choosing subject' (Cook 2009: 336), has continued to dominate thinking and debate on children as consumers in spite of the paradigm shift from socialization to social competence in childhood studies more broadly. This concern has resulted in an inordinate amount of time and energy being devoted to the construction of the dichotomous child consumer, who is simultaneously either exploited or empowered by market forces, depending on the research agenda. For example, critics of children's consumer culture have argued that the pressure on children to consume in order to maintain social links with their peers is relentless and exploitative (Linn 2004; Mayo & Nairn 2009; Schor 2004). A focus on children's talk-in-interaction about consumer commodities shows the continuing relevance and value of Mackay's contention (1975: 184) that an ethnomethodological framework 'makes available … children as beings who interpret the world as they do [and thus] transforms a theory of deficiency into a theory of competency' to current thinking on children as consumers. Addressing the child consumer through an interactional lens allows for a move beyond the empowered–exploited dichotomy. While the consumer-socialization perspective views consumer acts such as 'brand recognition', 'decision-making', 'evaluating', 'appraising', 'valuing', and indeed 'choosing' as static cognitive objects that children display with increasing levels of sophistication depending on the child's cognitive developmental stage, the interactionist approach used here views children's stated desires, preferences, and evaluations as dynamic 'interactional objects' (Wootton 2007) or 'interactional expressions' (Schegloff 2007) that are displayed competently and creatively by children across the chronological spectrum.

Don Slater (1997: 168) views consumption as an open-ended process. The meanings of goods are understood to be negotiated and not simply determined by producers. The work of product evaluation depicted in the extracts above supports this view, as product evaluation is shown to involve a number of social complexities. Firstly, the types of response provided to the request for a product evaluation must fit in with conversational conventions. Preferred responses can close down sequences, while dispreferred responses rarely do, as they require accounts. Secondly, the accounting device provides the participant with the opportunity to construct a consumer self within this socio-cultural context. Thirdly, stated evaluations and accompanying accounts invite other participants to support or challenge members' utterances, thereby creating opportunities to build allegiances or foster disputes.

To conclude, while marketing theorists and practitioners rely heavily on a developmental framework both to conceptualize and understand children as consumers as well as to target them and their parents effectively, an interactionist approach to understanding children as consumers sheds some light on the extent to which children as young as three or four are active in negotiating product-related meanings for their own social ends. That products can be understood in terms of age appropriateness appears highly significant for preschool consumers, but age-based meanings of products are malleable, as is demonstrated through talk-in-interaction in a social setting. The products discussed above, *Teletubbies* and *Barney*, are both targeted at the 'preschool market' (under-fives) but this market is differentiated further by toy marketers and children alike. A *Teletubbies* plush toy is described as 'suitable from birth' on the Toys "R" Us British website. A search for *Barney* on the same website reveals no fewer than 58 *Barney*-branded items, the vast majority of which are categorized as suitable for the 3- and 4-year-old and 5- to 7-year-old categories, with a substantial number of products also falling in the birth to 12 months and 12- to 24-month categories. The negotiation of product-related meanings by preschoolers for social ends in order to build aged consumer selves such as 'big boys' and 'big girls', to construct others as 'babies', or to build alliances or foster disputes with peers, demonstrates social competence on the part of children in using toys as social resources. While marketers may provide strong suggestions as to the age appropriateness of toys – for example, by depicting a 1-year-old with a *Teletubbies* plush toy in a shop cata-

logue – children display creativity and resourcefulness in expressing their views on products, and ultimately use these resources to
do age in a social context.

Notes

1 Preschool children are here defined as being between three and four years
old.

2 The activities comprised (*i*) a 'bingo' (match and win) game that used brand
logos, some of which were specific to children's cultures and some of which
were non-specific, in which the first player to match four quadrants was
declared a winner; and (*ii*) a creativity exercise, which involved the children
choosing laminated, velcro-backed cards taken from a toy catalogue with
which to decorate a felt-covered cardboard Christmas tree or lunchbox
depending on the time of year the groups were conducted. The selection
thus reflected a snapshot of the artefacts of consumer culture available at
the time the study took place.

3 All transcripts were produced using Transana – open source software for
the transcription of video and audio data (<http://www.transana.org/>).

4 CA (Sacks 1995a and b) is concerned with the intricacies of turn-by-turn
interaction and employs a special transcription system in an effort to produce highly textured transcripts.

5 Assessments are structured to invite particular next actions termed 'preferred'
(for example, the acceptance of an invitation) over other actions termed
'dispreferred' (for example, expressing disagreement) (Pomerantz 1984).
These terms are not intended to refer to the 'private desires or psychological proclivities of individual speakers'; they are descriptive of the way these
responses are 'done' in ordinary talk (Kitzinger & Frith 1999:302).

6 HIT Entertainment creates and distributes 'entertaining content and rich
characters', including *Barney and Friends, Bob the Builder*, and *Fifi and the
Flowertots*. Barney is listed as one of nine brands on the company website
and is described as a 'loveable huggable T-rex, a staple in preschoolers lives
… Barney uniquely addresses important socio-emotional and cognitive
skills in toddlers … Children see Barney as their trusted friend, one who
accompanies them as they grow and develop and learn about their ever-
changing world' (<http://www.hitentertainment.com/corporate/Barney.
html>, accessed 22 December 2011).

References

Billig, Michael (2001), 'Discursive, rhetorical and ideological messages', in Margaret Wetherell, Stephanie Taylor & Simeone J. Yates (eds.), *Discourse theory and practice: A reader* (London: SAGE).

Chin, Elizabeth (2001), *Purchasing power: Black kids and American consumer culture* (Minneapolis: University of Minnesota Press).

Cook, Daniel Thomas (2004), *The commodification of childhood: The children's clothing industry and the rise of the child consumer* (Durham, NC: Duke University Press).

– (2008), 'The missing child in consumption theory', *Journal of Consumer Culture*, 8(2) 219–243.

– (2009), 'Knowing the child consumer: historical and conceptual insights on qualitative children's consumer research', *Young Consumers*, 10/4: 269–82.

Douglas, Mary & Isherwood Baron (1996), *The world of goods: Towards an anthropology of consumption* (rev. edn., London: Routledge) (first pub. 1979).

Eder, Donna & Fingerson, Laura (2003), 'Interviewing children and adolescents', in James A. Holstein & Jaber F. Gubrium (eds.), *Inside interviewing new lenses, new concerns* (London: SAGE), 33–54.

Freeman, Olivia (2009a), 'Analysing focus group data', in J. Hogan, P. Dolan & P. Donnelly (ed.), *Approaches to qualitative research: Theory and its practical applications* (Cork: Oak Tree Press).

Goodwin, Marjorie Harness (2006), *The hidden life of girls* (Malden: Blackwell Publishing).

– (2007), 'Participation and embodied action in preadolescents girls' assessment activity', *Research on Language and Social Interaction*, 40/4: 353–75.

Gunter, Barrie & Furnham, Adrian (1998), *Children as consumers* (London: Routledge).

James, Allison & Prout, Alan (eds.) (1990), *Constructing and reconstructing childhood* (London: Falmer Press).

John, Deborah Roedder (1999), 'Consumer socialisation of children: A retrospective look at twenty-five years of research', *Journal of Consumer Research*, 26: 183–213.

Keller, Margit & Kalmus, Veronika (2009), 'What makes me cool? Estonian tweens' interpretative repertoires', *Young Consumers*, 10/4: 329–341.

Kitzinger, Celia & Frith, Hannah (1999), 'Just say no? The use of conversation analysis in developing a feminist perspective on sexual refusal', *Discourse & Society*, 10/3: 293–316.

Langer, Beryl (2002), 'Commodified enchantment: Children and consumer capitalism', *Thesis Eleven*, 69: 67–81.

– & Farrar, Estelle (2003), 'Becoming "Australian" in the global cultural economy: Children, consumption, citizenship', *Journal of Australian Studies*, 79: 117–126.

Linn, Susan (2004), *Consuming kids: Protecting our children from the onslaught of marketing and advertising* (New York: Anchor Books).

Mackay, Robert W. (1975), 'Conceptions of children and models of socialization', in Ray Turner (ed.), *Ethnomethodology: Selected readings* (Harmondsworth: Penguin), 180–93.

Martens, Lydia, Southerton, Dale & Scott, Sue (2004), 'Bringing children (and parents) into the sociology of consumption: Towards a theoretical and empirical agenda', *Journal of Consumer Culture*, 4(2):155–182.

Mayo, Ed & Nairn, Agnes (2009), *Consumer kids: How big business is grooming our children for profit* (London: Constable and Robinson).

McNeal, James (2007), *On becoming a consumer: The development of consumer behaviour patterns in childhood* (London: Butterworth-Heinemann).

Pomerantz, Anita (1984), 'Agreeing and disagreeing with assessments: Some features of preferred and dispreferred turn shapes', in J. Maxwell Atkinson & John Heritage (eds.), *Structures of social action: Studies in conversation analysis* (Cambridge: CUP).

Potter, Jonathan & Wetherell, Margaret (1987), *Discourse and social psychology: Beyond attitudes and behaviour* (London: SAGE).

Psathas, George (1995), *Conversation analysis: The study of talk in interaction* (London: SAGE).

Puchta, Claudia & Potter, Jonathan (2004), *Focus group practice* (London: SAGE).

Pugh, Allison J. (2009), *Longing and belonging: Parents, children and consumer culture* (Berkeley & Los Angeles: University of California).

Qvortrup, Jens, Bardy, Marjatta, Sgritta, Giovanni & Wintersberger, Helmut (1994) (eds.), *Childhood matters. Social theory, practice and politics* (Aldershot: Avebury).

Sacks, Harvey (1995a), *Lectures on conversation I* (Cambridge, Mass.: Blackwell).

– (1995b), *Lectures on Conversation Volume II* (Cambridge, Mass.: Blackwell).

Schegloff, Emmanuel A. (2007), *Sequence organization in interaction: A primer in conversation analysis* (Cambridge: CUP).

Schor, Juliet B. (2004), *Born to buy: The commercialised child and the new consumer culture* (New York: Scribner).

Seiter, Ellen (1993), *Sold separately: Parents and children in consumer culture* (New Brunswick: Rutgers University Press).

Slater, Don (1997), *Consumer culture & modernity* (Oxford: Polity Press).

Sparrman, Anna (2009), 'Ambiguities and paradoxes in children's talk about marketing breakfast cereals with toys', *Young Consumers*, 10/4: 297–313.

Ten Have, Paul (2007), *Doing conversation analysis: A practical guide* (London: SAGE).

Wærdahl, Randi (2005), '"Maybe I'll need a pair of Levi's before Junior High?" Child to youth trajectories and anticipatory socialization', *Childhood*, 12/2: 201–219.

Wootton, Anthony J. (2007), 'A puzzle about please: Repair, increments, and related matters in the speech of a young Child', *Research on Language and Social Interaction*, 40/2–3: 171–98.

Appendix

Transcription Conventions

The glossary of symbols provided below has been adapted from those provided by Psathas (1995) and Ten Have (2007). The majority of these symbols were first developed by Gail Jefferson.

	Symbol	Meaning
I - Sequencing	[	A *single left bracket* indicates the point of overlap onset.
	]	A *single right bracket* indicates the point of at which overlapping stops.
	=	*Equal signs* indicate *latching* that is there is no interval between the end of a prior and the start of a next part of talk.
II – Timed Intervals	(0.0)	The *number in parentheses* indicates the elapsed time in tenths of seconds of a pause in speech.
	(.)	A *dot in parentheses* indicates a very brief pause within or between utterances.
	Word	*Underscoring* indicates some form of stress, via pitch and/or amplitude.
III – Characteristics of Speech Production	:::	*Colons* indicate a prolongation of the immediately prior sound. Multiple colons indicate a more prolonged sound.
	-	A *dash* indicates a cut-off of the prior word or sound.
	. , ? ?, !	*Punctuation marks* are used to indicate characteristics of speech production; they do not refer to grammatical units.
	.	A *period* indicates a stopping fall in tone.
	,	A *comma* indicates a continuing intonation, the kind of falling-rising contour produced when reading items from a list.
	?	A *question mark* indicates a rising intonation.
	!	An *exclamation point* indicates an animated tone.
	↓ ↑	*Arrows* indicate marked shifts into higher or lower pitch in the utterance-part immediately following the arrow.
	WORD	*Upper case* indicates especially loud sounds relative to the surrounding talk.
	°word °	Utterances or utterance parts bracketed by *degree signs* are relatively quieter than the surrounding talk.
	>text<	*Right/left carets* bracketing an utterance indicate the enclosed speech was delivered more rapidly than usual for the speaker.
	<text>	*Left/right carets* bracketing an utterance indicate the enclosed speech was delivered more slowly than usual for the speaker.
	.hhhh	A *dot-prefixed row of hs* indicates an inbreath. Without the dot they indicate an outbreath.
	W(h)ord	A *parenthesised h, or row of hs within a word* indicates breathiness, as in laughter, crying, etc.
IV - Transcribers Doubts & Comments	( )	*Empty parentheses* indicates the transcribers inability to hear what was said and/or to identify the speaker.
	(word)	*Parenthesized words* indicates dubious hearings or speaker identifications.
	(( ))	*Double parentheses* contain transcriber's descriptions rather than, or in addition to, transcriptions.
	→	*Left margin arrows* indicate specific parts of an extract discussed in the text.

CHAPTER 10

Tweens as a commercial target group

Children and Disney filling the category

Ingvild Kvale Sørenssen

In the past few years, the television network Disney Channel has begun to cater more specifically to what is called the tween demographic. The term tweens is a marketing term usually used to indicate children aged 8–12, an age-group thought of as being 'in-be*tween*' children and teenagers. As Disney has defined and targeted this age-group as an audience, the question is how Disney as a producer constructs them as consumers, and, most importantly, how young people themselves construct this supposedly tween space. In this essay, I will first give short accounts of tweens as a concept and the theoretical frame for this research, before considering how Disney constructs this phase, and the ways in which a selection of Norwegian children considered to be tweens make meaning of this age-group. In the process, I will touch on the definition and usage of tweens by Disney Channel Scandinavia (that broadcast to the Nordic and Baltic states), and the ways in which the corporate view of the concept corresponds with how children aged 9–12 use and identify with the term.

What are tweens?

The term tweens originated in commercial marketing, and, as such, one cannot and should not ignore how the market addresses this group (Cook & Kaiser 2004). However, this is not to suggest that the market offers the correct definition, or indeed that such a correct definition exists; it is merely a starting point for an investigation of the term. Although the term tweens is derived from the market, it has found its way into other cultural spaces (Preston & White 2004: 126): take parenting books such as *Forstå barnet ditt: 8–12 år* ('Understand your child: 8–12 years') (Ulvund 2010), where the book-jacket blurb promises that the author will discuss 'tweens – om barn på vei til å bli ungdom og deres spesielle kjennetegn' ('tweens – about children becoming adolescents and their special characteristics') (ARK.no 2010). Another example is the book *Tweens: What to Expect From – And How to Survive – Your Child's Pre-Teen Years* (Clifford-Poston 2005). Similarly, the general media seem to be attuned to the term, as evidenced when Barack Obama was inaugurated and US newspapers used the term tweens about his two daughters (Fermino 2009; Freydkin 2009). The term tweens thus seems to have gained status as an everyday word, with no need to describe further what they are (or indeed *who* they are). In all these cases, the common denominator seems to be that they are distinct groups made up of 8–12-year-olds, but not set in relation to consumption.

Lately, research specifically investigating tweens has surfaced (Andersen et al. 2007; Bickford 2011; Clancy 2011; Gjødesen 2011; Guthrie 2005; Johansson 2007, 2010; Mitchell & Reid-Walsh 2005a; Pilcher 2011; Rysst 2010; Tufte 2011; Tufte & Rasmussen 2005; Wærdahl 2003, 2005; Willett 2005). When the term tweens is used in academic writing, it is often in relation to consumer culture. An example of academic research focusing specifically on tweens is the Danish book *Tweens – mellem medier og mærkevarer* ('Tweens – between media and brands') (Andersen 2011), based on the research project bearing the name 'Tweens – between media and consumption'. In other words, the intrinsic exploration of the term is based on the notion that tweens are consumers. In Lars Pynt Andersen's book, consumption is thought to arise in interplay with other factors, such as social context and economic resources, and that consumer identity is only a small part of tweens' identity. Even though the Danish research project concludes that tweens are more than mere consumers, I will argue that by focusing on consumption as a framework for understanding ostensibly tweenage children, the children in this category are constructed through the marketers' definitions first, and only secondly as social agents.

Although Disney's views as a producer play a prominent part here, when interviewing the children, consumption was not the main topic; rather, the focus was on how the informants performed age. By focusing on how the children who inhabit this age-group reflect on what it means to be not-yet-teenagers yet not-young-children, I sidestep having immediately to investigate the concept tweens as consumers: instead of discussing the term tweens in relation to consumption, my contribution to the field is how children talk and reflect on being in the age-group that Disney (and other market players) has defined as the tween target group. In order to gauge how Disney as a corporation constructs tweens and caters to the tween market segment, I interviewed the general manager of Disney Channel Scandinavia (hereafter GM) and the director of the toys division at Disney Consumer Products Nordic (hereafter DTD). The interviews took place at Disney's offices in Stockholm and Copenhagen in 2008. The interview guide consisted of questions about Disney's perceptions of tweens and what the company considers offering this target group.

To explore how young people placed in the tween category understand and construct meaning in the space between childhood and teenage, qualitative individual interviews with ten Norwegian girls aged 9–11, and five Norwegian boys aged 10–13 were undertaken. The interviews took place in private in the children's homes and lasted about one hour each.

Children's identities as being and becoming

Before turning to the analysis, it is worth considering the analytical framework by focusing on the identity and ambiguity of being and becoming. Notions of identity serve as an analytical tool when analysing how tweens as a target group are defined, both by Disney as a corporation and by members of the target group themselves. I make use of identity in this essay following Richard Jenkins (2004), and more particularly his suggestion that identity is a social issue – not a solo project of 'finding oneself' – that is continuously constructed through an internal–external dialectic, so that people perform identity based on both their external surroundings and themselves: 'What people think about us is no less significant then what we think about ourselves' (ibid. 19). Given this notion of the internal–external dialectic, the contextual and relational situation (or with whom people have dealings) will thus influence the type of identity people perform, so that in other words they have multiple identities with which they operate (Ackroyd & Pilkington 1999: 447). Thus they are thought to continuously construct their identities within a given relational context. As the concept of tweens is based on age, age performance also becomes an issue. Age can be seen as being part of one's identity, or as Ivar Frønes (1995: 190) puts it, 'To be older is not just a biological fact, it is, for children, a social strategy'. The age people do or perform can also be said to be a part of their identity performance.

In addition to identity, *being* and *becoming* are also important here, as this was expressed by both the Disney representatives and the child informants. Social studies of childhood have largely been founded on the notion of looking at children as beings, in contrast to perceiving them as adults-in-the-making, or 'becomings' (Qvortrup 1994). Lately, however, there has been a call to include both concepts when theorizing childhood. Both Nick Lee (2001) and Alan Prout (2005) argue that we need to recognize children as both being *and* becoming. Being can be seen as taking the children's lives seriously here and now. However, if children talk of themselves as becomings, why should we as researchers label them solely beings? The point here is that there is no reason why one cannot be both being *and* becoming, depending on the individual and the situation. Children, like adults, can be seen and experienced as both being and becoming (Bjerke 2011; Johansson 2010; Prout 2005; Uprichard 2008). One of the reasons for the double occupancy of both being and becoming is the way in which children are treated in different scenarios. Having multiple identities can thus mean acting and being perceived as a *being* in some relational contexts, and as a *becoming* in others. Hence, it can be said that an ambiguity of being and becoming is relevant for the tween group. With this in mind, I will now turn to Disney's perceptions and constructs of the tween target group.

Disney filling the category

Disney targets tweens as a segment since they deem it profitable. Market segmentation is a way of catering to niche interests while actually expanding a market share; it also seems to be the 'natural' progression of any commercial venture, and has historically been proven to generate more revenue (Cook 2004; Turow 1997). When I asked the Disney Channel Scandinavia GM why they had originally decided to segment and cater specifically for this target group, he told me that it was an audience largely underserved by other channels. GM also suggested that members of the tween age-group were watching television shows aimed at an older audience. According to the Disney Consumer Products Nordic DTD, 'It was Disney Channel who said we can do sitcoms for tweens, and we can expand our audience by focusing on tweens.' Hence, the reason Disney chose to focus on tweens as a target group and segment this specific group was that Disney believed it to be a lucrative opening in a profitable, underserved market. When interviewing GM in 2008, he said that the Walt Disney Company had targeted this group as tweens for the last 5–7 years.

When interviewed, the two Disney representatives drew on different ideas of what tweens were, mapping out a complex understanding of the term. Asked what characterized the tween audience, GM answered:

> I think character traits is that they got one leg in their childhood, and from a television channel perspective, they still very much watch some of those shows and enjoy the entertainment that we provide, but they are getting very curious about some of the slightly older shows, like the live action shows, and finding them very exiting.[1]

As an example of 'older shows', GM used the sitcom *Friends* as something Disney had found children in the tween category to be watching. Children in the tween category were thus thought of as drawing on different age performances through their television use, moving between shows for young children and shows aimed at an older audience. A reason for watching shows aimed at older people is worded here as 'getting curious about', implying an aspiration to be older, or can be seen as an act of anticipatory socialization. 'Anticipatory socialization', a term used by Randi Wærdahl (2003, 2005), can be described as the way people, including children, prepare for changes of identity and age. In relation to how anticipatory socialization works, Wærdahl argues: 'The sources of information could be anything from live role models (siblings, friends, peers), to adults and media messages' (Wærdahl 2003: 211). Media use can thus be seen as facilitating this aspiration or anticipation, acting as a source for their age performance. When asked if he believes that tweens aspire to become older, GM answered 'I think that's just a part of the DNA of tweens.' It is interesting that genetics are here used as an image. Behind his answer lies a clear biological perspective. The claim that it is in the nature of tweens, DNA to aspire to be older also indicates that it is universal, embedded in every individual tween's genes.

Generally, throughout the interviews the Disney representatives painted a picture of the essentialized tween. Both GM and DTD constructed the target group as a homogeneous group, and defined tweens as a unitary target group drawing on biology, developmental perspectives, and social context as a motivation to perform age.

> DTD: They are influenced by what teens are doing and wearing, and want to distance themselves from anything that their little sister might own or like. They still care what their parents think, but their friends hold greater importance in what they do and how they present themselves.

The emphasis on friends as important influences on tweens' lives corresponds with developmental psychology, where middle childhood is seen as a stage where children move from being very family-oriented to being more peer-oriented (Schultz Larsen 2003). From the perspective of developmental psychology, children in their tweens are becoming more aware of the social realm and increasingly occupied with how they think they are being perceived by others (Bunkholdt 2000).

DTD also said that music and new technology have an influence on how children in the tween years present themselves. By suggesting that children in their tweens seem to be influenced by technological advances, DTD was thus subscribing to a more social constructionist perspective. In this sense, the two Disney representatives drew on different theoretical standpoints to describe what drives tweens: a biological, developmental perspective, *and* a social constructionist perspective. These different perspectives are also found in market literature on tween children. Martin Lindstrom and Patricia B. Seybold (2004), for example, discuss the structural context of tweens, and attribute the changing notions of childhood to social change and technological advances. David L. Siegel et al. (2004), on the other hand, rely on developmental perspectives, mostly Jean Piaget's ages and stages, to construct and explain tweens. As the excerpts show, Disney draws on both of these notions when contemplating what drives tweens.

DTD and GM also differed in the way they defined tweens. Both talked about tweens as being in-between; however, where DTD saw them as moving forward in life, GM also focused on tweens moving back and forth between childhood and teenage. This moving back and forth was not present in the interview with DTD, who called tweens 'transitional tweens', reflecting a belief that tweens as a category are in a state of flux – in transition from childhood to teenage – and hence that they are moving forward. GM, however, emphasizes the fluctuation within the category; and fluctuation, as opposed to flux, allows for a more back-and-forth movement. GM and DTD thus described the concepts of being and becoming, if not in so many words, as trademarks of children inhabiting the tween years. The difference is in how the age performance or movement is talked about: tweens can be viewed as becomings or as beings. Hence transitioning tweens can be said to be becomings, as they are on their way forward in life. Yet, given that GM claims that fluctuation is a character trait of tweens, they are described as beings as well. In talking of tweens as transitioning, DTD discounted the idea that fluctuation is characteristic of tweens, instead focusing solely on the transition. GM's and DTD's portrayals of tweens are thus contradictory, while each still complements the other.

Children filling the category

Seeing that Disney was using the tween concept, I went into the field looking for how nominally tween children define their age. In the interviews, hobbies and likes and dislikes, including media use, at home and school were discussed, as was identity in relation both to older and younger children and to their peers. At the end of each interview, I asked the children whether they had come across the word tween and what it meant, in order to gauge whether the marketing term, which by then was appearing in newspapers and parenting books as well as academic texts, had reached the informants' vocabulary. Of the fifteen informants, only Ida (aged 10) and Katie (aged 9) had heard of the term.

> Ingvild: And I wonder, have you heard about tweens?
> Katie: Yes, it's like children who'll soon be teenagers.
> Ingvild: What does that mean?
> Katie: Like, people from 9–12, sort of.
> Ingvild: OK, would you say that you're a tween?
> Katie: Yes, would you?
> Ingvild: I don't know, I'm asking you.
> Katie: Mum would say that I'm one anyway, and I would too. I sort of think that I'm a child, and then I'll be a teenager, but then I think that the person I am, if I'm a tween or a child now, the person I am is Katie.

Katie here defines tweens as children 'who'll soon be teenagers', echoing the flux definition that DTD suggested – tween as transition. Even though Katie knows the term, she seems reluctant to describe herself as one, and instead defines herself as being in the same category as her younger brother, who is three: 'we are both children', she tells me later in the interview. Tweens for Katie thus seems to be a subcategory of the universal category of children. She is a child, and she announces that she is a tween and will become a teenager, implying that being a teenager is distanced both from being a child and from being a tween. She *is* a child and will *become* a teenager; she is not both at the same time. However, for Katie, it is not the label child, tween, or teenager that seems to be important, but rather a sense of a core identity. She articulates the notion that you go through life as the same person; becoming, yes, but always being, and thus the ambiguity of the two are always present. Accordingly, Katie resists being essentialized as a person within a category, focusing rather on herself as an individual.

Ida also knew the term, and, like Katie, did not think it applied to her or give the impression of having any connection with it. Ida told me that tweens meant age. Neither Ida nor Katie said that they used this label when talking to friends, for, as Ida told me, 'my friends already know how old I am', and using the term tween would be superfluous. When I asked where they had heard the term, Ida answered that she had heard it from her father, while Katie had heard it from her mother. This could imply that they were reluctant to use it because, rather than learning it from others, such as their peers, whom they thought inhabited the category, they had learned this somewhat forced definition from a group who were anything but their peers; in this case, their parents. The term tweens has not spread to or been internalized by the informants in this study. In addition, both Ida and Katie defined themselves as children. Tweens seem to be thought of as a subcategory within the category of children – quite the paradox.

While two informants recognized the term tweens, the rest of them often spoke of themselves as 'big children'. By doing so, they actively differentiated themselves from small children, usually aged 3–7, but also pointed out that they were not teenagers; they were still children. Several of the informants actually used the Norwegian term '*i mellom*', 'in-between', when describing themselves. While some of the informants talked about being in-between, they still put themselves in the category of children. This could be an expression of the potential safeness of childhood, while allowing for trying out or playing at being teenagers or even adults while they are still at a distance (Mitchell & Reid-Walsh 2005a). The informants could thus perform and do age by being in-between, and by being and becoming, all depending on the relational context, as will be seen.

Age as relational

Age can be said to be done by individuals; it is not merely a biological or natural given. Doing age can thus be seen as a strategy (Frønes 1995) that is played out by doing what is expected in a given situation. Acting like (or being) a child and acting like (or becoming) a teenager are socially and relationally dependent. The informants expressed the idea that sometimes they were being children and sometimes becoming teenagers; a fluctuation that seemed to depend on the social and relational context. Moreover, in isolation from others they would continue to draw on different age performances; for example by choosing which television programmes to watch.

The relational context seems to be important for determining the age identity – being children or becoming teenagers – they drew on. Some informants talked about how they would act like or be a child in one situation and a teenager in another. Ida expressed the ambiguity of being in-between, drawing on childhood and teenage in different contexts:

> Ida: At school we're more like teenagers; at home we're more like kids: we go out to play in the snow and stuff.

In the different contexts and relations of home and school, Ida draws on two different age categories. In the interviews, there were several instances when informants spoke about moving between or having several identities that could vary according to context and relations. As Jenkins (2004) suggests, identity is not merely a question of asserting one's identity, but this identity 'must also be validated (or not) by those with whom we have dealings' (ibid. 19). The way Ida talks about doing identity at home and school echoes Jenkins's notion (ibid.) that the internal–external dialectic as strategy and performance differs according to the context in which you find yourself. At school, Ida obviously feels that they are 'more like teenagers'. She does not say that they act or pretend, she says that they *are* more like teenagers. This opens for a multiplicity of identities as an individual and a member of this cohort. Ida and her peers do not, in Ida's words, become different people; rather, they have a plethora of repertoires, with a variety of attributes that they emphasize in different relational contexts. Ida does not use 'I', but rather 'we', when talking about how she and others act in the different contexts of home and school. In other words, their switching between acting like children and acting like teenagers can be viewed as a group identification trait. In the excerpt, Ida expresses that doing age is contextual and relational, and something which everybody does. Her account of drawing on different sets of identity in different contexts chimes with the point made by Steven Miles et al. (1998) that young people's experience of contemporary society is characterized by shifting identities.

Age was also said to be done in situations where they were alone, in addition to the relational context. In this setting, age performance cannot be about reading what is expected socially. In solitude, the internal–external dialectic was partially reduced to an internal dialectic, freeing them to perform age not according to what was expected, but rather depending on their mood.

> Ingvild: Does one outgrow Disney Channel?
> Suri: Well, it's sort of only for periods. Sometimes you want to be a little cool, and so you watch *The Voice* or MTV; and sometimes sort of childish, and so you watch Disney.

Although Suri here was 'free' from doing age based on external expectations, the internal–external dialectic is still present, as is evident from her remark that she sometimes felt more 'childish' – thus subscribing to a general, constructed notion of age-appropriate behaviour. The shifting age performance Suri portrays here was also described by other informants, and was very clear throughout my empirical data. Watching MTV one day and Disney Channel the next can be seen as evidence of children's double identity once they reach their tweens, with a foot in both childhood and becoming a teenager (Tufte 2011). Suri here echoes GM, who claimed that from a television perspective, children in their tweens have one foot in children's programmes and one in television aimed at an older age-group. When it comes to age as an identity performance, children in their tweens seem to occupy a 'free zone' when they are alone.

Through Suri's media usage, she is able to vary her age performance according to her inclinations, allowing her to play with teen culture from a safe distance and without commitment (Mitchell & Reid-Walsh 2005a: 3).

In addition to switching from one age identity to another according to mood or social situation, there is also the possibility of drawing on both simultaneously, without this being seen as contradictory – or even without it being recognized as simultaneous as such. When talking about a friend of hers, Susan told me that 'her style is Pokémon and Lady Gaga'. While we might look at this as falling somewhere between childhood and teenage, given that Lady Gaga represents youth culture and Pokémon represents childhood, for Susan, far from being fragmentary, this was a complete and whole style. Susan gives no impression that Pokémon and Lady Gaga belong to two different 'styles' or two different age performances; rather, they make up a style that is her friend's. According to Miles et al. 'the playing with identities from one situation to the next, whereby the individual draws upon different meanings at different times' (Miles et al. 1998: 83). Susan and her friend make an ensemble of things apparently not belonging to the same age performance. The use of consumer products or commercial symbols such as Lady Gaga and Pokémon can thus be considered examples of the interpretive and improvisational power that children can wield (Gabriel & Lang 2006). To follow Daniel Thomas Cook (2004), this can be seen as an example of how children 'creatively appropriate culture, including consumer culture, rather than having it imposed on them' (ibid. 148).

There is evidence of the tension between being and becoming in this empirical data. Informants expressed the notion that they inhabited a free zone where they could switch between being a child and becoming a teenager, playing with teen culture (Johansson 2005; Mitchell & Reid-Walsh 2005a). However, this seemed to be truer at home in an internal-dialectic situation than at school, where there was more of an external–internal dialectic situation (Jenkins 2004). Generally, although the informants talked about being in-between children and teenagers, they firmly placed themselves in the category of children. This being the case in the empirical data, I now conclude by discussing it as an academic idiom.

Concluding discussion

In this essay, I have described the way in which Disney constructs the term tweens, and how children inhabiting this phase perceive themselves and their age-group. The term tweens has started to leak into the public consciousness, and has also recently made its way into the academic vocabulary. However, while Disney actively makes use of the word, the children I interviewed did not use it.

Since my focus here has been on Disney and a number of children defined as being in their tweens, the data offers two different points of view to consider in describing children and consumption at a particular age. On the one hand, Disney, with its external point of view, constructs the age range as a recognizable group that can be targeted as a market segment. Disney defines the tween phase as being in a state of flux, yet even though the corporation acknowledges the complexities of the fluctuating transition children in their tweens seem to go through, they still essentialized 'tweens' as a homogeneous group. On the other hand, in the empirical material we find children who experience and construct their sense of being from 'the inside', and who paint a picture in which age performances vary according to setting. Moreover, while the children described performing age as relational and situated, the social context was not highlighted by the Disney representatives. That being said, there are similarities in the way the children and the Disney representatives present what it means to be a tween child. Most striking is that both talk about moving back and forth in age performances. Although the Disney representatives construed tweens at the intersection of being and becoming, they did not consider what might motivate this ambivalence.

In scholarly research, there has been a tendency to use the notion of tweens in three ways. Firstly, in adopting what was originally a marketing term, academics have also tacitly borrowed the marketers' definition of the notion, using it as a descriptive term. What is missing in this is any attempt to develop tweens as a theoretical concept. Secondly, research that makes use of the term tweens does so primarily in relation to consumption. By making use of the concept in this manner, academics may contribute to the essentializing of the child, or the tween, as nothing more than a consumer. Thirdly, researchers tend to discuss tweens using an etic approach – as outsiders discussing the individuals inhabiting a category – neglecting children's perspectives and understandings of this phase.

The field of social studies of children and childhood has traditionally been resistant to any categorization by age for fear of adopting a reductionist and essentiallist perspective on 'the child' (James, Jenks & Prout 1998; Lee 2001; Prout 2005). Yet I would argue that it is essential that we investigate categories such as tweens from the children's points of view if we are to understand how they make meanings and act in their everyday lives. Take the sociologist Barrie Thorne (1993), who started using the term 'kids' instead of children because this was the term that children used themselves: she argued that the term kids moved across the age divisions between 'infant, toddler, child and teen' (Thorne 1993: 9). By using the term kids, the category retains a dynamic characteristic that is more in line with how the participants see and understand themselves. This is echoed by the children in my study, who actively used children as a category as opposed to making use of the term tweens.

The concept tweens is constructed by marketers in general, and Disney in particular, as a category that is flexible in form and content. However, children in their tweens resist this classification because it might function as a hindrance: why commit to a category that might constrain their flexibility? The act of defining and categorizing a complex phase in life surrounds it with borders, however open those borders are meant to be. As in the case of the fluctuating tween, these borders constrain the individual's leeway. The term serves to define or name the complexity of the shifts between the different age performances; yet, paradoxically, the very naming and defining of this complexity can be experienced as a constraint on the individual. That said, however, Geoffrey C. Bowker and Susan Leigh Star Star argue that 'the only good classification is a living classification' (2000: 326). In other words, only time will tell whether the usage of tweens as a classificatory category will become common and internalized by those actually inhabiting the age-group.

Note

1 The interviews with GM and DTD were conducted in English, while quotations from interviews with the children are given in the author's translation.

References

Ackroyd, Judith & Andrew, Pilkington (1999), 'Childhood and the construction of ethnic identities in a global age', *Childhood,* 6/4: 443–54.

Andersen, Lars Pynt, Tufte, Birgitte, Rasmussen, Jeanette & Chan, Kara (2007), 'Tweens and new media in Denmark and Hong Kong', *Journal of Consumer Marketing,* 24/6: 340–50.

– (2011) (ed.), *Tweens: Mellem medier og mærkevarer* (Frederiksberg: Samfundslitteratur).

ARK.no (2010), *Forstå Barnet ditt, 8–12 år,* available at <http://www.ark.no/SamboWeb/produkt.do?produktId=4920263>, accessed 1 June 2012.

Bickford, Tyler (2011), *Children's music, MP3 players, and expressive practices at a vermont elementary school: Media consumption as social organization among schoolchildren* (Ph.D. thesis, Columbia University).

Bjerke, Håvard (2011), 'Children as "differently equal" responsible beings: Norwegian children's views of responsibility', *Childhood,* 18/1: 67–80.

Bowker, Geoffrey C. & Star, Susan Leigh (2000), *Sorting things out: Classification and its consequences* (New Baskerville: MIT Press).

Bunkholdt, Vigdis (2000), *Utviklingspsykologi* (Oslo: Universitetsforlaget).

Clancy, Sarah Jane (2011), *From childhood to tweenhood: An examination of the impact of marketing fashion to tweens on tween self-image and mother–child interactions* (Ph.D. thesis, McMaster University).

Clifford-Poston, Andrea (2005), *Tweens: What to expect from – and how to survive – your child's pre-teen years* (Oxford: Oneworld Publications).

Cook, Daniel Thomas (2004), *The commodification of childhood: The children's clothing industry and the rise of the child consumer* (Durham, NC: Duke University Press).

– & Kaiser, Susan B. (2004), 'Betwixt and be tween: Age ambiguity and sexualization of the female consuming subject', *Journal of Consumer Culture,* 4/2: 203.

Fermino, Jennifer (2009), 'Kids join in joyous celebration', *New York Post,* 20 January 2009, available at <http://www.nypost.com/p/news/politics/kids_join_in_joyous_celebration_istGjHM4j9bwNjwMfpbqDL4j9bwNjwMfpbqDL>, accessed 1 June 2012.

Freydkin, Donna (2009), 'All over Washington, a ball was had by all, or so it seems', *USA Today*, 20 January 2009, available at <http://www.usatoday.com/life/people/2009-01-19-inaugural-balls_N.htm>, accessed 1 June 2012.

Frønes, Ivar (1995), *Among peers: on the meaning of peers in the process of socialization* (Oslo: Scandinavian University Press).

Gabriel, Yiannis & Lang, Tim (2006), *The unmanageable consumer* (London: SAGE).

Gjødesen, Tessa (2011), 'Tweens mellem familie, venner og forbrug', in Andersen (2011), 77–128.

Guthrie, Meredith R. (2005), *Somewhere in-between: Tween queens and the marketing machine* (Ph.D. thesis, Bowling Green State University).

James, Allison, Jenks, Chris & Prout, Alan (1998), *Theorizing childhood* (Cambridge: Polity Press).

Jenkins, Richard (2004), *Social identity* (London: Routledge).

Johansson, Barbro (2005), *Barn i konsumtionssamhället* (Stockholm: Norstedts).

– (2007), 'Fashion and style in a commercial and cultural borderland', in Karin M. Ekström, Helene Brembeck & Magnus Mörck (eds.), *Little monsters: (de)coupling assemblages of consumption* (Zurich: LIT), 131–47.

– (2010), 'Subjectivities of the child consumer: Beings and becomings', in David Buckingham & Vebjørg Tingstad (eds.), *Childhood and consumer culture* (Basingstoke: Palgrave Macmillan).

Lee, Nick (2001), *Childhood and society: Growing up in an age of uncertainty* (Buckingham: Open University Press).

Lindstrom, Martin & Seybold, Patricia B. (2004), *Brandchild: Remarkable insights into the minds of today's global kids and their relationship with brands* (London: Kogan Page).

Miles, Steven, Cliff, Dallas & Burr, Vivien (1998), '"Fitting in and sticking out": Consumption, consumer meanings and the construction of young people's identities', *Journal of Youth Studies*, 1/1: 81–96.

Mitchell, Claudia, & Reid-Walsh, Jacqueline (2005a), 'Theorizing tween culture within girlhood studies', in Mitchell & Reid-Walsh (2005b), 1–24.

– (2005b) (eds.), *Seven going on seventeen: Tween studies in the culture of girlhood* (New York: Peter Lang).

Pilcher, Jane (2011), 'No logo? Children's consumption of fashion', *Childhood*, 18/1: 128.

Preston, Elizabeth H. & White, Cindy L. (2004), 'Commodifying kids: Branded identities and the selling of adspace on kids' networks', *Communication Quarterly*, 52/2: 115–28.

Prout, Alan (2005), *The future of childhood: Towards the interdisciplinary study of children* (London: RoutledgeFalmer).

Qvortrup, Jens (1994), 'Childhood matters: an introduction', *Childhood matters: Social theory, practice and politics*, 14: 1–24.

Rasmussen, Jeanette (2011), 'Tweens?', in Andersen (2011), 11–28.

Rysst, Mari (2010), '"I am only ten years old": Femininities, clothing-fashion codes and the intergenerational gap of interpretation of young girls' clothes', *Childhood*, 17/1: 76–93.

Schultz Larsen, Ole (2003), *Fem aldre: Udvikling fra fødsel til pubertet* (Århus: Systime).

Siegel, David L., Coffey, Timothy J. & Livingston, Gregory (2004), *The great tween buying machine: Capturing your share of the multi-billion-dollar tween market* (Chicago: Dearborn Trade Publishing).

Sørenssen, Ingvild Kvale & Mitchell, Claudia (2011), 'Tween-method and the politics of studying kinderculture', in Shirley R. Steinberg (ed.), *Kinderculture: The corporate construction of childhood* (3rd edn., Boulder: Westview Press), 153–67.

Tufte, Birgitte (2011), 'Tweens og medier', in Andersen (2011), 29–52.

– & Rasmussen, Jeanette (2005), 'Children and adolescents' use of the internet – with focus on tweens', in Birgitte Tufte, Jeanette Rasmussen & Lars Beck Christensen (eds.), *Frontrunners or copycats?* (Copenhagen: Copenhagen Business School Press), 118–35.

Turow, Joseph (1997), *Breaking up America: Advertisers and the new media world* (Chicago: University of Chicago Press).

Ulvund, Stein Erik (2010), *Forstå barnet ditt: 8–12 år* (Oslo: Cappelen).

Uprichard, Emma (2008), 'Children as "being and becomings": Children, childhood and temporality', *Children & Society*, 22/4: 303–313.

Wærdahl, Randi (2003), *Learning by consuming: Consumer culture as a condition for socialization and every day life at the age of 12* (Oslo: Universitetet i Oslo)

– (2005), '"Maybe I'll need a pair of Levi's before Junior High?": Child to youth trajectories and anticipatory socialization', *Childhood*, 12/2: 201–219.

Willett, Rebekah (2005), 'Constructing the digital tween: Market discourse and girls' interests', in Mitchell & Reid-Walsh (2005b), 278–93.

CHAPTER 11

Fashioning girls

Sue Jackson & Tiina Vares

Girls in late modern societies confront a tangled and complex landscape in which to construct identities around meanings of femininity. In popular culture, they are hailed as independent, self-choosing, self-managing subjects through discourses of 'girl power' and consumerism. The entanglement of these discourses produces significant meanings of self as 'empowered' through choosing and buying products. Both consumption and empowerment underscore contemporary postfeminist constructions of femininity – and these constructions collectively meld in the notion of 'new femininities' (Gill & Scharff 2011). The key significations of postfeminist modes of femininity most relevant to this essay are 'knowingness', girly hyperfemininity, and sexuality (Gill 2007a; McRobbie 2009). In the production of 'new femininities' consumption, empowerment and sexuality converge; fashion is an arena where the collision comes sharply into focus. It is the pre-teen girl's mobilization as a consumer of postfeminist popular culture and fashion that has generated widespread anxieties, some would argue moral panic, about girls being sexualized by the products marketed to them via postfeminist media (Egan & Hawke 2008). Specifically, the marketing of adult-styled, 'sexy' clothing to pre-teen girls has perhaps fuelled the most concern and response. Clothing such as G-strings, T-shirts with sexual messages (for example, 'Hottie'), tight crop-tops, and low-rise jeans blur distinctions between girls and women and 'produce sexuality as both thinkable and recognisable' (McRobbie 2008).

While a range of critical voices have risen against various aspects of this 'sexualized' pre-teen market (for example, academics, feminists, politicians), perhaps one of the loudest has erupted from a 'childhood innocence' discourse in which these pre-teen girls are constituted as vulnerable, easily influenced, and, importantly, asexual (see Egan & Hawke 2008). Thus, girls are required to tread a difficult, contradictory path between constituting self as fashionable, empowered, and sexually desirable through purchasing and wearing contemporary styles of 'sexy' dress, on the one hand, and maintaining identities as 'good', asexual girls, on the other. Emma Renold and Jessica Ringrose (2011) deploy the term 'schizoid subjectivities' to denote the contemporary, normative requirement for girls to work with such contradiction. As these researchers point out, there is a pressing need for research approaches that are capable of working with the complexities girls confront in such contradictory social messages. Our purpose in this essay is precisely to contribute such important knowledge about the ways in which girls navigate the contradictory requirements of an 'empowered' sexuality juxtaposed with 'good girl' femininity.

The present study builds on a small body of recent feminist critical research similarly seeking to further our knowledge about how girls manage and make sense of contradictory femininities (for example, Raby 2008; Ringrose 2010), but we do so more specifically in the context of contemporary debates about girls' sexualization through media consumption (Lerum & Dworkin 2009; Lumby & Allbury 2010). In previous studies, clothing emerges as a key signifier of sexual meaning, so that items such as 'thongs' and very short skirts may invoke identities as 'sluts'. Any apparent 'freedom' for girls to 'choose' the clothes they buy and wear, then, is constrained by the regulatory gaze of others and the unavailability of such 'freedom' within girls' positioning as 'children'. As Rosalind Gill (2007b) reminds us, agency within a consumer discourse needs to be understood within a Foucauldian framework wherein power is seen to work through the ability to structure our identities or sense of self. In the case of pre-teen girls, the powerful production of a highly particularized version of self – for example, the 'sexy', sassy girl (Brookes & Kelly 2009) – in postfeminist discourses contests with an equally powerful discourse of child innocence. The challenge for pre-teen girls is to successfully negotiate the precarious line between 'too sexy' and 'not sexy enough' in crafting their fashionable selves.

At this point, we need to clarify the way in which we use the term postfeminism in the essay, for, as Gill (2007) observes, it is variably understood and also widely contested in feminist debates. Somewhat unhelpfully, perhaps, these debates have centred on notions of postfeminism as, for example, a backlash, or as heralding a new progressive era in feminism. These conceptualizations rehearse dichotomies such as good–bad or progressive–regressive. In this essay, we use Gill's articulation (2007) of postfeminism as a sensibility that averts this kind of dichotomization. The conceptualization of a sensibility accords with a poststructuralist discursive understanding of postfeminism in that the term draws in the complex web of meanings of femininity within broader and overlapping contemporary social contexts of neo-liberalism and consumerism (Gill 2007; McRobbie 2009). Conceptualizing postfeminism through a feminist poststructuralist lens (Weldon 1987) is particularly useful in enabling us to interrogate the contradictions that underpin the ways in which power is deployed within a postfeminist sensibility. Empowerment, and the agentic subject produced within it, is the beating heart of postfeminism, animating three key articulations: neo-liberal knowingness (savvy) and the rhetoric of freedom and choice; sexuality in the figure of the hypersexualized woman who is always 'up for it'; and consumption of products designed not only to please the self but also improve it (McRobbie 2009). We have already alluded to how this amalgamation of empowerment, consumption, and sexuality within postfeminist discourses presents a complex and challenging social world for girls to navigate when juxtaposed with childhood discourses of innocence and asexuality (Egan & Hawkes 2008).

We wish to problematize notions of agency through fashion consumption, and also to interrupt a model that assumes girls' media consumption links in a straightforward way with clothing practices. We view girls' identity work in relation to fashion within a poststructuralist articulation of the 'self' as 'in process': fluid and shifting, yet also constrained by the effects of disciplinary power that requires us to self-regulate and self-monitor our compliance with dominant social norms. In this, we are drawing on Judith Butler's concept (1990) of subjectivation to understand girls as both actively producing identities that may transform or alter powerful discourses, for example, childhood or heterosexuality, and also as produced by such discourses. Within our framework, we hold consumer culture to function as a mechanism of self-regulation, providing the 'tools' or 'technologies' to construct oneself as an ideal subject – the 'know-how' and products to improve 'looks', popularity, and self-confidence. Incorporating these theoretical underpinnings, this essay draws on material from our current research project about girls' use of and engagement with 'tween' popular culture in their everyday lives. We present a detailed examination of the kind of identity work accomplished through the consumption of fashion, drawing on narratives of clothing practices and preferences produced in girls' video diaries. Our discursive approach enables us to highlight such complexities and ambiguities in self-production as fluid positioning across postfeminist discourses of femininity; neo-liberal discourses of individuality; and moral discourses of conventional femininity and childhood innocence, and specifically the asexual child (Egan & Hawke 2008). In so doing, our intention is to present an altogether more nuanced picture of the ways that girls' identity work is undertaken in the context of consumer culture. This approach crucially avoids dichotomizing arguments (Willett 2008) about girls as either subjected or agentic in relation to sexualized media, offering the potential to open up understandings about how agency and influence work through each other.

Fashioning on camera

The material we discuss in this essay is drawn from our current three-year research project, 'Girls, "Tween" Popular Culture and Everyday Life', on girls' use of and engagement with popular culture in their daily lives. A total of 71 girls participated in the first year of the project, recruited from three primary and two intermediate schools in two metropolitan sites in New Zealand: Christchurch (36 girls), and Wellington (35 girls). In 2008, approximately half of the girls were in Year 7 (ages 10–11) and half in Year 8 (ages 12–13).

In the second year of the project, 54 girls remained in the project, and of those who did not participate in 2009, most (12) were then in Year 9. Girls identified themselves as coming from diverse ethnic and socio-economic backgrounds. Their location in a New Zealand culture has much in common with Anglo-American societies, but also has its own unique features pertaining to, for example, its indigenous culture, its emphasis on outdoor lifestyles, and its (mis-) perceived sense of being a classless society.

Material for the project was gathered using focus groups and media video diaries; only video material is used in this essay. Following our project information session to Year 7 and Year 8 girls in each school, we subsequently met with interested girls, who had parental consent to participate. Meeting in discussion groups of mostly 7–8 participants, we worked with only one group in each location at any time. In the focus group sessions, we discussed wide-ranging topics related to the popular culture they used and engaged with. At the end of the discussion, we gave each girl a video camera and provided them with guidelines about the ethical use of the cameras and ideas for the kinds of recordings they might make. The key task for girls was to tell us on camera about the popular culture they engaged with daily, and we encouraged them to show us the media they used and how they used it. Video diaries were recorded for a one-month period. Although we suggested diaries be recorded for around 10 minutes every day, in the main the girls recorded less frequently but for much longer than 10 minutes. The girls used the cameras in different ways, including a direct narrative in which they addressed us through the camera lens; joint filming with other girls, where they engaged in media-related activities together; and showing us some form of popular culture while telling us about what they, and we, were looking at. At the end of the one-month video-recording period, the focus groups reconvened and the girls were invited to talk about their experiences of filming and what they had filmed. The focus group and video-recording procedure was repeated approximately 12 months later. Thus in the second year of the project, the original Year 8 girls had moved on to high school.

At the time of writing, all the material – focus groups and video diaries – has been transcribed. The initial thematic analysis has been completed and some more detailed discursive work has begun. We adopt a case-study approach, and use the video diary of one girl, Alicia, to demonstrate the kinds of strategies commonly deployed by girls in the video diary study to locate self as fashionably cool in postfeminist fashion terms, while carefully navigating its potentially sexy meanings.[1] Thus our aim in the essay is to problematize the binaries of agency and passivity and 'good/bad girls' by examining the ways that contradictory calls to sexual agency in a postfeminist discourse and to asexuality in a child innocence discourse are managed. In the following analysis we examine Alicia's negotiation of these discourses through two postfeminist subjectivities identified in our study – 'savvy girl' and 'girly girl' – and a third subjectivity fashioned in the contradictory spaces of the discourses that we have called mod(est) girl.

Fashioning a self

By way of background, the video diary guidelines issued to participants asked the girls to conduct a tour of their bedrooms as a way of beginning to tell us about themselves: their interests, the popular culture they used and liked, their families, and so on. We specifically mentioned that they might also like to do a 'tour' of their wardrobe and tell us about their clothes and accessories. Although not specifically referred to in our guidelines, in some diaries the girls also enthusiastically showed us their clothing purchases from shopping expeditions with friends or mothers. Typically, they would lay all the items purchased out on the bed and identify the shop from which the clothing had been bought. We want to emphasize that not all girls invited us to view their wardrobes or their recent clothing purchases, and neither did the topic of clothing appear in every girl's diary. Nonetheless, clothing featured regularly in the diaries to a varied extent and in various ways. As noted above, in this essay we use Alicia's video diary to enable us to provide a more detailed examination of how girls accomplished their identity work within the world of fashion (see also Jackson & Vares 2011; Vares, Jackson & Gill 2011).

'Savvy girl'

Of all of the girls in our study, twelve-year-old Alicia most ardently produced herself as a prolific consumer of clothes. A New Zealand/ Dutch girl from a middle-class family, she had the financial resources to fuel her expenditure on clothes, shoes, and accessories. As she told us: 'I like to go shopping, and when I go shopping, I have to spend something. I have to spend some money to buy something.' With these words, Alicia recognizes herself as a compulsive consumer; an identity mobilized by, and fashioned through, her participation 'in the world of goods' (McRobbie 2008). In her shopping narratives, she produced herself as a 'smart, savvy girl' who knew how to purchase fashion at a good price to create her own individual style. Like the women in *Sex and the City*, Alicia's appetite for buying clothes and shoes, which she represented as her particular passion, speaks to a contemporary discourse of (postfeminist) bourgeois femininity (Attwood 2005); one which, in part, draws together class, media, marketing, fashion, and the construction of a desirable self. Consumption, in postfeminist terms, brings into being an empowered self; for example, by making choices based on knowing about the product, its marketing and its value for money. We found that girls who identified themselves as ardent shoppers also positioned themselves as savvy about where to buy, what to buy, and whether the price was too high or a bargain. The kind of savvy we are referring to is best illustrated with two extracts from Alicia's diary:

> J Mall is doing this thing about 'Showtime', and [zooms in on the slogan and reads it out] 'The world is your stage' I think, something [*laughs*] and um, if you buy over $250-worth of stuff in J Mall, you get the new fragrance by Kylie Minogue only at [declares this loudly like a radio announcer] $20! Yeah, kind of cool. But in conclusion, you have to spend, 250, um, 250, '60 – you have to pa..., you have to buy – 270, you're wasting $270. [Camera now focused on A's reflection in the mirror – she gestures to emphasize her point.] You know me, how I love shopping – well I don't want to spend it on *that*.

Alicia's narrative is rich with savvy: celebrity knowledge in refer-
encing Kylie Minogue; media savvy about advertising strategies
(to save money you need to spend $250); and informed consumer
knowledge in recognizing value for money. Both her passionate
self-positioning as a consumer and her savvy analysis of the media
are recognizable in the 'smartness' and 'empowered consumption'
strands of postfeminist subjectivity (Gill 2007b). This empowerment
through consumption and knowingness also inflects the construction
of Alicia as savvy in the next example:

> This is on my Watchlist, I really wanna get it, it's from Supre,
> and it's three extra smalls, and it's what I fit, and um, yeah, and I
> wanna get that, so. And this is all, and that's all about it [shows us
> the webpage set-up] and the price for it now – what! Is $6! ... But
> um, anyway, that's Trade Me, and I don't spend all of my time on
> here, 'cos, I just try to find cheap bargains, but that's where I got
> my shoes for a very cheap, cheap price, for $6.90 when you actually
> get them in Foot Locker's for over $300, or round $200 to $300
> or even more than that.

The fashion marketplace is no longer constrained by materiality
but reaches globally across cyberspace. Acting as our guide on how
to shop for clothes on the Internet, Alicia logged in to her space
on the New Zealand auction site Trade Me and proceeded to use
the camera to show us items she had on the Watchlist for pending
auctions. In the extract, Alicia tells us of the top from Supre that
she 'really' wants. We would suggest that telling us where the top is
originally from is not incidental to Alicia's identity as a fashionable
girl: Supre is a fashion shop that targets teenage girls and women
in their twenties, and both its marketing and fashion styles can
reasonably be described as incorporating postfeminist constructions
of femininity as both 'girly' and 'sexy'. Its clothing sizes are small,
designed for very slim bodies, and so it is not surprising that Alicia,
a petite 12-year-old, fits their '3 extra smalls' size. Perhaps signifying
its 'tween' appeal, the shop was commonly mentioned as a shopping
destination in other girls' diaries. Alicia's constitution as a savvy girl
can be found in her ability to bargain shop – she purchased shoes

worth 'over $300, or round $200 to $300 or even more' for the small sum of $6.90. Again, the shop name has salience, recognizable to New Zealand consumers as one of the more expensive brand-name sports shoe-shops; Alicia's mention of it underlines the achievement of a 'bargain' and her identity as a savvy consumer.

'Girly girl'

Contrary to the assumptions in the sexualization debates that girls such as Alicia are very vulnerable to being seduced into buying the 'sexy' clothes worn by celebrities and depicted in various forms of media, girls in our study uniformly expressed preferences for casual and comfortable clothing conveying a 'tween' style: skinny jeans, boots, and long cardigans. Tight-fitting clothing was entirely absent from the girls' video-recorded attire, present only when critiqued in their narratives. These counter-sexualizing forms of dress appear in the following excerpt from Alicia's diary, filmed in her 'tour of the wardrobe':

> And then, I've got this one from Glassons [shows a grey sweatshirt with an old-style Mickey Mouse on the front]. This jersey, it's um, like, you know how you kind of wear those old baggy things and, yeah, this is kind of mine, and um, it says, 'It's a good day to play' and it's got Mickey Mouse 'cos I love Disney characters and all that; and this is kind of the baggy style as well, [a white sweatshirt with red-lettered 'Nike' on it] Nike Airforce, um, it's a jersey, a white jersey, it's quite big so I wear it as baggy [talks about souvenir T-shirts from Australia]. This is a jersey from Urban Angel [light pink, zip-up fleece top] and um, yup, and I got that from my brother [talks about Asian markets zip-up fleece top purchase]. And this is from Disneyland [a pink fleece top with an embroidered Tinkerbell on the back]. My mum's friend, T, she went to Disneyland, so I got that, but I'd – that's quite big as well, but I don't wear it.

A recurrent theme in the literature is the desire of tween girls to avoid signifiers of childishness; a theme that recurs in the sexualization anxieties about girls wanting to grow up too fast (Lamb &

Brown 2006). One way of reading Alicia's love of Disney characters is through a childhood innocence discourse (Egan & Hawke 2008), since in these moments she appears to happily position herself as a child. While the pink Tinkerbell fleece, with its strong significations of girly femininity, had been given to her, the Mickey Mouse T-shirt seems to be her own purchase. Its child significations are not only evident in the cartoon character himself, but also the message stating 'It's a good day to play'. Alternatively, however, we can also read Alicia's Disney passion within the contemporary movement of postfeminist celebration of 'girl', in which cuteness and girliness are elided and strategically marketed (McRobbie 2008). Alicia did not buy the Mickey Mouse T-shirt at a children's shop but at Glassons, a shop catering predominantly for older teens and young adult women (similar to Supre). We suggest this exemplifies the entwining of 'girl' and consumption (Harris 2004; McRobbie 2008), which functions to blur the distinctions between 'girl' and adult woman that have been implicated in the marketing of sexualized products to children (Lamb & Brown 2006; McRobbie 2008). However, Alicia's narration and display of her wardrobe seems to undermine notions of the sexually consumed, consuming girl; she prefers 'baggy' clothes, and actively resists 'wearing tight jerseys', as she says in the continuation of her narrative:

> I got this from Glassons [shows an indistinct black top on a hanger] and it's one of those tops that you strap up, like, here, you strap it up, like that; and this, this is kind of the baggy style as well [a grey-blue hoodie with indistinct, bright green lettering] uum, 'cos I don't like realing, weary, wear, really, really, sorry, really wearing tight jerseys, but um, it's from Jay Jays [she goes on to show and list similar purchases and an overall skirt, identifying the four shops where purchased].

Alicia's embrace of 'baggy' and concomitant rejection of 'tight' is, as noted earlier, typical of girls in our study. Girls frequently expressed preferences for comfortable clothing such as their 'fat pants', and on film they almost invariably appeared dressed in the style of clothing Alicia refers to: hoodies, fleece tops, and jeans or shorts. The importance of feeling comfortable in clothes has similarly been observed in other studies (for example, Buckingham et al. 2009), and is variously attributed to physical comfort, an avoidance of body display, or a 'sexy reading' of self, and not wanting to 'stand out' from peers. The salience of New Zealand culture needs to be noted here as well, since there is emphasis on casual, outdoor lifestyles that are embodied in casual styles of dress in leisure time. While the style of clothing perhaps does not conform to the sexy slink of postfeminist fashion, the majority of Alicia's shopping venues definitely target teen girls and young adult women, and their advertising clearly appropriates the production of a desirable self that is fashion-consuming, slim, attractive, and 'sexy' (see Brookes & Kelly 2009). In identifying herself as a shopper at such shops, Alicia is arguably positioned as a fashionable young woman within a contemporary postfeminist discourse. Moreover, the extent to which these same shops appeared in other girls' diaries suggests to us the notion that they function as a tweenage resource for constructing oneself as fashionably 'cool'.

'Mod(est) girl'

Although the clothing girls wore and talked about on camera seemed disconnected to 'sexy' postfeminist culture, it would be misleading to suggest that they were somehow disengaged from it. Rather, a compelling element of the girls' talk about fashion and clothing was the way in which they carefully negotiated body-revealing styles of dress that potentially could convey meanings of sexuality. So, for example, a strappy dress required a T-shirt underneath, sheer tops needed under-tops, short dresses had to team up with leggings. When girls did show us strappy dresses, they were explained as a special-occasion garment worn to a wedding, school disco, or similarly significant event. These uniform, recurrent codes of appropriate dress point strongly to normative rules for girls' exposure of their bodies, as several UK studies have also found (for example, Malson, Marshall & Woollett 2002; Ringrose 2008). We suggest the strong possibility that these practices of concealing, not revealing, their bodies are underpinned by moral panics about the sexualization of girls in which a discourse of childhood innocence constituting the asexual child is heavily incorporated (see Lumby & Allbury 2010; Egan & Hawke 2008; Jackson & Vares 2011). In other words, girls' practices of dress are subject to the regulatory discourses of girl–child sexuality.

In Alicia's diary, the management of dress that could potentially be read in terms of 'sexiness' blurred with her self-construction as a savvy girl – this time a girl with fashion sense who knew how to work with clothes in ways that rendered them both 'appropriate' and fashionable. In the following extract, she shows and tells us about her modifications to a top that she successfully bid for on Trade Me:

> The thing is, *this* top that I'm wearing right now, I̲ got it from Trade Me. But *when* I got it, I thought, I saw it and was like, it's too *big*! And so I was like, oh, my gosh! So *then*, [stands up straight to reveal her solution] *I* put it as a *dress* – with [pulls herself up on the kitchen workshop so we can see her legs] *leggings. Because* [gets down again] in *our* days, it's *not* cool to have a *long* dress, it's cool to have – [moves so can display] *short* drop – uh, *short* top made into a long *dress*, I mean, uh, uh, um, a *long* [grabs top] a long *top*, made into a *short* dress and *leggings. But* – yeah. If, if, if *you* have long dresses, it's ok, because – *you* guys are allowed to wear them. *Us* – you shouldn't be *seen* with long dresses on the street, [puts hand on chest] not *our* days.

As a dress, the too-big top threatens to violate a code of age appropriateness because of its shortness, and Alicia stresses emphatically and shows us by filming herself that it is worn with leggings. Alicia's modification of the top positions her as a creative, agentic 'problem-solver', allowing her to accomplish a fashionable identity (a short dress) without slippage into the 'sexiness' of a too-short dress. Elsewhere in her account of the purchase, she also shows how she further modified the garment by pinning the neckline so that it is not too big (or revealing) on her. Alicia's marking out the generational territory of fashion further underlines her constitution as a fashionable girl; girls like her need to be 'cool', unlike us older researchers, who can wear 'uncool' long dresses, implicitly positioning us outside fashion's address. However, this is a 'cool' that consistently speaks

to a moral modesty: in another section of her diary, Alicia explains
a top among some new purchases from Supre:

> but it's kind of like a dress top kind of thing, look at the patterns;
> it'll make me stand out in the crowd. But anyway, yeah I got that,
> it's not really a top, it's like a dress top, you only wear it with leg-
> gings, I tell you, you only wear it with leggings!

Here, Alicia draws the boundaries around standing out: obtaining
attention through bold patterns is permissible, but attention to a
pre-teen girl's exposed legs would not be. Such codes were commonly produced amongst girls, in both video diaries and focus
groups: in particular, low necks and short skirts or shorts without
leggings were deemed unacceptable, and risked readings of being a
'skank' or 'slut'. Gill's observation (2007a: 70) that young women's
clothing choices are 'invariably situated within moral rather than
political discourse' is useful in making sense of girls' careful attention to these sexual meanings of dress.

One of the claims in the moral panics about the sexualization
of girls is that in adopting 'sexy-styled clothing' girls are growing
up too fast. As the material we have discussed here indicates, we
found little evidence that girls were eagerly seeking maturity through
emulating sexiness. On the contrary, the girls in the focus groups
collectively embraced their 'in-between' tween identities, actively
distancing themselves from both younger girls and older teen girls.
Nonetheless, we wondered whether the transition to high school
for the Year 8 participants during the second year of the project
might bring a move towards a more sexualized self-positioning. Our
analyses of the second-year data are preliminary, and the questions
we have about changes require much more detailed examination
of the material; yet in focusing on Alicia's diaries, one example of a
shift in perspective over the year stood out, and this was in relation
to her choice of shoes. Alicia was an ardent shoe-shopper, and the
tour of her wardrobe in the first year revealed an extensive collection that ranged from her favourite Chucks to the shoes she had for
coral-walking during a Pacific island holiday. Alicia did not show or
tell us about high-heeled shoes in the first year of the project, and

this was a pattern across our material. Like tight-fitting clothing, exposed midriffs, and micro-skirts or -shorts, high heels, particularly stiletto heels, connote sexiness and also maturity (Holland & Attwood 2009). One way of reading the general absence of high heels in our material (unmentioned and potentially not owned) is through an age discourse: the inappropriateness of 'sexy' for 11–13-year-old girls. Supporting this possibility, Alicia's diary entry about shoes with a heel in the first year of the project corresponded to the careful management of clothes that might convey sexual meanings. In the next excerpt, she is showing us a pair of pink shoes that look like a pointy-toed version of ballet slippers:

> they're kind of like high-heeled kind of ones, [zooms in on them] like – well they haven't got a high heel, that's how high the high heel is – [picks up the shoe and turns it over so we can see the small heel] but they're really quite cool, they've got – they're pink, and they've got dots on them, like that, I wear – I don't really wear these anywhere except I'm going on a, you know, on, nice dinner with Mum and Dad and stuff, I'd maybe wear those.

On the one hand, these shoes convey the fashionability of post-feminist style – girly pink and the approximation of high heels denotes 'cool-ness' – while on the other, their simultaneous classification as 'not high', as we can see from the video recording, counters their reading as adult and potentially 'sexy'. Alicia is also careful to give a specific context for when she would wear these low-heeled shoes – going out with her parents; reserving even low heels for a special occasion – which works to shore up her location as a child. The contrast to Alicia's commentary about high-heeled shoes in the second year of the project is striking:

> [Camera pans to shoe selection] And I have, a pair, a pair of high *heels*, and here they *go* – oh, wait a second [camera shows carpet, then her high-heel-shod foot comes into view]. You, you were just looking into the, floor but here they *are*. [Sticks out a foot – she is wearing a black, elegant, strappy, formal-looking stiletto with a jewel detail. Her toenails are painted a coral colour.] Ow, *flash*! [Stands

up and looks down at the shoe.] *Pretty* cool – and they *are* pretty *high*. [Raises the camera to the mirror to show herself in cardigan and pyjama bottoms, wearing one high-heel shoe and grimacing.]

This time the heels are emphasized in her narrative, and the video image confirms a strappy, stiletto-style shoe: what was inappropriate when she was nearing 13 now appears to be appropriate. Alicia appreciates their contemporary fashionability as both 'pretty *high*' and '*pretty* cool'. Moreover, Alicia's attention to nail varnish exemplifies the kind of technology of self that is invoked in constituting an agentic, self-improving subjectivity. At the same time, however, Alicia's performance on camera resonates with parody, wearing high heels with her pyjama bottoms and pulling a face in an exaggeratedly comic way to convey the awkwardness of balancing on the spindly heel.

Concluding discussion

In this essay our aim has been to illuminate the challenges girls face in finding ways to manage the contradictory calls to agency in post-feminist terms as a consumer of 'sexy' fashion, on the one hand, and the call to the moral preservation of the 'good', asexual girl–child, on the other. Using Alicia's video diary extracts to highlight some of the key patterns and findings in our material, we have shown how a location in consumer discourse may enable a savvy and agentic subjectivity within the terms of postfeminist empowerment. Alicia's navigation of the auction site Trade Me to purchase clothing showed her skills in managing technology and money and operationalizing her knowledge of the market. Such sophistication, however, intersected with her location as a child; a position deployed in both the girly constructions of post-femininity and the moral child innocence discourse. Preference sometimes outweighed postfeminist fashion, as in the baggy clothing or hoodies; at other times, Alicia's clothing invoked the child (witness the 'cute' girliness of a Mickey Mouse top purchased at a 'girly' fashion shop); at still other moments, though, a location in a child innocence discourse constrained her to adopt 'sexy' clothes, and it was at these times that we caught glimpses of the careful kind of negotiation required of girls in a postfeminist-styled marketplace. For example, Alicia's narrative about her 'dress top' showed how moral boundaries operate to code dress as appropriate or inappropriate for girls of her age. On the other hand, it was in this tension between (postfeminist) fashionability – the short dress, the low neck – and moral discourses of girlhood, incorporating the 'good girl' and 'childhood innocence', that Alicia was able to find a space of creative agency, modifying her 'dress top' to fit and making it modest by pinning the neck and wearing it with leggings. In so doing, she could accomplish both fashionably 'cool' and 'proper' femininity. We suggest that such practices highlight, in the manner of Michel Foucault's concept (1990) of the technologies of self, the active fashioning of self within the boundaries afforded by the dominant discourses. Thus, in the context of contemporary debates about girls' sexualization, the detailed, discursive kind of examination we have presented here may be a way of avoiding homogenizing assumptions about girls' practices, and instead opening up understandings about how girls manage the pushes and pulls of contemporary and conventional femininity in fashioning a sense of self.

Acknowledgements

We wish to thank the girls who gave their time, energy, and enthusiasm to this project. We feel enormously privileged. We also wish to acknowledge the Royal Society of New Zealand for its financial support of the project.

Note

1 All the informants' names in the essay are pseudonyms.

References

Attwood, Feona (2005), 'Fashion and passion: Marketing sex to women', *Sexualities*, 8/4: 392–406.
Buckingham, David, Willett, Rebecca, Bragg, Sara & Russell, Rachel (2009), 'Sexualised goods aimed at children', report to the Scottish Parliament Equal

Opportunities Committee (2008–09/01/EOC), available at <http://archive.
scottish.parliament.uk/s3/committees/equal/reports-10/eor10-02.htm>,
accessed 1 June 2012.

Brookes, Fiona & Kelly, Peter (2009), 'Dolly girls: Tweenies as artefacts of
consumption', *Journal of Youth Studies*, 12/6: 599–613.

Butler, Judith (1990), *Gender trouble* (London: Routledge).

Egan, R. Danielle & Hawke, Gail (2008), 'Girls' sexuality and the strange
carnalities of advertisements: Deconstructing the discourse of corporate
paedophilia', *Australian Feminist Studies*, 23: 307–22.

Foucault, Michel (1990), *The history of sexuality*, Vol. 1, trans. Robert Hurley
(New York: Vintage).

Gavey, Nicola (2011), 'Feminist poststructuralist discourse analysis revisited',
Psychology of Women Quarterly, 35/1: 183–8.

Gill, Rosalind (2007a), 'Postfeminist media culture: Elements of a sensibility',
European Journal of Cultural Studies, 10: 147–66.

– (2007b), 'Critical respect: The difficulties and dilemmas of agency and
"choice" for feminism: A reply to Duits and van Zoonen', *European Journal
of Women's Studies*, 14: 69–80.

– & Scharff, Christina (2011) (eds.), *New femininities: Postfeminism, neo-
liberalism and identity* (London: Palgrave).

Harris, Anita (2004), *Future girl* (London: Routledge).

Jackson, Sue & Vares, Tiina (2011), '"Media sluts": Girls' negotiation of sexual
subjectivities in "tween" popular culture', in Gill & Scharff (2011), 134–46.

Lamb, Sharon & Brown, Lynne (2006), *Packaging girlhood* (New York: St
Martin's Press).

Lerum, Kari & Dworkin, Shari (2009), '"Bad girls rule": An interdisciplinary
feminist commentary on the report of the APA task force on the sexualization of girls', *Journal of Sex Research*, 46/4: 250–63.

Lumby, Catharine & Allbury, Kath (2010), 'Too much? Too young? The sexualisation debate in Australia', *Media International Australia*, 135: 141–52.

Malson, Helen, Marshall, Harriet & Woollett, Anne (2002), 'Talking of taste:
A discourse analytic exploration of young women's gendered and racialised
subjectivities in British urban, multicultural contexts', *Feminism & Psychology*, 12: 469–90.

McRobbie, Angela (2008), 'Young women and consumer culture', *Cultural
Studies*, 22: 531–50.

Raby, Rebecca (2010), '"Tank tops are OK but I don't want to see her thong":
Girls' engagements with secondary school dress codes', *Youth & Society*,
41/3: 333–56.

Renold, Emma & Ringrose, Jessica (2011), 'Schizoid subjectivities? Re-theorizing teen-girls' sexual cultures in an era of "sexualization"', *Journal of Sociology*, 47/4: 389–409.

Ringrose, Jessica (2008), '"Every time she bends over she pulls up her thong": Teen girls negotiating discourses of competitive, heterosexualised aggression', *Girlhood Studies*, 1/1: 33–59.

Vares, Tiina, Jackson, Sue & Gill, Rosalind (2011), 'Preteen girls read "tween" popular culture: Diversity, complexity and contradiction', *International Journal of Media & Cultural Politics*, 7/2: 139–54.

Willett, Rebecca (2009), '"What you wear tells a lot about you": Girls dress up online', *Gender and Education*, 20/5: 421–34.

CHAPTER 12

Children, 'sexualization', and consumer culture

Sara Bragg, David Buckingham, Rachel Russell & Rebekah Willett

In recent years, there has been growing concern about the sexualization of children, and specifically about the effects of commercial marketing and media in this respect. It has been raised at the level of public policy, both in the US and Australia; in Britain, the previous Labour government commissioned a major 'assessment of the impact of the commercial world on children's well-being' (Buckingham 2009), a report on sexualization conducted by a celebrity psychologist (Papadopoulos 2010), while the coalition government that came to power in 2010 launched yet another review – covering both topics – led by Reg Bailey, Chief Executive of the Christian charity the Mothers' Union (DfE 2011). There have been campaigns, such as 'Let Girls be Girls' by the influential parenting website Mumsnet; publications for parents (for example, Carey 2011); and newspaper or magazine articles on this theme, which regularly garner hundreds of responses via online forums. Many voices, in short, are raised to comment on the issue of sexualization.

In this essay, we reflect on a recent research project through which we contributed our own academic perspectives, and, through our mediation, those of children and parents, to these public debates. The project was funded by the Equal Opportunities Committee of the Scottish Parliament, which had been lobbied about the issue; it focused on 'sexualized goods' – clothing, cosmetics, toys, and branded merchandise such as Playboy – and involved a retail survey and work with Scottish parents and young people.[1] Here, we discuss what our research findings suggest about how such goods might be consumed and interpreted in specific contexts, and how they challenge some common assumptions about children, sex, and commercial-consumer culture. Space does not permit a detailed account of our methods and results, which can be found in the full report online (Buckingham et al. 2010).

At the same time, in this essay we consider how we attempted to challenge some of the terms of the debate, partly by calling on discourses of academic expertise and evidence, partly by constructing the public, as represented by our research participants, as sensible, knowledgeable and measured in their responses. Implicitly, and sometimes explicitly, we counterposed their 'good sense' to the 'moral panic' about sexualization. For instance, our executive summary stated that we aimed to provide '*concrete empirical* evidence on the marketing of [sexualized] goods', and 'some *in-depth analysis* of the perspectives of children and parents, in the interest of promoting a *more informed* debate' (our emphasis). These statements imply our own neutrality or disinterest, our concern to facilitate debate rather than engage in advocacy, and, moreover, they offer a diagnosis: that existing public debate is insufficiently 'informed' because it lacks 'evidence', and because such evidence as does exist has not been adequately 'analysed'. These positions are not unproblematic, as we will show. At the end of the essay, we reflect on the governmentality of contemporary practices of ethical self-formation in relation to both our research and the topic of sexualization itself.

Sexualized goods and the question of 'evidence'

Our research began with a highly critical review of the previous reports on sexualization (for example, Papadopoulos 2010; APA 2007; Australian Senate 2008). We identified significant flaws in their approaches: weak, inconsistent, and circular definitions of key terms; partial and unsophisticated analyses of media texts; and an uncritical reliance on psychological studies, especially laboratory experiments and large-scale correlational surveys, to support claims about audience responses. It was noted that they largely ignore research on the social and cultural contexts of sexuality, on how sexual meanings are established and negotiated and on how children and young people interpret and use sexual content, or indeed fail to engage with feminist and cultural studies more broadly. Most previous work has been concerned with media and advertising, rather than sexualized goods; almost all of it has used adult research subjects, often conveniently available US university students, rather than children; and it tends to concentrate on girls rather than boys, which, we suggested, was 'symptomatic of wider anxieties surrounding girls' sexual agency that appear to underlie much of the public debate' (Bragg et al. 2011: 281). Our critique was informed by a considerable body of academic literature and research that has dissected the sexualization discourse and attempted to analyse rather than moralize the contemporary mainstreaming of sex (for example, Attwood 2009, 2006; Buckingham 2009; Buckingham & Bragg 2004; Duschinsky 2010; Duits & van Zoonen 2011; Egan & Hawkes 2008; Lumby & Albury 2010; Russell & Tyler 2005; Willett 2008), just as academics have over the decades exposed the weaknesses of 'media effects' – claims in relation to violence and other themes (for example, Barker & Petley 2001; Gauntlett 1995). Nonetheless, we had few illusions about the capacity of these arguments, however well-founded, to displace popular convictions. After our report's publication, we individually had lengthy discussions with the makers of a BBC television documentary on sexualization, and Rachel Russell eventually appeared in it, commenting on young people's perception of specific goods. However, the presenter's questions about research evidence were directed not to Russell, but to Justine Roberts, the co-founder of Mumsnet and a vocal campaigner. The latter confidently, albeit fallaciously in academic terms, asserted that existing studies demonstrated various negative effects on girls, even conceding that such studies were few in number 'so far', as if an avalanche of further proof was soon to follow.

The first stage of our research also involved a retail survey of Scottish shops, using a broad five-point coding schema to capture different dimensions of sexualized goods aimed at young people under the age of 16. We began with a deliberately broad and inclusive categorization in the expectation that it would yield material we could further interrogate in our audience research, as follows:

(*i*) Goods that seem to make reference to sexual practices through images, words, or humour (including the use of ambiguity or in-nuendo; for example, 'blow me' and an image of a fan).

(*ii*) Goods that appear to make reference to sexual contexts through images, words, colours, styles, or items: that is, where the familiar-ity with the item stems from culturally sexualized contexts – for example, stripping (shiny gloves and stilettos), burlesque (feather boas), or 'sexy' lingerie (lace, red, black, and purple).

(*iii*) Goods that emphasize body parts and shapes that might be culturally associated with adult sexuality; for example, eyes, lips, breasts, cleavage, curves, legs, bottom, skin, and groin.

(*iv*) Goods that duplicate styles currently considered 'high fashion' for adults. This includes goods marketed in a way that combines items from a potentially sexual adult context with images, words, or practices (for example, play) associated with childhood, in such a way as to normalize them as children's goods; for example, Hello Kitty 'Sexy Little Mints', sweets that carry potential sexual connota-tions by virtue of their name and image.

(*v*) Goods that contain a reference to gender stereotypes; for exam-ple, by over-emphasizing physical attractiveness, associating females with love and intimacy, or associating males with aggressiveness and dominance, through words, images, symbols, or activities (Bragg et al. 2011: 282).

This broad coding identified several products that might be described as both sexualized and for children, ranging from Playboy station-ery to cosmetics kits in toyshops, as well as various clothing items, including bikinis, animal print underwear, boob tube dresses, and low-slung trousers. However, many of the shops surveyed contained no examples whatsoever of such goods. We concluded that:

> while there are undoubtedly some 'sexualized' goods aimed at children, there are relatively few of them, and their availability is limited. Children might purchase goods in contexts surrounded by sexual imagery and products, but such products are not necessarily aimed at them. (Buckingham et al. 2010: 5)

Implicitly, our measured tone and content was intended as a rebuke to those who claim that such goods are commonplace, but it is well known that negative findings are under-reported, easily eclipsed by single memorable cases such as a 'paedo bikini' or a 'pole-dancing kit for children'.[2]

However, the survey did furnish many examples of gender stereotyping on an active–masculine, passive–feminine axis, and quantities of appearance-related goods for girls such as cosmetics, hair accessories, purses, handbags, and so on. In addition, children are bound to encounter a much wider range of goods than those specifically targeted at them. Proximities blur the distinctions between adult, youth, and child, as when we found child-oriented products such as fake cartoon tattoos placed next to novelty items aimed at the 'hen night' market. Age markers can also be blurred by the nature of the products themselves: many clothing items aimed at young people are copies of adult fashions, and, conversely, make-up products are packaged as toys for younger ages. Shops with a cross-generational target group can be identified as 'aspirational' spaces (Russell & Tyler 2005). They do not appear to target children or young people explicitly, and do not attach explicit age markers to products, so they may be used in constructing a potentially desirable adult identity; whilst the presence of very small clothing sizes (such as US sizes 4–6 for women) and our background interviews with industry contacts suggest that young people are the target market by default for such shops.

Such evidence could have been (and often is) used to make more sensationalist claims, but we have restricted ourselves to acknowledging the shifting boundaries between child and adult identities, citing our own previous work (Buckingham & Bragg 2005) to suggest that 'the transition from child to adult status is becoming more ambiguous and complex than perhaps was the case in earlier times' (Buckingham et al. 2010: 40). Even without the other qualifiers, the function of 'more' in that statement is rather unclear – suggesting that features of the consumption landscape have changed, albeit without giving particular historical evidence, in a way that allows them to be read as contributors to 'genuine' anxieties as well as to unfounded 'panics'.

Parents and young people
talking about sexualized goods

Our research also sought out the views of parents and young people, using open-ended, participatory, and deliberative methods that aimed to avoid being overly intrusive (although discussions were nonetheless intimate at times; see Bragg 2012). We accessed young people aged 12–14 through schools in three different areas of Scotland, devising and observing three lessons related to sexualization that were taught by English and Media Studies teachers as part of the normal timetable, and following up with two short friendship-based group discussions in each school. We also conducted nine parent focus groups in 2–3-hour-long sessions, involving 35 women and 8 men, recruited partly through the schools and partly through the research team's own contacts. There was a mix of class backgrounds and parent types, including single parents and a lesbian mother, ages and numbers of children, and religious affiliations, and four participants from minority ethnic backgrounds. In these focus groups, we invited personal experiences of the issues involved, and provided stimuli for discussion such as images of children and of some of the products collected in the retail survey. Our methods did not give direct evidence of actual practices in which parents or children engage, but nonetheless they did convey the various discursive resources – for example, in ideas about 'good parenting', 'peer pressure', and so on – on which they drew in making sense of, contesting, and renegotiating sexualized goods.

In writing up our findings, we emphasized the 'nuanced and thoughtful responses' offered by our participants, and how these 'illustrated the complexity of the issues at stake', thereby implying that other commentators on the issue were by contrast strident and crude; and elsewhere we have argued that the Bailey Review (DfE 2011), for instance, manipulated its survey questions to produce 'evidence' of acute concern by '9 out of 10 parents' (Bragg & Buckingham, forthcoming). To some extent, our own approach 'summoned' precisely the reflective, deliberative selves we claimed to 'find': thus we explicitly encouraged parents to consider dilemmas and differences of view, and as the research progressed, we put to them significant issues that had emerged from previous groups. Yet it is also worth noting that while we prepared in advance some statements about sexualization, intended to prompt debate, and focused on what we imagined might be neglected, complex ideas, we never needed to use them, since the issues were invariably – and better – covered during discussions of relevant experiences. In some ways, then, we *under*estimated the capacities of participants, and *over*estimated the uniqueness of the insights generated by academic analysis. The two proved closer than we anticipated; an observation that should trouble the division also found in many moral panic studies between the perceptive scholar and mystified audience or public (Hier 2011).

Developmental and democratic childhoods

Among the participants, the topic of sexualization inevitably evoked far more general ideas about the nature of childhood, adolescence, and parenthood. Whilst childhood was universally agreed to be a time of fun, experimentation, and play, parents and young people differed between and amongst themselves over whether this should be labelled 'innocence' and what place (sexualized) consumer products might have within it. Growing up was conceived as a series of natural stages of development towards adulthood, in which children should gradually assume greater responsibilities. Parents generally claimed to subscribe to broadly democratic ideals of childrearing, in which they respected children's individuality or even rights to make their own decisions and express themselves. Beginning secondary school at 11 or 12 was seen as a watershed moment in desiring and deserving these rights:

> Girl: because when you go to high school you do want more responsibilities and you've kind of got an idea what to wear and what not to wear. (School 1 interview)
> Mother: Going to secondary school … they're a bit bewildered when they first arrive and they quickly learn … And it is at a time when their bodies are changing quite quickly so it all seems to come together. So I'd say really that once they get to secondary school they're kind of off and launched. (Parent group 2)

Cultural, social, and biological changes are presented in these statements as natural, congruent, and complementary, whilst being
strikingly dependent on a relatively context-specific age of transition between schools. Different educational arrangements – such as
middle schools covering the years between 9 and 13, still common
elsewhere in the UK – would conceivably generate quite different
perceptions of developmental milestones. Parents themselves identified contradictions in the claim that contemporary children are
'growing up too soon'; one commenting that by the age of 14 she
herself had left school, had a job, and was running a household,
whilst her youngest daughter who was now that age could barely deal
with her own laundry, in common with her peers, as other parents
also observed. Another mother in the same group acknowledged the
competing demands she placed on her own 13-year-old daughter:

> You want them to grow up in some ways but not in others. I want
> her to be more responsible and act in a more mature way when it
> comes to helping around the house, but I really don't want her to
> grow up too fast when it comes to her self-image and the way she
> dresses and the kind of influences that she's subjected to. (Parent
> group 1)

Nonetheless, the developmental models of childhood to which our
participants generally subscribed suggest that parents should promote children's ability to exercise choice, because this is crucial to
healthy maturation; and in practice, the main arena in which such
essential skills were rehearsed was that of personal consumption.
Herein lies a dilemma: parents are often exhorted to be proactive
about 'saying no' to sexualized goods, yet these are generally a matter
of clothes, hairstyles, cosmetics, and media, all of which are com-
paratively trivial. Moreover, inappropriate choices in these respects
can be construed as part of predictable, natural, adolescent rebellion
or even as a step on the way to developing crucial decision-making
capacities: both young and older participants referred to 'making
our/their own mistakes'. Unsurprisingly, then, parents claimed to
prefer negotiation and compromise, or, if that failed, devious tactics
whereby clothes shrank in the wash, or toys and other items myste-

riously went missing. These approaches, they suggested, in practice proved more manageable and liveable than confrontation or diktat. They repeatedly stated that they would not risk alienating their children or jeopardizing relationships over an issue that was ultimately 'not worth the battle', especially since 'there are worse things they could be doing'. Other tropes such as 'peer pressure' – perceived as unavoidable and hugely important in adolescence – or 'getting it out of their system' were also cited as reasons why parents might permit purchases of which they disapproved in principle. In sum, our findings suggested that most parents are less concerned about 'sexualization' than campaigners typically claim; and that there are competing moral logics involved in responses to sexualized goods, in which parents may have good reason for not taking action.

The contested meanings of sexualized goods

Attempts to define what is a sexualized product were highly contested by our participants, who argued that goods had no inherent sexual connotations or functions, and/or redescribed them as 'fun', 'fashion', 'play', and even 'learning'. Parents' descriptions of children returning from nurseryschool wearing nail polish or receiving make-up as birthday presents suggested that such goods had become a routine part of the experience of childhood, rather than its antithesis as campaigners have argued. Parents also rejected the notion that their own children were becoming sexualized, emphasizing their lack of sexual intent even when consuming such problematic products as thongs or high-heeled shoes. Yet such arguments reflect – without resolving – the many contradictions and ambiguities in the notion of sexualization itself, particularly in regard to children's state of mind or understanding, and indeed parents' potential for self-deception.

Young people were equally insistent that the meaning of clothing shifted according to context (party, school disco, or beach), combination (leggings could be 'tarty' if not worn with a long top; very short skirts or shorts were less sexual if worn with thick leggings or tights; make-up and hair gel could be 'too much' or 'just right'), how fashionable it was, and perspective. As a girl from School 2 stated, 'something that might be sexy to someone else, might not be to others'. For the young people, demonstrating their knowledge of the nuances of style was a way of challenging the idea that they were the ignorant or passive victims of sexualization. Some parents recognized and even enjoyed their children's expertise in the codes of contemporary youth culture: 'they can spot a brand from fifty paces!'

At the time of our research, Playboy-branded goods – from home furnishings, fashion accessories to stationery – were highly contro-versial; their popularity amongst young people making them an icon of childhood sexualization. The schoolchildren repeatedly declared that they were fully aware of the bunny logo's sexual meanings, connected with 'Hugh Hefner', the 'lassies in the mansion' [the television series *The Girls Next Door*], and sexual exploits, although some were embarrassed to explain this and many were critical of the women involved. 'The lassies were flaunting and I think that's totally disrespectful', declared one girl in School 1, her friend add-ing, 'They have no self-respect'.

At the same time, students insisted that the logo had become popular with their age-group purely because of fashion or as 'a cute pink bunny' – and indeed that it was now falling out of favour. Many deemed it 'childish', citing in evidence its popularity with younger siblings, or described it in derogatory (class-based) terms: 'tacky', 'minging', 'tarty', 'chavvy', and 'neddy'. Taking such views at face value provided some ammunition against the argument that Playboy was glamorizing the sex industry for younger generations, and we presented them accordingly in our report. However, there is more going on than this, especially as a number of these young participants were sporting examples of the very goods that they disdained in the presence of researchers, providing a tantalizing glimpse of an issue worth further investigation.

Parents too were undecided about the Playboy logo, heatedly debating not only how far it was inherently associated with the sex industry, but also the ethics of explaining this to children. One mother argued cogently that this would itself impinge on their in-nocence: 'you don't want to force them to think about things that they're innocently thinking [is] a nice pink bunny ... . Just allow them to be children for that bit longer' (Parent group 4). Her por-trayal of children's blissful ignorance contrasts starkly with the young people's assertions of their sexual knowingness, of course. Nonetheless, by echoing Mumsnet's 'Let Girls be Girls' slogan mentioned in the introduction, her point shows that neither shared popular sentiment about childhood, nor laying claim to the authority of a 'parent' identity, guarantee support for the same policies or stances in relation to sexualized goods.

Regulation of goods and the dilemmas of individual responsibility

Students rejected outright the notion of regulating sexualized goods for their own age-group, although rather predictably they were prepared to consider it for younger groups. Whilst some parents indicated that they would like support in dealing with what they saw as commercial exploitation, they too were aware of its potential pitfalls, resistant to what they saw as top-down, state-led regulation, and sceptical about actual implementation. Sexualized products might be a (largely unspecified) problem for a 'small minority' of 'irresponsible' parents and young people, they argued, but they were best seen as a matter of individual choice, meaning it was up to parents to take action on sexualized products should they so choose. The Bailey Review referred to above (DfE 2011) derived many of its recommendations from such arguments; focusing, for example, on how businesses might assist parents wishing to register offence, feedback, or criticism.

However, emphasizing personal choice and responsibility does little to help us understand the difficulties and complexities of consumption. Individualized strategies are limited in several ways: they entail problematic distinctions between responsible 'citizen-consumers' who navigate choices successfully, and 'others' whose consumption is undisciplined and disordered (Harris 2004; Hayward & Yar 2006; Tyler 2008). They assume that individuals are truly free to choose, when a striking feature of our discussions was how circumscribed parents were: by economic means; by notions of good parenting and peer pressure; by children's nagging, emotional blackmail, and/ or devious tactics; by choices made by other people or institutions. Individually, they might oppose pamper parties, Bratz dolls, or the

SITUATING CHILD CONSUMPTION

phenomenon of final-year primary school proms involving adult-style eveningwear, limousine hire, and so on. However, they did not think it necessarily right to refuse gifts of this nature or to exclude their children from social occasions. The mainstreaming of sex means that, as one mother remarked, 'I don't have any control over [my daughter's influences] because they're not just me, they come from everywhere' (Parent group 1). Negotiating contemporary consumption-oriented childhoods thus seemed to be experienced more as an imperfect balance between giving consent and feeling compelled, which one mother of a 12-year-old daughter succinctly formulated as 'buy[ing] into what might not be my choice' (Parent group 8).

The language of choice, and indeed of the sexualization of *child-hood*, obscures issues of gender in particular – the focus on what *girls* buy, do, wear, and play with. As one mother commented – expecting and receiving agreement from others – 'Well you don't need to worry about a wee boy dressing to look older and looking tarty or anything' (Parent group 7). Boys' potentially sexualized consumption practices were generally viewed with amusement rather than alarm, with considerable hilarity occasioned by the trend for underpants showing above low-slung trousers or their use of hair gels and deodorants ('you smell them before you see them!'). If anything, boys' attention to grooming was viewed as a good thing, which 'encouraged hygiene'.

Meanwhile, the process of negotiating sexualized consumption seemed far from benign for girls, involving perpetual self-scrutiny in order both to align themselves with peers deemed worthy of emulation, and to ensure they maintained a distance from degraded and undesirable others. Class-based connotations in reading potentially sexual products as 'tasteful' or 'slutty' have invidious consequences for working-class girls in particular (Egan & Hawkes 2008; Tyler 2008). For instance, despite a general sense that defining a sexualized product in the abstract was well-nigh impossible, participants were simultaneously convinced that some forms of female attire invited particular male attention or behaviour. Few wanted to name this as sexual assault, although some young people stated outright that some girls were 'asking for it' whilst denying that they personally believed this. Parents' formulations were careful and even tortuous: 'You wonder', speculated one mother, 'if some of them [male paedophiles or rapists] see as if though they've kind of been *given permission*, in a sense, if they see girls going around dressed like that' (Parent group 5, our emphasis). Another remarked, 'I'm not suggesting that they deserve anything if they're dressing like that but I think it does send out the wrong messages' (Parent group 3). Such connections implicitly condoned male violence, rationalizing it as a consequence of girls' choices and actions. The tendency to blame both the victim and her mother was expressed poignantly, even if not perhaps entirely consciously, by one mother who had herself been assaulted as a teenager and who remarked: 'I think as well you would worry if you'd agreed to something, then *it* happened and it was *your fault as well*' (Parent group 5, our emphasis).

Concluding discussion

Our intervention in the public debates about sexualization involved some perhaps typical academic manoeuvres that highlighted its complexities. We emphasized how our research participants resisted the 'sexualization narrative': parents by denying that their children were sexualized; young people by asserting they were knowledgeable and in control rather than victims. We pointed to polysemy, the postmodern premise that meaning depends on context and interpretation, to suggest the difficulties of identifying sexualized products. We stressed contradictions, such as equally valid rationales for taking different stances in relation to consumption, and argued that both the availability of these goods and degree of parental concern might have been overestimated. We contextualized the debate, relating it to 'broader' concerns, assumptions, and judgements about the nature of childhood and of children's knowledge and understanding, about good or bad parenting, about sexuality, and about the relations between social class, sexuality and taste. We cautioned against misrepresenting and vilifying other people. We highlighted the genuine difficulty of providing simple 'solutions' at the level of public policy, for instance in the form of regulation; and the inadequacies of arguments based primarily on individual choice, particularly their invidious consequences for women in relation to sexual violence.

When it was presented to the Scottish Parliament Equal Opportunities Committee, consumer-rights advocate Ed Mayo commented tartly that it was 'a wonderful piece of academic research' and went on to condemn its failure to 'come off the fence' or be clear about 'where the responsibility lies', whilst a member of the Scottish Parliament bluntly called it a 'cop-out'. Our argument that the problem is the discourse about sexualization led us to oppose formulating policy based on such a questionable notion: to policymakers, whose question concerned 'what to do about sexualization', our position was an inadequate non-outcome. Their responses scripted us as intellectuals cushioned from the pressing concerns of the 'real' world; one might offer a counter-narrative in which political demagoguery disrespects academic integrity, but this would be too facile. The following year, for instance, saw the start of the Slut Walks movement, which protests at the idea that women's clothing provides an excuse for sexual assault. It offers what we did not; an example of how positive action might begin from resisting the discourse and assumptions of sexualization.

Secondly, another way of framing and understanding public debates about sexualization is in terms of governmentality. This concept, first explored by Foucault (1991), has been used to consider the historical shift from overt rule and prescription by external authorities to the current tendency of advanced or neo-liberal democracies to regulate the 'conduct of conduct' and to foster individual responsibility-taking (see, for example, Rose 1999). In a particularly relevant discussion, Sean Hier (2011) proposes that we should conceptualize moral panic as a 'volatile instance' of these longer-term processes. Reading sexualization in terms of 'responsibilization strategies within and beyond the state' (Hier 2011: 526) directs our attention away from isolated controversies and instead to how the public debates function more broadly as practices of ethical self-formation or work on the self, by the self – in which, moreover, our own research and analysis participate, rather than standing wholly apart as we and the policymakers implied. In responding in whatever capacity to sexualization, individuals can be seen to constitute themselves as reflexive, responsible subjects who make their motivations and experiences available for public investigation, and who manage risk through particular forms of conduct, such as closely monitoring their own, their children's, and/or others' dress, sexual demeanour, consumption, activities, and public behaviour. Such practices of self-problematization are increasingly compulsory in contemporary society and occur in relation to other topics too, of course; but the example of sexualization illuminates something of their unrelenting nature and their tendency to obscure gender, class, and other social inequalities.

Notes

1 The authors would like to thank Dr Nika Dorrer, the researcher on the 'Sexualized goods aimed at children' project, for her invaluable support and contributions.
2 *The Sun*, 14 April 2010, available at <http://www.thesun.co.uk/sol/homepage/news/2931327/Primarks-padded-bikini-tops-for-kids-condemned. html>, accessed 4 November 2011; the pole-dancing kit was marked for adults, but apparently featured under 'Toys and games' on the Tesco Direct website, 24 October 2006 <http://www.dailymail.co.uk/news/article-412195/Tesco-condemned-selling-pole-dancing-toy.html>, accessed 4 November 2011.

References

American Psychological Association (2007), *Report of the APA task force on the sexualization of girls* (Washington, DC: APA).
Attwood, Feona (2006), 'Sexed up: Theorizing the sexualization of culture', *Sexualities*, 9: 77–94.
— (2009) (ed.), *Mainstreaming sex: The sexualization of Western culture* (London: I.B. Tauris)
Australian Senate (2008), *Sexualization of children in the contemporary media* (Parliament of Australia), available at <http://www.aph.gov.au_senate_committee_eca_ctte_sexualization_of_children.report_c01.pdf>, accessed 25 June 2012
Barker, Martin & Julian, Petley (2001) (eds.), *Ill effects: The media /violence debate* (London: Routledge).
Bragg, Sara, Buckingham, David, Russell, Rachel & Willett, Rebekah (2011),

'Too much, too soon? Children, "sexualization" and consumer culture', *Sex Education*, 11/3: 279–92.

– (2012), 'What I heard about sexualization: Or, conversations with my inner Barbie', *Gender and Education*, 24/3: 311–316.

– (forthcoming), 'Global concerns, local negotiations and moral selves: Contemporary parenting and the "sexualization of childhood" debate', *Feminist Media Studies*.

Buckingham, David & Bragg, Sara (2004), *Young people, sex and the media: The facts of life?* (Basingstoke: Palgrave Macmillan).

– (2005), 'Opting into (and out of) childhood: Young people, sex and the media', in Jens Qvortrup (ed.), *Studies in modern childhood: Society, agency and culture* (London: SAGE), 59–77.

– (2009) *The impact of the commercial world on children's wellbeing: report of an independent assessment for the Department of Children, Schools and Families and the Department of Culture, Media and Sport* (Annesley: Department for Children, Schools and Families), available at <https://www.education.gov.uk/publications/standard/publicationDetail/Page1/DCSF-00669-2009>, accessed 1 June 2012.

– Russell, Rachel & Willett, Rebekah (2010), *Sexualized goods aimed at children. Report for the Scottish Parliament Equal Opportunities Committee* (The Scottish Parliament), available at <http://archive.scottish.parliament.uk/s3/committees/equal/reports-10/eor10-02.htm>, accessed 1 June 2012.

Carey, Tanith (2011), *Where has my little girl gone?* (Oxford: Lion Publishing).

Cook, Daniel Thomas (2004), *The commodification of childhood: The children's clothing industry and the rise of the child consumer* (Durham, NC: Duke University Press).

DfE (2011), *Letting children be children: Report of an independent review of the commercialisation and sexualisation of childhood* (London: Department for Education).

Duits, Linda & van Zoonen, Liesbeth (2011), 'Coming to terms with sexualization', *European Journal of Cultural Studies*, 14/5: 491–506.

Duschinsky, Robert (2010), 'Feminism, sexualization and social status', *Media International Australia*, 135: 94–105.

Egan, R. Danielle & Hawkes, Gail L. (2008), 'Endangered girls and incendiary objects: Unpacking the discourse on sexualization', *Sexuality & Culture*, 12/4: 291–311.

Foucault, Michel (1991), 'Governmentality', in G. Burchell, C. Gordon & P. Miller (eds.), *The Foucault effect: Studies in governmentality* (Chicago: University of Chicago Press), 97–104.

Gauntlett, David (1995), *Moving experiences: Understanding television's influences and effects* (London: John Libbey Media).

Harris, Anita (2004), *Future girl: Young women in the twenty-first century* (London: Routledge).

Hawkes, Gail L. & Egan, R. Danielle (2008), 'Developing the sexual child', *Journal of Historical Sociology*, 21/4: 443–65.

Hayward, Keith & Yar, Majid (2006), 'The "chav" phenomenon: Consumption, media and the construction of a new underclass', *Crime, Media, Culture*, 2/1: 9–28.

Hier, Sean P. (2011), 'Tightening the focus: Moral panic, moral regulation and liberal government', *British Journal of Sociology*, 62/3: 523–41.

Lumby, Catharine & Albury, Kath (2010), 'Too much? Too young? The sexualization of children debate in Australia', *Media International Australia*, 135: 141–52.

Papadopoulos, Linda (2010), *Sexualisation of young people: Review* (London: Home Office Publications), available at <http://webarchive.nationalarchives.gov.uk/20100406223726/http://www.homeoffice.gov.uk/documents/Sexualisation-of-young-people.html>, accessed 25 June 2012

Rose, Nikolas (1999), *Governing the soul: The shaping of the private self* (2nd edn., London: Free Association Books).

Russell, Rachel & Tyler, Melissa (2005), 'Branding and bricolage: Gender, consumption and transition', *Childhood*, 12/2: 221–37.

Tyler, Imogen (2008), '"Chav mum, chav scum": Class disgust in contemporary Britain', *Feminist Media Studies*, 8/1: 17–34.

Willett, Rebekah (2008), 'Consumer citizens online: Structure, agency and gender in online participation', in David Buckingham (ed.), *Youth, identity and digital media* (Cambridge, Mass.: MIT Press), 49–70.

CHAPTER 13

'The Littlest Arms Race'?

War toys and the boy consumer in Eighties' Canada

Braden P.L. Hutchinson

Toys are perhaps the oldest and most enduring commodities mar-keted *to* and *for* children, independent of adult oversight. They have repeatedly been identified as essential to children's nature even when certain toys, whether air rifles or fashion dolls, have sparked intense controversies about child consumption. The war-toy con-troversy in Canada in the 1980s is an informative case-study that offers substantial insights into the logic of toy critics, the repre-sentation of male child consumers, and the suitability of a moral panic framework for scholarship on child consumption. War toys in particular have arisen as a matter of contention among adults and children on several occasions since the First World War in Canada and other Euro-American countries, sparking alternative toy fairs, public demonstrations, and awareness campaigns aimed at curtail-ing the consumption of violent playthings (Loewen 1987; Voice of Women Fonds, 1959–1987[1]). Though discontinued in 1977, Hasbro's relaunch of the G.I. Joe 'action figure' in 1982 offered former campaigners in the peace and feminist movements a new target for their anti-war-toy efforts (Jaffe 2006; Kay Macpherson Fonds, 1950–1993 & Conseil de la Sculpture de Quebec Fonds, 1965–2000[2]). The wide-ranging impact of this conflict is discern-ible in the toys, news stories, and archival material of the period. Though war-toy critics gained momentum during the first half of the Eighties, by the end of the decade a backlash had begun in the media, which criticized the use of war toys and boy consumers in adult debates over cold-war politics as a mischaracterization of boys' consumer behaviour and a threat to parental authority. Ultimately, the Eighties' war-toy debate led to an altogether different outcome than earlier campaigns, as war-toy critics fought a losing battle against manufacturers, marketers, and their allies. Though it would fall short of its stated objectives of banning war toys from Canadian shops or curtailing their sale, the anti-war-toy efforts would have a profound effect on the prevailing understanding of boys' toy consumption in Canada throughout the decade.

Innocence, agency, and moral panic

It is tempting to join the anxious refrain of war-toy critics and historians such as Gary Cross (1997: 2, 188) who have criticized Eighties' toys in general as 'pied pipers leading our children away from us', heralding children's freedom from adult guidance and thus making efforts to monitor and control child consumption all the more urgent. Certainly, it is difficult to dispute the argument that toys in the 1980s were marketed to children more intensively and extensively than ever before. However, bold assertions such as Cross's regarding the ultimate effect of advertising on children's consumer behaviour and their relationships with adults do not adequately address children's subjectivity or the role of agents outside the toy industry. Studies by Nicholas Sammond (2005) and Heather Hendershot (1998) of the media texts attached to these and other toys have pointed out that claims of market manipulation 'infantilize' consumers (Hendershot 1998: 3), offering 'the comfort of identifiable villains (or heroes) and an easy framework within which to imagine programs of social correction and control' (Sammond 2005: 358). On the other hand, over-emphasizing the agency at work in child consumption takes consumer desire and the behaviour it inspires for granted, claiming for it only a limited socio-economic significance (Cook 2004b: 148).

Consequently, those interested in inserting children's agency (or the possibility of it) back into studies of controversies over child consumption, but without abandoning a critical position in their assessment of consumer practice, might consider adopting the moral panic framework to analyse concerns about child consumption.

Though studies addressing moral panics have offered important insights into the political effect of controversies on myriad issues, the reductionism of this approach poses problems of its own. In her study of the construction of sexual psychopathy in Ontario, the Canadian historian Elise Chenier (2008: 44–45) claims that 'postwar culture was much more complex than the moral panic model allows … [it] characterizes popular responses to certain social problems as "disproportionate" to the actual problem, "irrational" and in some accounts, "hysterical".' When taken to its logical conclusion, moral panic can lead to the re-inscription of patriarchal stereotypes about women's irrationality; the privileging of the media as the central force at a time when media scripts were often activist-generated; and the lumping together of groups involved in the 'moral panic' under the rubric of conservatism, when more complex ideological backgrounds are actually at work (ibid. 47–48). Equally troubling is the realist epistemology that underpins moral panic's claim of dis-proportionality, which holds that a 'true' or 'actual' way things are exists, independent of how they are perceived by actors. Moral panic thus claims interpretive authority for the scholar at the expense of the historical actors' ability to define the social place and function of debates, allowing for only limited investigation of the motivations of those supposedly doing the panicking. Obviously, the implications of this approach can be as infantilizing and one-dimensional for the critics being studied, as other approaches can be for child consumers.

By surveying the cold-war and gender politics that surrounded children's toys, the discourse of war-toy critics, and the backlash against the anti-war-toy movement, this essay puts forward a different approach to studying debates about the child consumer. This 'third way' stresses the need to move beyond analyses of consumption that see it as either wholly liberating or as evidence of the corruption of children's pristine innocence (Cook 2004b). As Daniel Thom-as Cook suggests, at the centre of analyses of child consumption should be a recognition that 'the battles waged over and around children's consumer culture are no less than battles over the nature of the person and the scope of personhood in the context of the ever expanding reach of commerce' (ibid. 149). I would add that these struggles often coalesce a series of social and political struggles, not always immediately or explicitly economic, that mobilize childhood in the name of 'broader' political ends. In the particular instance of the debate about war toys in Canada in the Eighties, it was the political issue of cold-war rearmament that brought children, their playthings, and their consumer lives to the centre of adult conflicts.

War toys and the cultural politics of empire

In 1980, with the election of Ronald Reagan and the acquiescence of Pierre Trudeau's Liberal government to the testing and deployment of American cruise missiles on Canadian soil, it was clear to the peace movement that the cold war was heating up. Reagan and his neo-conservative advisers expanded American military intervention throughout the developing and developed world with the aim of winning the cold war. This 'change in method rather than aims' of America's cold-war policy was directed at modernizing America's arsenal and recruiting radical allies, which 'for their own reasons were willing to let left-wing regimes bleed' (Westad 2007: 345–356, 331). However, according to Robert Kagan, then employed by the State Department, the cold war of the Eighties was also a 'domestic battle for the American soul', meaning that children, and by extension their material worlds, could form an important front in the cold-war fight (ibid. 345). In many respects, Kagan's declaration was nothing new. As Sharon Stephens (1997) has demonstrated, American cold-war activities were often justified by injunctions to protect consumer-centred domesticity and the children ensconced within it from the Soviet enemy. Kagan was simply reiterating the American state's commitment to indoctrinating children and their families with anti-Communist and militaristic values.

According to Robert Parkinson, CEO of Hasbro Toys at the time, the toy industry was more than doing its part on the domestic front: 'We can take pride in America – that's what this toy says: that we're Americans and we're going to protect ourselves. G.I. Joe is what he says he is – a real American hero. This G.I. Joe is a rapid deployment team, and he's going to need a lot better helicopters than the ones we used in Iran' (Woods 1983: 6).

Heralded by Parkinson as a much needed corrective to the 'excesses' of the Sixties and Seventies, Hasbro's revamped 'paramilitary world policeman' was envisioned as a projection of American military power into the consumer market (Woods 1983: 8, 10). Hasbro's relaunch of the toy included a record-setting $4 million advertising campaign, made possible by the Reagan administration's repeal of US laws on advertising to children in 1980 and the complete absence of any such regulations in the smaller, subsidiary Canadian market – with the lone exception of Quebec's 1980 Consumer Protection Act (*Marketing* 1981). By 1982, the bilingual run of G.I. Joe comics and action figures had found their way into Canada. Launched in Europe as the nationally ambiguous 'Action Force', the Canadian variant was still called G.I. Joe, though the 'Real American Hero' tag line was dropped. While all the American Joes were American-born, the Canadian versions featured both Canadian- and US-born G.I. Joes. According to the 'File Cards' included with the dolls, Grunt, Back-Stop, Scarlett, and Snow Job were all racially white and all born in various parts of Canada. Snow Job

age 1. Scarlett File Cards, original and Canadian variant. ©Hasbro and Braden Hutchinson.

Image 2. Back-Stop and Snow Job File Cards, Canadian variant. ©Hasbro and Braden Hutchinson.

was born in the geographically confused location of 'Yellowknife, Yukon', Scarlett hailed from Grande Prairie, Alberta, while Grunt was Quebec-born. Back-Stop, introduced in 1987, was specifically designed to be of Canadian extraction. According to his File Card, he was forced to flee to the US from Quebec after injuring too many opposing players in Junior League hockey (see Image 1 and 2). This was in contrast to the multi-ethnic make-up of American Joes, which though mostly white, included stereotyped dolls of African-American and indigenous origins. Furthermore, the G.I. Joe vehicles and accessories, emblazoned with the American flag south of the border, were decorated with Canadian flags for their trip north (Andrew Bene Collection, 1977–2008³) (see Image 3). The comics and the dolls both sold exceedingly well, with total North American sales of the toys exceeding $40 million in 1982 (Woods 1983). The Canadian release of G.I. Joe invited Canadians to imagine themselves as racially homogeneous allies in the American cold-war fight.

Banning toys in place of disarmament

By Christmas of 1983, signs of an emerging debate were evident. Ms. Sosonowsky, a college instructor and member of the newly formed anti-war-toy organization Kids and Guns, expressed her dissatisfaction in a letter to Hasbro, co-signed by twelve separate anti-nuclear proliferation groups: 'Today when the very existence of life on this planet is threatened by an escalating arms race your Christmas offerings of death and destruction are particularly offensive' (Godley 1983). According to a satirical editorial in the *Globe and Mail* (1983) titled 'More Bangs for a Buck', the cold war had found its way into Canadian homes: 'With any luck it will be six, maybe seven o'clock on Christmas morning before the first missile leaves its plastic silo on its cunningly calculated trajectory to your left nostril ... the passion for imaginative incineration has never been greater.' Nonetheless, sales of G.I. Joe soared in 1983 yet again. A Tops In Toys manager, Ruth Kirby, remarked to the *Calgary Herald* that the blistering sales meant 'we're forever ordering to fill up' (Zacharias 1983).

By the mid-Eighties, G.I. Joe had ceased to be the only target of

Image 3. G.I. Joe vehicles, Canadian variant. ©Hasbro and Braden Hutchinson.

anti-war-toy groups. Toys such as Nukies also displayed the strategic convergence of the patriotism of toy company CEOs and Reagan's foreign policy imperatives. The *Montreal Gazette* (1985a) described Nukies, launched by a Florida toy company that year, as 'soft [and] cuddly' nuclear devices. These WMDs in miniature came with ownership cards that declared the purchaser a certified nuclear power with 'spheres of influence, the right to set up puppet dictatorships and all the rights and powers of a thermonuclear power' (ibid.). They consciously articulated a justification for recent US incursions in Latin America and elsewhere in the world, and displayed the

Reagan administration's by then familiar revival of American global hegemony through the stockpiling of weapons and weapon systems. Operation Dismantle, an anti-proliferation peace group, took a hard line on the arrival of Nukies in Canada, threatening 'to spray paint the things on the store shelves' (*Montreal Gazette* 1985b). Letters were written to Prime Minister Brian Mulroney and Consumer Affairs Minister Michel Côté demanding the toys be banned from Canada. As Jim Stark, president of Operation Dismantle, stated: 'If we can ban toys that could harm children physically, I dare say we can ban toys that would harm them psychologically. Any parent who would tuck their child into bed with a toy nuclear bomb should be reported to the Children's Aid [Society]' (*Montreal Gazette* 1985a). Despite the aloofness of the federal government from the issue, major toy retailers in Canada decided to bow to the demands of critics and forgo ordering the controversial toys.

Similar criticism of the violent, sexist, and racist Rambo line of toys manufactured by Coleco could be heard from the Business and Professional Women's Club of Montreal, the Canadian Mental Health Association, and the Canadian Arab Federation (Farber 1985; Barber 1986). In 1985, forty like-minded editorial cartoonists from the US and Canada came together with peace groups, women's organizations, health professionals, and journalists to launch an anti-war-toy cartoon campaign between 10 and 24 December. Their cartoons depicted male children being turned into soldiers and committing destructive acts due to the effects of war toys (*Montreal Gazette* 1986; Landsberg 1985, 1986).[4]

While many may have agreed with Donna Smith (1989: 117) that the effect of these toys was 'more diffuse and less concentrated than in the United States', they may equally have worried that 'the same images and languages are inside our heads and must influence our perceptions and behavior'. Taken together, the obvious and intentional realism of these particular toys clearly shows a strong link between the politics of the adult world and the production of playthings for children. Canadian and American children and their parents were invited by American-based toy companies to participate in empire-building second-hand by consuming toys that were clearly imbued with the values of Reagan's cold-war imperialism.[5]

According to Helen Brocklehurst (2006), children have often been central actors and objects in global politics and issues of national security. Consequently, it is not surprising that peace activists and women's organizations in Canada, having failed to block the testing and deployment of cruise missiles in Canada, would try to attain small victories in the fight against the 'military industrial complex' by attacking its presumed cultural equivalent, the 'television-toy manufacturers' complex' (French 1987). Dorothy Smith (1989) would later explain the frustration experienced by Canadian women peace activists in particular: 'For us in Canada, these effects [of cold-war rearmament] are intensified because of our military and economic relations to the United States ... we are always having to react to what has already been set in motion' (ibid. 93). Negotiating American cold-war imperialism through children's toys perpetuated a sense of purpose and achievement within certain ranks of the peace and women's movements, despite the continuous frustration of their efforts to achieve real disarmament. Success at combating war toys tended to persuade Canadian peace organizations and feminist activists that they could influence the outcome of American military imperialism and the patriarchal structures that purportedly underpinned it. They would influence global politics by targeting its domestic and intimate manifestations, namely the consumption of war toys by boys.

The rhetoric of maternal feminism

While we may have a clear sense of what concerned war-toy critics, the question still remains as to why boy consumers became the central targets of their criticism. Aside from the gendered marketing used to promote several of the toys specifically to boy consumers, the intense struggle between the feminist movement and an emergent anti-feminist counter-movement also influenced the shape of anti-war-toy efforts. Spearheaded by groups like R.E.A.L. Women, founded in 1983, the language of the anti-feminist counter-movement clearly borrowed from the language of maternal feminism and the peace movement, which stressed women's special role in safeguarding children due to their status as reproductive beings

(Dubinsky 1985; Steuter 1992). For the anti-feminist movement, the biological capacity to give life was central to the logic of their campaigns against abortion and homosexuality and in favour of a return to traditional gender roles (Dubinsky 1985). However, as Rod Bantjes and Tanya Trussler (1999) have shown in their study of activism against uranium mining in Nova Scotia, maternal rhetoric also creates discursive space for women to press feminist claims as 'mothers' or 'wives' against right-wing adversaries and experts. For the feminist and peace movements, children's toys offered an acceptable area of female expertise that could not be characterized by the anti-feminist counter-movement as anti-family. However, their efforts to highlight the dangers of war toys and assert their authority over boy consumers relied on the gender essentialism inherent in a maternal feminism that stressed the nurturing and life-affirming qualities of women and the militaristic and violent nature of men (Labelle 1986; Gagnon 1986; Rabinovitch 1989; Smith 1989).[6]

Pathologizing male children's desire

The anti-war-toy discourse shows a clear tendency to pathologize the demand of young boys for war toys through the use of what Linda Singer has called the logic of epidemic. According to Singer, epidemic logic is defined by:

> the production of anxiety follow[ed by] the isolation of some phe-
> nomena which have reached quantitatively undesirable proportions,
> anxieties ... are then to be allayed by specific measures or larger
> strategies aimed at addressing the problem. (Singer 1993: 29)

This epidemic logic is evident in the use of the term 'war toy' to describe the toys considered above, as well as those that were suggestively violent but replicated few aspects of contemporary warfare, including Teenage Mutant Ninja Turtles, Masters of the Universe, and Transformers. This conflated definition encouraged the convergence of immediate anxieties about nuclear proliferation and the broader feminist concern about masculine violence. Consequently, the pathologization of boys' consumer desire for war toys rested upon two mutually reinforcing representations of the male child consumer. Firstly, male children were represented by war-toy critics as innocent victims corrupted by the market. Secondly, critics stressed the negative developmental effects of 'war toys' on male children, claiming their use would lead to an increase in violent behaviour. The anti-war-toy case rested on claims that boys did not have the capacity to participate in the consumption of war toys due to their inherent innocence as children, but also because of their inherent tendency to violence as males.

In addressing the issue of boys' consumer desire, the Canadian Toy Testing Council (CTTC) and the Consumer Association of Canada (CAC) were particularly taken by the logic of fundamental child-hood innocence in their demand for federal legislation to govern toy marketing. According to the CTTC and CAC, the marketing of these toys was 'frightening' and generated an insatiable demand among boys that would invert power dynamics within the family. In the words of the CAC, 'It puts a real strain on parents who want to give their children everything they can' (*Calgary Herald* 1985a). Julie Creighton, executive director of the CTTC, was even more explicit about the dangers of consumer desire in boys when she declared that such advertising to children was 'an unfair marketing practice which is an unethical exploitation of the family through children' (*Calgary Herald* 1985b). In a feature by Cathy Mauk (1990) titled 'We're Mutant Turtles, You're Powerless Parents', the inability of boys to control their desires and the helplessness of parents was brought home more forcefully: '[We] come in cardboard and plastic pack-ages printed with a command that went straight to your little ones' hearts: "Collect us all!" … you will one day succumb and buy your child "just one" Ninja Turtle.' The Canadian Council of Children and Youth spokesperson Brian Ward was similarly concerned about boys' competence as consumers: 'Adults are able to make a rational, responsible and reasonable choice as a consumer. What seven-year-old can?' (Barber 1986: 39). Claims that war-toy consumption was embedded in more complex family dynamics, like that of 7-year-old Christian De Freitas, who stated that 'kids like toys … [and] don't have to worry about how much they cost, because we're not the ones who buy them', were conveniently recoded as evidence that boys 'want it all' (Semenak 1990).

To combat the problem of boys' consumer desire, several experts offered advice to parents, stressing their role in regulating the consumer lives of male children. The Winnipeg School Board approved a flyer distribution by the Building Peace Through Play Committee to educate parents about the danger of war toys, including their advertising 'tricks' (*Winnipeg Free Press* 1985). Janice Robertson, director of the Alberta Children's Hospital, had similar advice: 'You are in control of what comes into your home. You should not feel pressure to purchase toys that are in opposition to your beliefs and values. It is time parents took control,' (Birnie 1986; *Montreal Gazette* 1990).

Though critics recognized boys as desirous, this recognition did not result in an understanding of boys as agentive. The inherent innocence of boy consumers *as children*, so the logic went, made it impossible for them to develop 'healthy' consumer desire along the lines of adults. The infiltration of these market forces into the heart of domesticity occupied by male children threatened to invert parental authority over boy consumers, as 'toy-hungry children' would subvert the rational consumption of parents (Barber 1986: 39).

Combating the boy consumer

However, the status of boys as not only children but also males raised another set of concerns about the effect of the war toys themselves on their behaviour and development. In this respect, the incapability of boys to comprehend the distinction between play and reality was a frequent line of argument used by critics of war toys. Boys were often depicted as being susceptible to a monkey-see, monkey-do relationship to their toys as a result of inherent tendencies towards violence as males. Early childhood educator Sarah Meritt felt that the very design of the toys invited violence: 'the weaponry and physiques of these toys strongly suggest that praise goes to the person who uses the most violence and has the most strength' (Barber 1986: 38). The child psychiatrist Joanna Santa Barbara (1991), member of Canadian Physicians for the Prevention of Nuclear War, stated:

[Toys teach that] ... War is a game, an exciting adventure ... Killing is acceptable, even fun ... Violence or the threat of violence is the only way to resolve conflicts ... The world is divided into 'goodies' and 'baddies' ... The bad guys are devoid of human qualities and their destruction is desirable. (ibid. 8–9)

Percy Barsky, the Medical Director of Children's Homecare in Winnipeg and supporter of warning labels on war toys, stated that 'the result of becoming absorbed in these fantasizing games [with action figures] puts the kid into a separate world where he doesn't have any sense of reality ... and will actually goad him into performing violent acts, and often fatal acts' (*Calgary Herald* 1985a).

At protests staged outside toy shops by peace organizations and women's groups, a similar logic was detectable. According to the British Columbia-based New Westminster Peace Council spokesperson Beverley Mill, war toys had a hidden agenda: 'Really what it's doing is conditioning children into losing their fear of real guns and real violence. The good guys get the bad guys but the message is annihilate your enemy, not negotiate or find another way' (Armstrong 1987; *Globe and Mail* 1986). As Rose Dyson (1992) saw it in her article on war toys for *Peace Magazine*, 'It is easy to conclude that a significant portion of the modern economy is based on ideological child abuse ... It is no accident that we have rising levels of violence, suicides, mean world outlooks, crime, racism, and intolerance.' According to Pacijoue's teaching aid 'Cessez le Feu':

If, through television, film and toys, we provide a child with stories of doctors and nurses, we can expect that they will learn healing. If we provide him with stories of carpenters and tools, we can expect that he will build things. And if we glorify violence, we can expect that will carry over to the home, the classroom and the neighbourhood. (Auger 1987: 3)

When brought together, concerns about boys' consumption as children and their use of war toys as males worked as a powerful argument specifically designed to pathologize boys' consumption, cast war toys as an epidemic, and support assertions of female authority over male child consumers.

Backlash and transformation

While the efforts of war-toy activists continued into the 1990s, it was clear by 1985 that a backlash had begun against war-toy critics, ultimately prompting a shift in emphasis among activists. Toy companies had offered some resistance to the characterization of their toys by critics, but such statements were infrequent and not particularly compelling (*Calgary Herald* 1985b; Farber 1985). Conversely, the backlash spearheaded by journalists was more effective, offering to readers the persona of an agentive child consumer, exercising genuine consumer desires with competence. Yet those journalists in the media who were most responsible for promoting this interpretation made a point of emphasizing the role of parental guidance in children's consumer lives. While certainly agents, the boy consumer of the backlash was not autonomous.

The *Toronto Star* (1988) editorial 'Toys into Ploughshares' took the occasion of the alternative toyfair held in Toronto to satirize the centre-left, middle-class, and urban ideology of war-toy critics.[7] While Julie Creighton, Kay Macpherson, and others attacked the seemingly nihilistic satire of the *Toronto Star* editorial board, many other journalists offered more moderate yet similar critiques of war-toy critics (Kay Macpherson Fonds, 1950–1993). As Jack Spearman (1987) put it in his op-ed: 'So many people underestimate the intelligence of kids. They are a lot smarter than overprotective adults give them credit for.' Shelley Fralic's (1986) criticism of the anti-war-toy movement was decidedly less measured:

> War toys are hell … [the war-toy critics'] message is packed with emotion and motherhood … it's a different battle today, these self-appointed experts say. Today's toys are more violent, more concerned with nuclear power, more real. They will lead our children into the path of nuclear acceptance, into a new military consciousness being fostered by right-wing warmongers. Today's toys, they say, need

censoring ... War toys are hell but we'll decide what goes under the Christmas tree. (Fralic 1986)

The backlash characterized concerns about war toys as a dispropor-tionate moral panic that threatened parental authority. At the root of both moderate and more extreme backlash commentators was a fundamentally different understanding of boys' consumer activities. The backlash characterized boys as competent consumers, subjected to symbolic violence at the hands of war-toy critics. Rather than an image of the threatened innocent, possessing of innate, but dormant, violent impulses, it is of the semi-autonomous consumer agent able to negotiate the complex world of commodities with the aid of parents, as subordinate members in a patriarchal, heterosexual nuclear family.

The backlash that began in the press gained additional credence in the final days of the cold war. As the Iron Curtain was finally raised in 1989 and the Soviet Union began disintegrating, ultimately ceasing to exist altogether in 1991, the anti-war-toy movement's case that their efforts were relevant to world peace stood on increasingly unsteady ground. However, in the final weeks of 1989 the prospects of a Canadian society free from violence would seem much less promising, as a result of domestic, rather than international, events. On 6 December, Marc Lepine walked into the École Polytechnique in Montreal and shot 24 women and 4 men who attempted to go to the aid of his female targets: 14 women were killed and 14 men and women injured in an explicitly anti-feminist and misogynistic outburst of violence and terror. The shooting, popularly dubbed the Montreal Massacre, prompted outrage across Canada and elsewhere, finally putting the anti-feminist counter-movement of the 1980s on the defensive. In this context, feminist and peace organizations switched strategies, as they began to emphasize domestic violence against women and the need for gun control, rather than nuclear and military proliferation, in their effort to sustain the fight against war toys and reclaim the initiative from their opponents.

The case of Pacijoue is instructive in this regard. While the Mon-treal-based organization began its efforts with the connection between war toys and world peace, by the end of the decade it had shifted focus to the connection between war toys and domestic violence. One of its main educational outreach projects was the collection of donated war toys (defined in the broadest sense) from elementary school children. It was undertaken by sending out lesson plans on disarmament to primary school teachers, encouraging them to address the issue of world peace in class. The culminating activity was the donation by each pupil of a war toy to the teacher, who would then pass it along to Pacijoue. As part of the exercise, children were encouraged to use peer pressure on those who were reluctant to donate toys. Though some children and parents perhaps willingly gave their toys, such lessons also applied the authority of the school and the possibility of social shame in order to coerce donations from children and their families.[8] Initially begun as part of UN Disarmament Week in October 1988, after a number of subsequent collections Pacijoue found themselves in possession of tens of thousands of war toys that they planned to use for the construction of a world peace monument in Montreal focused on disarmament.[9] However, the search for funding for the monument and flagging interest of the city council meant that the prospects of the monument being erected by the autumn of 1989 or spring of 1990 seemed bleak.[10] After the events of 6 December 1989, the Pacijoue-proposed monument received increased interest and financial backing. In the end, 6 December 1991 was chosen as the date for the unveiling of the monument, to mark both the second anniversary of the Montreal Massacre and the first National Day of Remembrance and Action on Violence Against Women and related White Ribbon Campaign. The 12,000 war toys were embedded in the monument to peace, while another 6,000 were placed in a similar monument erected in Quebec City (*Toronto Star* 1990). Astutely, journalists followed Pacijoue's cues and situated the monument in the context of the Montreal Massacre rather than the peace movement. Lepine, one journalist pointed out, 'was in many ways a typical boy: He played at war while his sister played at dolls' (Picard 1991). Diane Savard, President of Pacijoue, drove home the new emphasis on domestic violence: 'We can't just bury our heads in the sand. We have to look at society's role in creating Marc Lepine's – and change society … Our message at Christmas is: Don't give violence as a gift' (Picard

1991). While Kathleen McDonnell (1994) has stressed the connection of Pacijoue's efforts to build the monument to moral panics about media violence, the historical context of the monument's conception shows that a general concern about violence obscured more complex and shrewd political calculations on the part of Pacijoue in shifting the meaning of the monument to suit the changing circumstances of a post-Soviet world.

The peace monument in Montreal demonstrates the clear pathologization of male children's consumer desire for war toys along the lines outlined above. However, it also demonstrates that in the face of a media backlash and the end of the cold war, critics actively switched strategies in order to further their cause. By connecting their efforts to the issue of violence against women rather than world peace, war-toy critics demonstrated that their efforts were specific and intentional – if ethically questionable – and not the result of a moral panic. However, this change was also indicative of a feminist movement, preoccupied with reclaiming lost ground from their political adversaries, moving on to other issues. Sexual and domestic violence would ultimately become the main focus of the White Ribbon Campaign. War toys and their boy consumers were increasingly peripheral to the main efforts to raise awareness and ultimately prevent domestic and sexual violence.

Concluding discussion

In an effort to fight one of the few aspects of American cold-war imperialism under the control of Canadian adults – war toys – feminists and peace activists intentionally shifted the landscape of the conflict from the institutions of formal politics to the economic and intimate spaces of the market and the family in an effort to gain the upper hand. Drawing heavily on maternal feminism, war-toy critics developed an essentialist representation of boy consumers as both innocent children and potentially violent men in support of their claims that war toys were dangerous. Though the intention was to politically undermine American cold-war policy, the use of war toys and boy consumers as tools placed both at the symbolic centre of struggles about the future of world peace and gender equality. In their symbolic struggle for political and personal peace, the resulting pathologization of boys' consumer desire for war toys enacted a different kind of violence on very real boys. In response, the media backlash emphasized the competence of boy consumers to navigate complex consumer issues under the guidance of the nuclear family, claiming that the anti-war-toy campaigners were, alternatively, fuelling a moral panic. For war-toy critics, boys and their playthings were just collateral damage; for those involved in the backlash, they constituted intentional casualties. The accusations of moral panic by the media backlash led to the dismissal of the sincere and very serious political concerns at the root of the anti-war-toy efforts. Examples such as the Eighties' war-toy debate in Canada should give us pause. It behoves us to consider the ramifications – ethical, moral, and political – of the opportunistic mobilization of the consuming child by popular movements, irrespective of their ideological pedigree. The Canadian example clearly demonstrates that the theoretical framework of moral panic, while a powerful tool for political struggle, offers a truncated view of conflicts over child consumption, hiding the strategic and tactical rationale that underlies the deployment of children and their material objects in order to achieve large-scale political objectives. Characterizing the use of children to further political struggles as moral panic highlights the violence – symbolic and real – of these actions. However, moral panic serves to limit the possibility of acknowledging the often rational and calculated deployment of children by ideologically complex actors and groups for specific and diverse political ends.

Notes

1 Library Archives Canada (LAC), MG28–I218, Vol. 7 File 2, Vol. 16 File 13–16 & Vol. 46 File 9–10.
2 (LAC), MG31-K36 Vol. 4 File 13 & Bibliotheque et Archives Nationale du Quebec (BANQ) Gatineau, P233-S7-SS1-D27.
3 Andrew Bene Collection [Private Archive], Ottawa, ON.
4 'Newspaper cartoonists declare war on war toys, 1986' (Kay Macpherson Fonds, LAC, 1950–1953).
5 Historians of the nineteenth century such as Joanna de Groot (2006) and Kristin Hoganson (2007) have described the domestication of empire and

the second-hand engagement with it through consumption in the British and American contexts, respectively.

6 Concerns about war toys did extend to girls, if to a lesser extent. While violent toys targeted at boys were seen as a problem by critics, those same individuals would often complain that equally violently themed playthings for girls were problematic because they looked too much like Barbie dolls, not because they encouraged violence. The case of She-Ra, He-Man's female warrior counterpart, is instructive in this regard (see Zwarun 1985).

7 Carey French (1987) makes a similar point by satirizing the middle-class bias of the war-toy controversy: 'It's your typical yuppie family fuss. Dad, 41, a bespectacled banker with a receding hairline and a Bay Street suit, is clutching a pot-bellied wrestler doll. Mom, 38, a jean-suited high school teacher, is clutching a box of Fisher-Price play dinnerware ... Dad is sulking ... he is secretly worried that 5-year-old Patrick ... is growing up a wimp ... Mom figures that, if the kid gets his hands on any of the stuff he sees on kids' TV shows, he will turn out to be Charlie Manson.'

8 Des jouets de guerre pour la paix [lesson plan]. 'Conseil de la Sculpture de Quebec Fonds' (1965–2000), BANQ.

9 'Conseil de la Sculpture de Quebec Fonds' (1965–2000), BANQ.

10 Gagnon to Fainstat, 30 January 1989, 'Conseil de la Sculpture de Quebec Fonds' (1965–2000), BANQ.

References

Andrew Bene Collection (1977–2012), Ottawa, ON, Andrew Bene Collection [Private archive].

Armstrong, John (1987), 'New Westminster group sets sights on war toy ban', *Vancouver Sun*, 26 November, A12.

Auger, Christophe (1987), *Cessez le feu: Guide pedagogique jouets militaires* (Montreal: Fide).

Conseil de la Sculpture de Quebec Fonds (1965–2000), Bibliotheque et Archives Nationale du Quebec, Gatineau, PQ, P233-S7-SS1-D27.

Bantjes, Rod & Trussler, Tanya (1999), 'Feminism and the grass roots: Women and environmentalism in Nova Scotia, 1980–1983', *Canadian Review of Sociology and Anthropology*, 36/2: 179–97.

Barbara, Joanna Santa (1991), 'What to do about war toys at home and beyond', *The Ploughshares Monitor*, 12/3: 8–9.

Barber, John (1986), 'Warfare in toyland', *Maclean's*, 15 December, 99/50: 38–40.

Birnie, Peter (1986), 'Good vs. evil on Santa's new toy list', *Calgary Herald*, 10 November, F1.

Brocklehurst, Helen (2006), *Who's afraid of children? Children, conflict, and international relations* (Aldershot: Ashgate).

Calgary Herald (1985a), 'Toy marketing more than just child's play', 8 November, C8.

– (1985b), 'Toy council seeks grant to examine marketing', 10 November, D2.

Chenier, Elise (2008), *Strangers in our midst: Sexual deviancy in postwar Ontario* (Toronto: University of Toronto Press).

Cook, Daniel Thomas (2004a), *The commodification of childhood: The children's clothing industry and the rise of the child consumer* (Durham, NC: Duke University Press).

– (2004b), 'Beyond either/or', *Journal of Consumer Culture*, 4/2: 147–53.

Cross, Gary (1997), *Kids stuff: Toys and the changing world of American childhood* (Cambridge, Mass.: Harvard University Press).

Dubinsky, Karen (1985), *Lament for a 'patriarchy lost'? Anti-feminism, anti-abortion and R.E.A.L. Women in Canada* (Toronto: Canadian Research Institute for the Advancement of Women).

Dyson, Rose (1992), 'Toyland as terror zone', *Peace Magazine*, 8/2: 6–7.

Evans, Sara M. (2003), *Tidal wave: How women changed America at centuries end* (New York: The Free Press).

– (2009), 'Feminism in the 1980s: Surviving the backlash', in Gil Troy & Vincent J. Cannato (eds.), *Living in the Eighties* (New York: OUP), 85–97.

Farber, Michael (1985), 'Rambo-toy foes are up in arms', *Montreal Gazette*, 2 October, A3.

Fralic, Shelley (1986), 'Cease fire, war toy critics told', *Vancouver Sun*, 13 December, B2.

French, Carey (1987), 'Toying with children', *Globe & Mail*, 19 December, D5.

Gagnon, Nathaly (1986, Fall), 'Le movement pacifiste au quebec: Reflexion d'une militante', *Atlantis*, 12/1: 60–63.

Globe and Mail (1983), 'More bangs for a buck', 22 December, A22.

– (1986), 'Shops under attack by demonstrators for selling war toys', 1 December, A21.

Godley, Elizabeth (1983), 'War on war toys', *The Vancouver Sun*, 2 December, B1.

Groot, Joanna de (2006), 'Metropolitan desires and colonial connections: Reflections on consumption and empire', in Catherine Hall & Sonya O. Rose (eds.), *At home with the empire: Metropolitan culture and the imperial world* (New York: CUP), 166–90.

Hendershot, Heather (1998), *Saturday morning censors: Television regulation before the V-Chip* (Durham, NC: Duke University Press).

Hoganson, Kristin L. (2007), *Consumers' imperium: The global production of American domesticity, 1865–1920* (Chapel Hill: University of North Carolina Press).

Jaffe, Deborah (2006), *The history of toys from spinning tops to robots* (London: Sutton Press).

Kay Macpherson Fonds (1950–1993), Library and Archives Canada (LAC), Ottawa, ON, MG31 K36, Vol. 4 File 13.

Labelle, Gilles (1986), 'Politique, masculinite et violence', *Atlantis*, 12/1: 35–45.

Landsberg, Michelle (1985), 'Toys bring sinister new meaning to "triumph of the skies"', *Globe and Mail*, 7 December, K7.

– (1986), 'The merchants of superkill no longer know that they are mad', *Globe and Mail*, 1 February, A2.

Loewen, Candace (1987), '"Mike hears voices": Voice of women and Lester Pearson, 1960–1963', *Atlantis*, 12/2: 24–30.

Marketing (1981), 'Irwin toy battle heats up; more charges expected, 86/9: 2.

Mauk, Cathy (1990), 'We're mutant ninja turtles, you're powerless parents', *Globe and Mail*, 18 April, A7.

McDonnell, Kathleen (1994), *Kid culture: Children, & adults & popular culture* (Toronto: Second Story Press).

Montreal Gazette (1985a), 'Peace group set to shoot down toy nuclear bomb', 20 July, A7.

– (1985b), 'Cruise missiles coming to Canada', 20 July, A7.

– (1986), 'Newspaper cartoonists declare war on war toys', 4 December, G16.

– (1990), 'Advice to Moms and Dads – you can just say no', 25 November, D1.

Parr, Joy (1999), *Domestic goods: The material, the moral and the economic in the postwar years* (Toronto: University of Toronto Press).

Picard, Andre (1991), 'Plastic guns, G. I. Joe gone to graveyard', *Globe and Mail*, 6 December, A8.

Ribinovitch, Susan (1989), 'Shootout on the new frontier: The return of the warrior', in Janice Williamson and Deborah Gorham (eds.), *Up and doing: Canadian women and peace* (Toronto: Women's Press), 127–137.

Sammond, Nicholas (2005), *Babes in tomorrowland: Walt Disney and the making of the American child* (Durham, NC: Duke University Press).

Semenak, Susan (1990). 'We want toys and we don't care what they cost because we don't have to pay for them.' *Montreal Gazette*, 25 November, D1.

Singer, Linda (1993), *Erotic welfare: Sexual theory and politics in the age of epidemic* (London: Routledge).

Smith, Dorothy E. (1989), 'Gender, power and peace', in Williamson & Gorham (eds.) *Up and doing: Canadian women and peace* (Toronto: Women's Press), 93–100.

Smyth, Donna E. (1989), 'Getting tough and making sacrifices: The language of war in the 1980s', in Williamson & Gorham (eds.), *Up and doing: Canadian women and peace* (Toronto: Women's Press), 116–26.

Spearman, Jack (1987), 'Toys won't turn your kids into killers', *Calgary Herald*, 15 December, A4.

Stephens, Sharon (1997), 'Nationalism, nuclear policy and children in Cold War America', *Childhood*, 4/1: 103–123.

Steuter, Erin (1992), 'Women against feminism: An examination of feminist social movements and anti-feminist countermovements', *Canadian Review of Sociology and Anthropology*, 29/3: 288–306.

Strong-Boag, Veronica (1996), 'Independent women, problematic men: First- and second-wave anti-feminism in Canada from Goldwin Smith to Betty Steele', *Histoire sociale/Social history*, 29/57: 1–22.

Toronto Star (1988), 'Toys into ploughshares', 24 November, A6.

– (1990), '6,000 Donated War Toys a Monument for Peace', 29 April, A25.

Voice of Women Fonds (1959–1987), Library Archives Canada (LAC), MG28–I218, Vol. 7 File 2, Vol. 16 File 13–16 & Vol. 46 File 9–10.

Westad, Odd Arne (2007), *The global Cold War* (Cambridge: CUP).

Williamson, Janice & Gorham, Deborah (1989) (eds.), *Up and doing: Canadian women and peace* (Toronto: Women's Press).

Winnipeg Free Press (1985), 'War toy message backed for schools', 11 December, 3.

Woods, William Crawford (1983), 'The littlest arms race', *Harper's Magazine*. 266/1595: 6, 8, 10–11.

Zacharias, Yvonne (1983), 'War toys', *Calgary Herald*, 18 November, C9.

Zwarun, Suzanne (1985), 'Toy makers working hard at trivialization of women', *Calgary Herald*, 4 March, A16.

CHAPTER 14

Nobody panicked!

The Fifties' debate on children's comics consumption

Helle Strandgaard Jensen

Even if gangster comics have sometimes directly inspired the young to commit criminal acts, it is fortunately not the case that one becomes a criminal by default by reading about crime. What is worse is, however, the way in which the modern consumption of comics – and not only the Bang! Bang! type – hinders reading development and a sense of language, damages children's creativity and imagination, and leads them to reject the fine literature that the libraries have to offer.[1]

This clear dismissal of comics as an appropriate medium for children was part of an article written in 1953 by Lorentz Larson, a Swedish teacher and esteemed expert on children's literature.[2] It was in the early 1950s that the Scandinavian debate about children's comics consumption began in earnest, and Larson was one of its central actors (Jensen 2010; Knutsson 1995). The quote captures one of the dominant arguments in the debate's massive rejection of comics as a desired medium for children: comics were seen to drive them away from appropriate literature. For Larson, the popularity of the comics was also a personal blow, as he had spent much of his professional life promoting the virtues of appropriate children's literature, which he believed was of 'vital importance' for the 'development of [the child's] soul' (Larson & the Women's International League for Peace and Freedom 1954: 13; for Larson's career, see Nilson 1969).

From a present-day point of view, Larson and many of his contemporaries' anxiety over children's comics consumption can seem irrational and backward.[3] The distance to the past and past views on comics is further emphasized by the almost canonical status that superheroes such as *Superman* and *Batman* have gained in popular culture today – these modern classics were despised by Larson and other debaters. It is not only in popular outlines of Fifties' conservatism that the period's debaters are viewed as overreacting. The frequent academic categorization of the Fifties' comics debates, and other seemingly similar debates, as instances of moral or media panics has also contributed to a scholarly condescention towards the viewpoints of the Fifties' debaters as panicky, backwards and irrational (Drotner 1992: 60; Knutsson 1995; Springhall 1998: 162). In contrast to the panic approach, I argue for the value of trying to understand the rationales and experiences that went into the past debaters' conceptualizations of children's media consumption, based on the specific context in which they occurred. Thus the analysis aims to move beyond the understanding of the Fifties' debaters as irrational and panicky and see their opposition to children's comics consumption as based on their professional experiences and expectations.[4]

To write a history of the Scandinavian comics debate that focuses on its mundane elements presents an alternative to the moral/media panic approach. This alternative, and its focus on the specific socio-cultural contexts of the debate, is important in the context of this book, because past debates on children's (media) consumption often occur as contested reference points in present-day debates, whether implicitly or explicitly (see, for example, Buckingham 2000; Drotner 1999; Juncker 2006; Livingstone & Drotner 2008). Historicizing these reference points by showing their complex rationales in close relation to their specific socio-cultural context makes them a multifaceted backdrop for today's discussions on children and consumption – instead of the simple counterpoles they often become in historical analyses that use the panic approach (for further discussion of this problem, see Buckingham & Jensen, forthcoming). Thus, by trying to engage with the debates on their own terms, a more positive dialogue with the past and its different understanding of children and media should be possible – something that also might help to counter today's often polarized discussions about the relationship between children and consumption (see further, Buckingham 2011; Buckingham & Tingstad 2010; Cook 2004).

Moral panic and the mundane alternative

Public debates in the Fifties about child consumption of comics have often been seen as classic instances of moral or media panic (Barker 1984; Critcher 2008; Drotner 1999; Knutsson 1995; Petersen & Sørensen n.d.).[5] In the form of a specific theoretical approach, moral panics originate from Stanley Cohen's *Folk Devils and Moral Panics* of 1972 (Cohen 2002; Rowe 2009). The approach suggests a way of studying heated popular debates fuelled by the mass media, in which social and cultural power-holders stigmatize groups of people or phenomena by labelling them as deviant and subversive, and by doing so sustain their own hegemonic position. Since the 1970s, the approach has become popular in many fields, including childhood and media studies (see, for example, Livingstone & Drotner 2008; Messenger Davis 2010). However, despite the widespread usage of the moral or media panic approach, its utility as a tool for studying popular debates about children's media consumption is questionable.

Two points of criticism of the panic approach as used in childhood and media studies are particularly important here. The first relates to *disproportionality*. The panic approach implies that the reactions of the debaters were not commensurate with the threat represented by the object of attention; this is why they are classified as panicky, after all. In panic-inspired analyses of the Fifties' comics debates, the debaters have been seen as overreacting to the threat this medium represented to children's psyches and reading abilities (Critcher 2008; Knutsson 1995; Springhall 1998). The problem here is how we decide on the existence of this mismatch. On what grounds can we justify a comparison of a present-day analysis of comics with that of the 1950s debaters', as for instance John Springhall and Martin Barker have done (Springhall 1998: 127; Barker 1984)? This epistemological problem is particularly evident in analyses of past debates, as our judgement of the *too* panicky reaction stems from our own present perspective. Temporal distance will sometimes mean that the phenomenon in question has very different connotations, as is the case with the superhero comics. This distance makes our assessment of disproportionality even more difficult.

The second point of criticism relates to the *displacement* that the debates are seen as creating. The claimed disproportional reaction by participants in moral panics often leads researchers to conclude that the debates are really about something other than they claim to be (Critcher 2008; Drotner 1992; Springhall 1998). The debaters are seen as wittingly, or unwittingly, using the debates as displacements for something else; as 'scapegoats' to counter unwanted effects of 'modernity', often in the shape of cultural democratization (Springhall 1998: 147; Drotner 1999: 597). What the moral/media panic approach tells us, then, is that we cannot trust the reasons that the participants themselves give. The debaters are in some cases seen as using a scapegoat, for instance the comics, to enforce a generational order, a certain cultural hierarchy, or a particular political agenda (Critcher 2008; Barker 1984; Springhall 1998). In other cases the object of debate is seen as a target of emotional projection (Drotner 1992, 1999). These explanations for the different agents' reasons for engaging in the debates are seen as concealed behind the motives uttered by the subjects themselves. It is up to the researcher to uncover the *real* motives (for instance sustaining existing generational, cultural, or political hierarchies) on the basis of her own judgement of the phenomenon the subjects reacted to. This makes it very difficult to take the utterances of the debaters seriously and engage in an analysis of viewpoints that are different to those of today.[6] The same problem can be seen as applying to the understanding of current views that are different to those which dominate our own fields – whether stemming from other academic traditions or popular beliefs (Buckingham & Jensen, forthcoming).

Understanding past debates

Instead of studying the Fifties' comics debate as a moral panic, the following analysis treats the debaters' conceptualizations of children's comics consumption as rational acts. This rationality is to be found in a relationship between the different debaters' utterances and their socio-cultural and professional experiences of how the world worked. This includes, for example, their understandings of childhood, child psychology, the benefits of reading and education, and so on. This approach is inspired by two different texts. One is Barbara Rosenwein's essay (2002) 'Worrying about Emotions in History'. Here, Rosenwein proposes that emotions should be seen as social constructs instead of as irrational, untrammelled expressions, and thus turns her back on the way in which the history of emotions has normally been written with strong teleological undertones; something that has led to interpretations of people in the past as being more irrational and hysterical. Rosenwein's project is interesting as an alternative to the moral panic approach, because it helps to clarify the logic of the very strong reactions towards comics in the 1950s in their specific socio-cultural context, rather than dismissing them as irrational or inexplicable.

The other work we can turn to in order to understand the way in which comics were deemed inappropriate reading material for children is Peter Harder's essay 'Conceptual Construal and Social Constructions' (Harder 2011). In this work, Harder explains how conceptualizations interact with social forces, which together shape the way the world works. This means that understanding is situated in Nature and that conceptualizations 'live or die depending on feedback from the environment' of which they are part (Harder 2011: 659). Seeing conceptualizations in this way means that the reactions to comics in Fifties' Scandinavia must be understood as results of a two-way process between the individual debaters and their environments; for example, their socio-cultural or professional background. Here I will concentrate on relating the different debaters' understandings of children's comics consumption to their professional environment.

The suggestions on how to understand meaning-making as a dialectic process emphasize the importance of its situated nature. The present essay focuses on Scandinavia, and how the region's shared ideas of democratic education, children's relation to media, and the role of the state in the expanding welfare societies provided common ground for the dismissiveness towards comics in the 1950s. Hence, though the lives lived by Scandinavian children in the various countries may have diverged in several respects, the commonalities were many when it came to ideas about the role of the media in children's lives. The evidence of a high degree of transfer between the Scandinavian countries regarding this specific topic can be found in the sources themselves. New Nordic research also emphasizes precisely this potential for the transfer of ideas in the region: 'With its historically tight political and cultural links between the five countries, and relatively open borders, numerous trans- and bilateral agreements, we can talk about a very high Nordic density of transitional institutions and organizations' (Petersen 2011: 42).[7] Furthermore, specific research has pointed to the shared mindsets on pedagogy, education, and children's mental health in Scandinavia in the 1950s (Andresen et al. 2011: ch. 6; de Coninck-Smith 2002: 18).

The following analysis makes use of source material consisting of articles from newspapers, journals, and popular magazines, as well as treatments in book form and various official reports from Denmark, Sweden, and Norway.[8] Armed with this varied material, I tackle a broad public arena in which opinions on comics were constructed and contested, and in which no authority *per se* dominated, as this was an issue that concerned children's private media consumption. The private nature of the consumption necessarily conceptualizes it as a power struggle between state, market, family, and children. In this struggle, no professional, political, or socio-cultural view of the matter had the natural advantages it might otherwise have had in an institutional setting. I see this wide set of relations of power, resistance, and authority as a public struggle over consumption politics regarding children's media consumption, and in doing so have been inspired by Martin Daunton and Matthew Hilton's study of the ways in which the acceptance or dismissal of the consumption of certain commodities change over time (Daunton & Hilton 2001). By viewing notions of children's comics consumption as consumption politics, it speaks to the broader history of the Scandinavian welfare states and relations between market and state, between different professional groups, and between private and public spheres.

Books or comics?

In 1952, the Danish magazine for substitute teachers and student teachers published a special issue on children's reading (*Unge pædagoger* 1952). The aim of the publication was to prompt a debate about the popular press. The contributors belonged to the professional groups that dominated the comics debate: schoolteachers, psychologists, nursery teachers, and librarians. The editorial posed children's attraction to so-called poor-quality magazines, romances, and comics as a puzzle that fell to the modern educator to solve. The solutions suggested by the contributors mainly consisted of making children interested in what librarians and teachers had singled out as 'quality literature' (ibid. 3–4). The parallels between this argument and the one advanced by Larson quoted above are conspicuous: children's interest in comics posed a threat to their consumption of appropriate literature. This potential lack of contact with what were defined as good books was not only seen as a threat to the individual child, but to society as a whole, for literature was thought an important way of passing on cultural and moral values (Larson 1953; Nordisk kontaktudvalg 1957; Sørensen 1953; *Unge pædagoger* 1952; Winther 1954).

It is striking how disdain for comics was closely tied to the promotion of good literature, as this suggests more generally how relations between the media and children were understood in this period. The pairing of books and comics as good and bad media has been noted in previous studies of the Fifties' comics debate (Kauranen 2008; Knutsson 1995); and it should be noted that film and television were viewed similarly, as can be seen in this quote from a leading figure in Danish education, the head teacher Christian Winther: 'the comics problem is not an isolated phenomenon, but closely connected to not only inappropriate book series ... but also films, radio, and television' (Winther 1954: 854). Hence comics were seen as part of a larger group of media that children consumed, and their deviant status stemmed from the significance ascribed to the other media. This system of meaning associated with the various media for children is important, as it shows why, for example, teachers and librarians threw themselves into the debate – the fight against comics was also a fight for good literature (see Buttenschøn 1954; Larson & the Women's International League for Peace and Freedom 1954; *Unge pædagoger* 1952; Nordisk kontaktudvalg 1957). To understand the aversion to comics we must therefore also understand how the supposedly suitable alternatives were conceptualized, and by whom.

Children's reading habits had been of great interest to Scandi-navian educators and librarians during the 1940s and early 1950s (Birkeland, Risa & Vold 2005; Weinreich 2006), when several studies had been conducted to identify what children read in their leisure time (Larson 1947; *Ungdomskommisionen* 1952; Bejerot 1954; Sletvold 1953; Deinboll 1942). These studies had revealed the vast discrepancy between what children read and what educa-tors wanted them to read. The focus in Scandinavian educational circles on the perceived gap between ideal and actual consumption coincided with the growing international attention paid to children's mass media consumption. The convergence between international and Scandinavian interests can be seen as one of the reasons why (superhero) comics in the mid-1950s became the focus of atten-tion in Scandinavian debates about children's media consumption.

In the early 1950s, UNESCO had commissioned several reports on children and media. Of special interest here is the one entitled *The Child Audience: A Report on Press, Film and Radio for Children* (Bauchard 1953). The report and its conclusions on comics were repeated in Scandinavian articles in subsequent years (Bejerot 1954), particularly the way in which it singled out superhero comics as inappropriate because 'by undermining or warping the traditional values of each country, the superman myth is becoming a kind of international monster' (Bauchard 1952: 37–8). According to the Norwegian advisory committee on comics, which had been estab-lished on a UNESCO initiative in 1953, *Batman, Superman,* and other superhero comics were the worst possible reading for children, as they inspired hatred, violence, sexism, and racism (Problemet tegneserier 1954). The views of the committee were clearly influen-tial in Scandinavia, as there were repeated references to its work in 1953 and 1954 in both the Swedish and Danish teachers' unions' magazines (*Folkeskolen* 1953–4; *Svensk Skoltidning* 1953–4).

The teachers' point of view

Teachers held a special status in the Scandinavian comics debate. Not only were they very active when it came to writing articles in newspapers on the subject, but they were also recognized as experts on children's reading (*Folkeskolen* 1953–4; *Svensk Skoltidning* 1953–4; By 1953; Fransson 1953, 1954; Larson 1953, 1954a, 1954b; Norsk Skuleblad 1953; Nørvig 1952, 1953; Winther 1954, 1955). The influence of an educational perspective on the comics debate can also be seen, for example, in the power that the Norwegian Ministry of Ecclesiastical and Educational Affairs had over the conceptualization of appropriate literature. Every year, delegates from the Ministry awarded a prize for the best Norwegian children's book and drew up lists of appropriate books. Possessed of the authority to determine what reading material was good for children, educators also sought to have the last word on what was bad. However, the expertise ascribed to teachers in the question of children's comics consumption did not only refer to their institutional role, but also to the leading role in the future of welfare society that comprehensive schools were accorded in this period (Andresen et al. 2011; de Coninck-Smith 2002; Sjöberg 2003).

Democratization was a key word in the Scandinavian educational and pedagogical milieus following the Second World War (de Conick-Smith 2002: 18; Tuhen & Vaage 2004; Qvarsebo 2006). The experience of the War was interpreted as calling for the new comprehensive school systems to bring up children to be democratic citizens, and the comprehensive school became a central institution in the ideal of the democratic welfare society (Sjöberg 2003: 54; Andresen et al. 2011). This required teachers and other professional educators to play a more active role in children's enculturation processes, rather than leaving their upbringing to parents to tackle alone (Sandin & Halldén 2003: 10). This drive for the involvement of educators in children's moral upbringing resonates with the teachers' involvement in children's comics consumption at home. It also indicates why superhero comics were often singled out as being particularly pernicious: the way in which Batman, Superman, the Phantom, and the rest solved problems was not particularly democratic, but rather, it was argued, was violent and uncompromising (see, for example, Hansen 1955: 258). The comics were seen as a potential threat to the willingness to obey the laws of the land, as the Danish schoolteacher Anne Marie Nørvig was quoted saying in a Norwegian report in 1954 (Arbeidsudvalget for Statens Folkeoppplysningsråd 1954).

Nørvig is a good example of the type of teacher who was involved in the comics debate. She had trained as a psychologist and had a special interest in the interrelationship between the educational and private spheres concerning childrearing (de Coninck-Smith 2002). Nørvig was worried that parents, who often, she wrote, cared a great deal about their children's nutrition, were too little concerned with the moral 'sustenance' of the comics their offspring 'devoured' (Nørvig 1953). Because of this potential neglect of children's upbringing, she saw an increased need of professional guidance for parents to help them meet the challenges of the new welfare society. In the same way as Larson in the quote above, Nørvig refuted a direct causal link between children's comics consumption and their views on crime. However, like other psychologists of the period, she was afraid that children who were vulnerable because of their social position or their general personal insecurities would be influenced by what she saw as the poor morals of superhero and crime comics (ibid.; Arbeidsudvalget for Statens Folkeoppplysningsråd 1954, quoting Nørvig; Florander 1955). This influence, according to Nørvig, had to be recognized and addressed by professionals who worked with children.

Nørvig's concern for the effect of comics on children's morals can be viewed as part of a larger shift in the educational system from physical to mental wellbeing and governance in the 1950s (Andresen et al. 2011: ch. 6; Qvarsebo 2006). In the Nordic child welfare services, mental health problems, particularly neuroses, caused by the child's environment were a great concern, thus ensuring that the relationship between family and society was of central interest. The emphasis on nurture rather than nature can also be seen in the comics debate. With a focus on nurture, the idea of prevention became important, for, given the social nature of mental health problems, they could be prevented by improving children's surroundings (Andresen et al. 2011: 330). The sometimes shrill warnings about the potential ill effects that comics might have should be understood in this light, as there was a 'growing fear that faulty upbringing or certain childhood experiences could once again derail democracy in its entirety' (ibid. 331). In this battle for true democracy and efficient, productive citizens, mental hygiene was the most important weapon.

The strength of the reaction to comics – particularly the superhero variety – on the part of psychologists and psychiatrics such as the Swedish child psychiatrist Nils Bejerot should be understood in this light, since according to this logic such comics posed a serious threat to children's mental health. The comics, according to Bejerot and many of his contemporaries, were a 'relevant mental hygiene and cultural problem' that should be prevented, even though there might be uncertainty about its precise effects (Bejerot 1954: preface).

Children's mental health and vulnerability

Bejerot was to become an influential figure in the Scandinavia comics debate with the publication of his book *Barn–Serier–Samhälle* ('Children–Comics–Society') in 1954 (for its favourable reception, see, for example, Nordisk kontaktudvalg 1957). In it, he distinguished between the types of comic he thought were innocuous – *Donald Duck* and its Swedish equivalent *Tuff & Tuss* – and the harmful, deviant crime and horror comics such as *Hopalong Cassidy* and *Batman*. This latter group, Bejerot argued, was racist, sexist, and celebrated 'character traits' that teachers, parents, and society 'officially worked against' (Bejerot 1954: 100). Inspired by his American role model, the psychiatrist Fredric Wertham, Bejerot drew a more direct behaviouristic line than did many teachers between the comics and the effect he thought they had on children. The crime and violence in the series would thus in his eyes lead straight to a more violent society. The high esteem in which Bejerot's assessment of the comics problem was held must be seen in the light of the rising status of scientific and psychological research at the time, even if only as a rhetorical strategy (Qvarsebo 2006: 191). The type of knowledge that the medical profession represented when it came to, say, studies of media effects was highly valued at this point (Luke 2005). The urgent tone with which Bejerot entered the comics debate can thus be seen as stemming from his own professional beliefs, but also from the way in which the kind of scientific knowledge he represented was thought of at this time.

   Part of Bejerot's critique was tied to the capitalist, and particularly American, spirit in which he said the comics were produced

(Bejerot 1954). As with other Scandinavian debaters such as Denmark's Tørk Haxthausen, Bejerot stood on the left of the political spectrum. However, taking the political affiliation of the debaters as a whole, generally speaking all shades of political opinion were represented – and the hard, capitalist side of American culture, which the comics were seen to represent, came under attack from both Left and Right. The way in which comic books were produced was one of the main points in the criticism against them: their production was seen as ruled only by the laws of profit (Bejerot 1954; Nordisk Kontaktudvalg 1957; Statens Folkeoppplysningsråd 1954). Criticism of US production values thus seems to have had more to do with a rejection of the vulgar fixation on money and the exploitation of young, vulnerable consumers, than with strictly political motives – although this might have been the case for some debaters (Bejerot 1954; By 1953; Gemeten 1953; for Danish anti-Americanism in general, see Petersen & Sørensen n.d.).

The criticism of manufacturers' exploitation of children in a single-minded pursuit of profit was repeated in relation to popular book series and popular films. These media products were seen as being created in 'factories' far removed from all artistic processes (By 1953; Gemeten 1953). This view of comics and other products of popular culture as things born out of pure capitalism could not be further from views on the art of writing a good children's book. Good children's books were at this time seen as both aesthetically sober and carefully adapted to the child's psyche (see, for example, Weinreich 2006). Conceptions of artistic hierarchies, with unique art at the top and mass-produced trash at the bottom, were thus re-evoked and sustained by the debates about children's comics consumption. Teachers' presumed insight into cultural quality and its transmission to future generations added to their credibility in matters regarding children's leisure-time media consumption.

Besides the production of comics, the way in which they were consumed and distributed was also viewed as problematic. Appropriate children's books were mentioned as being the ones read in the library or at school (see, for example, Sørensen 1953); comics, on the other hand, were described as being read in the playground, in the school toilets, in the street, or at home. Consumption was

strongly associated with peer culture – comics were something children bought themselves or borrowed from friends (see, for example,
Nørvig 1953). Children's independent agency in this matter was
seen as leading them to consume inappropriate media. This was in
strong contrast to the consumption that was controlled by adult
professionals such as librarians, who controlled and supervised the
consumption of appropriate books.[9]
 The association of children's independent consumption with their
subsequent inappropriate choices can also be observed in adult views
on their choices of films or popular books. When the psychologists
of the day looked at what led children to choose 'trash' films, they
saw the main reasons as being peer pressure and a lack of parental
interest (Siersted 1953; Granat 1953; Germeten 1953). The reason
children chose inappropriate media was thought to be ignorance of
what was good for them. Children were seen as unwittingly drawn
to, or tricked into, the consumption of comics by evil marketers or
peer pressure. Interestingly, however, at the same time as children
were seen as being completely incapable of making appropriate
choices on their own, they were understood to be powerful consumers. Adult debaters seldom missed a chance to express their indignation about the huge amount of money they thought children
had at their disposal (Larson & the Women's International League
for Peace and Freedom 1954). The combination of a powerful yet
easily impressionable consumer was a threat that the professionals
who worked with children could not disregard, and to which their
counterstrike was education and the promotion of good books.

Concluding discussion

The history of the Fifties' comics debate presented here differs from
the way this controversy has been narrated in the moral/media
panic stories. This difference is a result of how past views of comics
have been historicized, linking the period's concrete conceptualizations of children and media to the specific socio-cultural environment of the professionals who uttered them. Of course, the story
told here shares some of its plot line with the stories told using a
panic approach; the view, so important to the debate, that comics

were a potential threat to cultural hierarchies is evidence of that. However, the likes of Nørvig, Bejerot, and Larson did not use the debates about comics as cover for other socio-cultural agendas, as the panic stories would have us believe (see, for example, Critcher 2008; Drotner 1999; Springhall 1998). Indeed, the professional environment of these debaters and their understanding of how relationships between children and the media worked makes their vigorous fight against comics, and particularly superhero comics, appear quite logical. Obviously, the debaters promoted their specific professionalism by joining the debate, but rather than being a question of displacement, I suggest we should read this as being one with their professional duty.

The social and political expectations of the educational system in the Scandinavian welfare states were enormous in the Fifties. This pressure can be seen as a factor that pushed teachers to the forefront in the battle against the (superhero) comics, as they thought children's comics consumption might ruin their professional efforts – and thus the future of society. The expertise which teachers were thought to possess regarding children's leisure-time reading was to their advantage in an age when the professional environment in education was changing. The introduction in the post-war period of new professions in the areas of the welfare system related to children could have posed a threat to the teachers' authority. However, through their engagement in various questions about children's leisure-time media consumption – and the ways in which their views converged with those of child psychologists and psychiatrists – their continued centrality was ensured in matters concerning children's wellbeing. Thus we can take the Fifties' comics debate to be a specific example of how children's leisure-time media consumption can form an arena where different professional definitions of children's best interests converge and clash. The hegemony of a certain group, for example different professions, marketers, or adults in general, in defining what a good childhood is, and subsequently the right to control children's practices, can be sustained or challenged in this kind of debate.

The various debaters' participation in the debate about comics can be seen as reflecting the way in which threats to children and Scandinavian society were conceptualized at a given moment. The debate was an arena where specific problems – in this case, comics – were addressed in ways that drew upon the period's dominant discourses regarding children, childhood, and media. The relationship between the view of children as future citizens and the debaters' professional understanding of what this required in terms of education made them oppose comics as an appropriate medium for children. Carefully selected books were perceived as much more suitable for children, as they were believed to be a potentially edifying factor in their lives. The understanding of how such media worked in relation to children – as (direct) conveyers of cultural norms and values – made that relationship a central concern in debates about upbringing and education. The belief that comics, particularly superhero comics, gave undemocratic and violent norms currency can thus be seen as the reason educators and psychiatrists opposed them. Comics, by virtue of significance attributed to the concepts of media and children, were a natural focus of debate about the future of society as a whole.

Notes

1 Larson 1953: 10. Professionally translated from Swedish to English. Unless stated otherwise, quotes in Swedish, Norwegian, and Danish have been translated into English by the author.
2 For the great respect for Lorentz Larson's work on children's reading in educational milieus in Scandinavia during this period, see, for example, Winther 1955; Nilson 1969; Holm 1969.
3 See, for example, Kirsten Drotner (1992, 1999), Martin Knutsson (1995) and John Springhall (1998) for accounts of the Fifties' comics debate in which the debaters have been seen as responding negatively to children's comics consumption for irrational reasons (Drotner 1999), or because they were old-fashioned and did not understand the medium (Knutsson 1995; Spinghall 1998).
4 The overall argument of this article has previously been presented in 'Why Batman was Bad: A Scandinavian debate about children's consumption of comics and literature in the 1950s', *Barn* 20/3 2010: 47–70. *Barn* is published by the Norwegian Centre for Child Research at the Norwegian University of Science and Technology, Trondheim.
5 The labels moral panic and media panic have also been used to characterize many other debates about children's media consumption, such as those

about Nick Carter in Sweden in the beginning of the twentieth century (Boëthius 1989), anything from 'Penny Gaffs to Gangsta Rap' (Springhall 1998), as well as films in the 1930s and videos in the 1980s (Critcher 2008). Though not within the scope of this essay, it must be noted that the same epistemological problems apply to the use of the moral/media panic approach in these analyses as in the case of the panic approach to the Fifties' comics debates.

6 That notwithstanding, Ulf Boëthius' analysis of the Swedish debates about Nick Carter at the turn of the twentieth century is an example of how a moral panic approach can be combined with a detailed historical analysis of the political and professional interests involved in these types of debate (Boëthius 1989). However, Boëthius' comparison of the Nick Carter debates with the Nazi regime's attack on 'degenerate art' shows how the theoretical framework is open to the risk of presentist conclusions (Boëthius 1989: 328).

7 Scandinavia refers to Denmark, Norway and Sweden; the Nordic countries comprise those plus Iceland and Finland. The potential for the high level of transfer noted for the Nordic countries can be said to be even greater for Scandinavia because of the three countries' linguistic proximity, which means that translation is not necessary before textual transfer.

8 The primary source material comprises 807 newspaper or periodical articles and several popular books and official reports. The vast majority of the articles were published between 1953 and 1957 in Denmark, Sweden, and Norway. They were identified through a systematic evaluation of the three countries' national printed and digital newspaper and journal indices for these years (Dansk Tidsskrifts Index and Dansk Artikel Index for Denmark; Svensk Tidningsindex and Svensk Tidskriftsindex for Sweden; Norsk Artikelindex and A-tekst, the national newspaper database, for Norway), and of the references these published sources contain.

9 The centrality of the library as an alternative space, offering appropriate alternatives, has also been noted by Ralf Kauranen as an element in the Finnish comics debate (Kauranen 2008).

References

Andresen, Astri, Gardarsdottir, Olöf, Janfelt, Monika, Lindgren, Cecilia, Markkola, Pirjo & Söderlind, Ingrid (2011), *Barnen och välfärdspolitiken: Nordiska barndomar 1900–2000* (Institutet för framtidsstudier; Stockholm: Dialogos Förlag).

Barker, Martin (1984), *A haunt of fears: The strange history of the British horror comics campaign* (London: Pluto).

Arbeidsudvalget for Statens Folkeopplysningsråd (1954), *Instilling i tegneseriesaka* (Flisa: Flisa Aksindenstrykkeri).

Bauchard, Philippe (1952/53), *The child audience: A report on press, film and radio for children* (Paris: UNESCO).

Bejerot, Nils (1954), *Barn–Serier–Samhälle* (Stockholm: Kulturfront).

Birkeland, Tone, Risa, Gunvor & Vold, Karin Beate (2005), *Norsk barnelitteraturhistorie* (2nd edn., Oslo: Samlaget).

Boëthius, Ulf (1989), *När Nick Carder drevs på flykten* (Södertälje: Fingraf).

Buckingham, David (2000), *After the death of childhood: Growing up in the age of electronic media* (Cambridge: Polity Press).

– & Tingstad, Vebjørg (2010), *Childhood and consumer culture* (New York: Palgrave Macmillan).

– (2011), *The material child: Growing up in consumer culture* (Cambridge: Polity Press).

– & Helle Strandgaard Jensen (forthcoming), 'Beyond 'media panics': Reconceptualising public debates about children and media', *Journal of Children and Media*.

Buttenschøn, Ellen (1954), 'De misbrugte læsere', *Aarhus Stiftidende*, 6 June.

By, Sverre (1953), 'Fritidslesnad for barn og ungdom', *Norsk Skuleblad*, 17/18: 200–202.

Cohen, Stanley (2002), *Folk devils and moral panics* (3rd edn., London: Routledge).

Cook, Daniel Thomas (2004), *The commodification of childhood: The children's clothing industry and the rise of the child consumer* (Durham, NC: Duke University Press).

Critcher, Chas (2008), 'Making waves: Historical aspects of public debates about children and mass media', in Livingstone & Drotner (2008), 91–104.

Daunton, Martin & Hilton, Matthew (2001), *The politics of consumption: Material culture and citizenship in Europe and America* (Oxford: Berg).

Davies, Marie Messenger (2010), *Children, media and culture* (Maidenhead: Open University Press).

de Coninck-Smith, Ning (2002), 'Det demokratiske børneopdragelsesprogram: Anne Marie Nørvig om børn, forældre og familie i USA og Danmark 1930–1955', in Mads Hermansen & Arne Poulsen (eds.) *Samfundets børn* (Århus: Klim), 13–34.

Deinboll, Rikke (1942), 'Folkskolanarnas leseinteresser I–II', *Norsk Pedagogisk Tidsskrift*, 35: 129–139 & 176–183.

Drotner, Kirsten (1992), 'Modernity and media panics', in Michael Skovmand and Kim Schrøder (eds.), *Media cultures: Reappraising transnational media* (London: Routledge), 42–62.

Drotner, Kirsten (1999), 'Dangerous media? Panic discourses and dilemmas of modernity', *Paedagogica Historica*, 35: 593–691.

Florander, Jesper (1955), 'Kulørte argumenter', *Dansk Pædagogisk Tidende*, 8/3: 188–211.

Fransson, Evald (1953), 'Serielitteraturen – ett uppfostringsproblem', *Folkskolan*, 7: 198–208.

– (1954), 'Serielitteraturen ett upforstringsproblem', *Norsk Pedagogisk Tidskrift*, 48: 14–24.

Germeten, Else (1953), 'Barn og film'. *Norges barnevern*, 30/10: 73–5.

Granat, Barbro (1953), 'Våra barn och bion', *Arbetarbladet*, 19 & 27 March.

Harder, Peter (2011), 'Conceptual construal and social constructions', in Mario Brdar, Stefan Thomas Gries & Zic Fuchs (eds.), *Cognitive Linguistics: Convergence and Expansion* (Amsterdam: John Benjamins).

Holm, Carl (1969), 'Lorentz Larson 75', *Skolbiblioteket*, 15/4: 218–19.

Jensen, Helle S. (2010), 'Why Batman was Bad: A Scandinavian debate about children's consumption of comics and literature in the 1950s', *Barn*, 20(3): 47–70.

Juncker, Beth (2006), *Om processen: Det æstetiskes betydning i børns kultur* (Copenhagen: Tiderne Skifter).

Kauranen, Ralf (2008), *Seriedebatt i 1950-talets Finland: En studie i barndom, media och reglering* (Åbo: Åbo Akademis förlag).

Knutsson, Magnus (1995), 'Seriemagasinet mot Barnboken: En moralpanik ut kultursociologisk perspektiv', *Bild & Bubbla*, 40/1: 30–35.

Larson, Lorentz (1947), *Ungdom läser: En undersökning över läsintresserna hos barn och ungdom i åldern 7–20 år* (Gothenburg: Elander).

– (1953), 'Barn och Serier', *Svensk Skoltidning*, 49: 10–12.

– & the Women's International League for Peace and Freedom (1954), *Barn och serier* (Stockholm: Almqvist & Wiksell).

Livingstone, Sonia & Drotner, Kirsten (2008) (eds.), *International handbook of children, media and culture* (London: SAGE).

Nilson, Margot (1969), 'Lorentz Larson hedersdoktor', *Skolbiblioteket*, 15/3: 90–3.

Nordisk kontaktudvalg (1957), *Nordisk kontaktudvalg vedrørende børns og unges læsning* (Betænkning af 16. juni, 1957; Betænkning 217, 1958).

Norsk Skuleblad (1953), [Editorial no. 12], *Norsk Skuleblad*, 18/12: 3.

Nørvig, Anne Marie (1952), 'Et internationalt problem – Tegneserierne', *Vår Skola*, 38/34: 517–21.

– (1953), 'Hvorfor synes børn om seriehæfter?', *Politiken*, 27 November.

Petersen & Sørensen (n.d.), *Americanisation and anti-Americanism in Denmark, ca. 1945–1970. A pilot study* (Working paper 1, Ameridanes/Arbejdspapir 1,

Amerikansk på Dansk), available at <http://static.sdu.dk/mediafiles//Files/Om_SDU/Institutter/Ihks/Projekter/Amerikansk%20paa%20dansk/Artikler/PilotstudieFinalVersion.pdf>, accessed 28 August 2011.

Problemet tegneserier (1954), *Utgreiing til Statens Folkeopplysningsråd fra Det Rådgivande Utvalg Angående Tegneserier* (reprinted in *Norsk Pedagogisk Tidskrift*, 38: 2–13).

Qvarsebo, Jonas (2006), *Skolbarnets fostran: Enhetsskolan, agen och politiken om barnet 1946–1962* (Diss.; Linköping: Tema Barn, Linköping University).

Petersen, Klaus (2011), 'National, Nordic and trans-Nordic: transnational perspectives on the history of the Nordic welfare states', in Pauli Kettunen & Klaus Petersen (eds.) *Beyond welfare state models: Transnational historical perspectives on social policy* (Cheltenham: Edward Edgar Publishing Limited), 41–64.

Rosenwein, Barbara H. (2002), 'Worrying about emotions in history', *American Historical Review*, 107/3, 821–45.

Rowe, David (2009), 'The concept of the moral panic: An historio-sociological positioning', in David Lemmings and Claire Walker (eds.) *Moral panics, the media and the law in early modern England* (New York: Palgrave Macmillan), 22–40.

Sandin, Bengt & Halldén, Gunilla (2003) (eds.), *Barnets bästa: en antologi om barndomens innebörder och välfärdens organisering* (Eslöv: B. Östlings förlag/Symposion).

Siersted, Ellen (1953), 'Hvorfor skal børn se noget skidt?', *Politiken*, 10 February.

Sjöberg, Mats (2003), 'Att fostra ett skolbarn. Den nya skolan och barndomens förändring 1950–1970', in Sandin & Halldén (2003), 53–99.

Sletvold, Sverre (1953), 'Barn og tegneserier', *Prismet. Tidsskrift for Skole og Heim*, 4: 173–4 & 179–82.

Sørensen, Elenora (1953), 'Gennem barnets fritidslæsning skabes værdier for samfundet', *Vejle Amts Avis*, 17 February.

Springhall, John. (1998), *Youth, popular culture and moral panics. Penny Gaffs to Gangsta-Rap, 1830–1996* (New York: St Martins).

Thuen, Harald & Vaage, Sveinung (2004), *Pedagogiske profiler: norsk utdanningstenkning fra Holberg til Hernes* (Oslo: Abstrakt forlag).

Ungdomskommisionen (1952), *Ungdommen og fritiden: betænkning* (Copenhagen: J. H. Schultz).

Unge pædagoger (1952), *Unge pædagoger* (Copenhagen: Unge Pædagogers Forlag).

Weinreich, Torben (2006), *Historien om børnelitteratur: Dansk børnelitteratur gennem 400 år* (Copenhagen: Branner & Korch).

Winther, Christian (1954), 'Børnene og den 'kulørte' litteratur', *Folkeskolen* 71/32: 854–60.

– (1955), 'Kampen mod Superman og Fantomet', *Information*, 5 February.

About the authors

Sara Bragg is an Academic Fellow and Lecturer in Child and Youth Studies at the Department of Childhood, Development and Learning, the Open University, London, UK. Her research interests and topics include cultural studies approaches to education, child and youth cultures, sexualities, consumption, young people as media audiences, student/youth 'voice' and participation, and 'creative' learning and research methods.

David Buckingham is Professor of Media and Communications at the School of Social Sciences, Loughborough University, UK. His research focuses on children's and young people's interactions with electronic media, and on media education. He recently led an independent assessment for the UK government on 'the impact of the commercial world on children's wellbeing' and has completed projects on learning progression in media education, childhood, 'sexualization' and consumer culture, young people, the Internet, and civic participation. His most recent book is *The Material Child: Growing Up in Consumer Culture.*

David Cardell is a Ph.D. candidate at the Department of Thematic Studies – Child Studies, Linköping University, Sweden. His research focuses on how children and families make use of amusement parks, and how visits are conducted, as well as incorporated into everyday life situations. Cardell's theoretical interests are politics–pleasure and consumption–management relations. He also has an interest in commercial youth sports and spectacular leisure activities, such as indoor play spaces.

Daniel Thomas Cook is Associate Professor of Childhood Studies and Sociology at Rutgers University, Camden, New Jersey, and editor of the journal *Childhood*. He is the author of *The Commodification of Childhood*, editor of *Symbolic Childhood*, and *Lived Experiences of Public Consumption*, and has written a number of articles and anthology contributions on consumer society, childhood, leisure, and urban culture.

Shosh Davidson is a Ph.D. student at the Department of Educational Leadership and Policy, in the Faculty of Education at the University of Haifa, Israel. She studies children and consumer culture in different domains of life, such as the family and school. She has also been engaged in ethnographic work on the commercial involvement of a retail corporation in schools as part of its 'corporate social responsibility' policy.

Olivia Freeman is Lecturer in Consumption Studies and Communications at the Dublin Institute of Technology, Ireland. Her research focuses on children's consumer culture, advertising and marketing to children, gender and consumption. Freeman has a strong interest in the theoretical and practical aspects of conversation analysis and discourse analysis. Her work has been published in the area of language and interaction as well as the field of consumption. Freeman is also Co-Director of the DIT Centre for Consumption & Leisure Studies and the Discourse Analysis Group at DIT.

Braden P.L. Hutchinson is a Ph.D. candidate and Teaching Fellow at the Department of History, Queen's University, Canada. His research focuses on the history of toys in Canada, 1860–1990, examining controversies about toy consumption and the place of the child consumer among middle-class, working-class, gendered, and racially 'othered' Canadians. He is also interested in the shifting boundaries and meanings surrounding 'good' and 'bad' toys and consumer behaviours, and their generative influence on disciplinary projects aimed at educating the consumer desire of Canadian children and their parents.

Sue Jackson is Senior Lecturer at the School of Psychology, Victoria University of Wellington, New Zealand. She is known for her research and publications on young women's negotiation of sexuality, the ways sexuality is represented in girls' popular culture, and how girls make sense of media representations of femininity and sexuality. Currently, her research centres on a four-year project with co-researcher Tiina Vares entitled 'Girls, "Tween" Popular Culture and Everyday Life', supported by the New Zealand Royal Society Marsden Fund.

Ingvild Kvale Sørenssen is a Ph.D. candidate at the Norwegian Centre for Child Research, Norwegian University of Science and Technology, Trondheim, Norway. Her research focuses on the construction of tweens through consumers and media goods, focusing especially on Disney Channel. In particular, she applies a cultural studies approach, looking at different stakeholders' construction of tweens as a category.

Rachel Russell is Lecturer in Social Sciences at Glasgow Caledonian University's School for Business and Society, and Co-Director of the Caledonian Centre for Equality and Diversity, UK. Her research interests are focused on equality and diversity, and young people's engagement with popular and consumer culture.

Tobias Samuelsson is an Assistant Professor at the Department of Thematic Studies – Child Studies, Linköping University, Sweden. His research focuses on children and their interplay with surrounding social, cultural, and material frames. Samuelsson is currently taking part in the research project 'Culture for and by children', in which he studies children's visits to science centres and the way these places are enacted as places for children. Samuelsson also has an interest in children's everyday life, with a particular focus on their work.

Bengt Sandin is Professor at the Department of Thematic Studies – Child Studies, Linköping University, Sweden. His publications focus on children and childhood in a historical perspective, from the early modern period to the late Swedish welfare state, and including studies on early modern education and state-building, child labour, street children, educational media politics, and welfare politics and the history of child psychiatry in Sweden. Sandin is a co-editor of the recent anthologies *Understanding Literacy in its Historical Contexts:*

Socio-Cultural History and the Legacy of Egil Johansson, and *Neither Fish nor Fowl: Educational Broadcasting in Sweden 1930–2000*.

Johanna Sjöberg is a Ph.D. candidate at the Department of Thematic Studies – Child Studies, Linköping University, Sweden. Her research focuses on children and consumption, studying laws and regulations surrounding advertisements for children, as well as the visual positioning of children in print advertisements. Sjöberg is interested in how notions and ideals of children and childhood are created visually.

Anna Sparrman is Associate Professor and Senior Lecturer in Visual Culture at the Department of Thematic Studies – Child Studies, Linköping University, Sweden. Her research focuses on the intertwinement of children, childhoods, visual (material) culture, sexuality, children's culture, and consumption from a contemporary, everyday perspective. Her research also includes visual research methodologies. Sparrman is currently research leader for the project 'Culture for and by children', which studies amusement parks, children's museums, theme parks, and science centres.

Helle Strandgaard Jensen is a Ph.D. candidate at the Department of History and Civilization, European University Institute, Florence, Italy. Her research focuses on public debates about children's media consumption in Scandinavia, c.1950–1985 She investigates the history of children's television, the Fifties' Scandinavian debates about comic books, and the concept of 'girl power'. She is part of the Platform for a Cultural History of Children's Media (PLACIM) network based at Maastricht University.

Tiina Vares is Senior Lecturer in Sociology at the University of Canterbury, Christchurch, New Zealand. Her research interests lie in the areas of gender, sexualities, the body, and popular culture with a focus on the reception of popular cultural texts. She is currently working within the research project 'Girls, "Tween" Popular Culture and Everyday Life', supported by the New Zealand Royal Society Marsden Fund.

Rebekah Willett is Assistant Professor of Library and Information Studies at the University of Wisconsin–Madison, USA, where she teaches courses on young adult literature, multicultural literature for children and young adults, informational divides, and online participatory cultures. Willett's research interests focus on children's media cultures, especially issues of gender, play, literacy, and learning. Her publications include work on playground games, amateur camcorder cultures, young people's online activities, and children's story-writing.

Steve Woolgar is Professor and Chair of Marketing, and Head of Science and Technology Studies (STS) at the Said Business School, University of Oxford, UK. His research interests span a range of theoretical questions and perspectives in STS, and their implications for social theory. Current projects include (with Dan Neyland) mundane governance – the ways in which ordinary objects and technologies are implicated in social regulation and control; (with Tanja Schneider) the emergence of 'neuromarketing'; and (with Malte Ziewitz) the rise of web-based ratings systems and evaluation technologies. Woolgar is co-editor of the forthcoming anthologies *Globalization in Practice*, *New Representation in Scientific Practice*, and *The Turn to Ontology in STS?*

Viviana A. Zelizer is Lloyd Cotsen '50 Professor of Sociology at Princeton University, USA. She specializes in historical analysis, economic processes, interpersonal relations, and childhood. Zelizer has published books on the development of life insurance, the changing economic and sentimental value of children in the US, and the place of money in social life. Two of her recent publications are *The Purchase of Intimacy*, and *Economic Lives: How Culture Shapes the Economy*.